Twayne's Filmmakers Series

Frank Beaver, Editor

Martin Scorsese

Martin Scorsese on the set of his critical and popular success, *GoodFellas* (1990). Warner Brothers. The Museum of Modern Art/Film Stills Archive.

MARTIN SCORSESE

Les Keyser

TWAYNE PUBLISHERS
An Imprint of Simon & Schuster Macmillan
NEW YORK

Prentice Hall International
LONDON · MEXICO CITY · NEW DELHI · SINGAPORE · SYDNEY · TORONTO

Twayne's Filmmakers Series
Martin Scorsese

Copyright © 1995 Simon & Schuster Macmillan
All rights reserved. No part of this book may be reproduced or transmitted in any
form or by any means, electronic or mechanical, including photocopying,
recording, or by any information storage or retrieval system, without permission
in writing from the Publisher.

Twayne Publishers
An Imprint of Simon & Schuster Macmillan
1633 Broadway
New York, New York 10019-6785

Library of Congress Cataloging-in-Publication Data
Keyser, Lester J., 1943–
    Martin Scorsese / Les Keyser.
        p.   cm. — (Twayne's filmmakers series)
    Includes bibliographical references and index.
    ISBN 0-8057-9315-1. — ISBN 0-8057-9321-6 (pbk.)
    1. Scorsese, Martin—Criticism and interpretation.   I. Title.
II. Series.
PN1998.3.S39K49   1992
791.43'0233'092—dc20   92-26784
                                                                        CIP

The paper used in this publication meets the minimum requirements of American
National Standard for Information Sciences—Permanence of Paper for Printed
Library Materials. ANSI Z3948-1984. ∞™

10 9 8 7 6 5 4 3 2   (hc)
10 9 8 7 6 5   (pb)

Printed in the United States of America

For Catherine
"I will get Peter Quince
to write a ballad of this dream;
it shall be called 'Bottom's Dream,'
because it hath no bottom."

CONTENTS

FOREWORD

Of all the contemporary arts, the motion picture is particularly timely and diverse as a popular culture enterprise. This lively art form cleverly combines storytelling with photography to achieve what has been a quintessential twentieth-century phenomenon. Individual as well as national and cultural interests have made the medium an unusually varied one for artistic expression and analysis. Films have been exploited for commercial gain, for political purposes, for experimentation, and for self-exploration. The various responses to the motion picture have given rise to different labels for both the fun and the seriousness with which this art form has been received, ranging from "the movies" to "cinema." These labels hint at both the theoretical and sociological parameters of the film medium.

A collective art, the motion picture has nevertheless allowed individual genius to flourish in all its artistic and technical areas: directing, screenwriting, cinematography, acting, editing. The medium also encompasses many genres beyond the narrative film, including documentary, animated, and avant-garde expression. The range and diversity of motion pictures suggest rich opportunities for appreciation and for study.

The Twayne Filmmakers Series examines the full panorama of motion picture history and art. Many studies are auteur-oriented and elucidate the work of individual directors whose ideas and cinematic styles make them authors of their films. Other studies examine film movements and genres or analyze cinema from a national perspective. The series seeks to illuminate all the many aspects of film for the film student, the scholar, and the general reader.

Frank Beaver

PREFACE

Recent literature about Hollywood has offered sad exposés of failed dreams, blighted careers, corporate shenanigans, and a production system in disarray, as deals, dollars, and drugs rule Tinseltown. David McClintick, for example, in *Indecent Exposure* details the financial chicanery endemic to the megabuck business of dreammaking[1] while muckraker Bob Woodward documents the debilitating effect of cocaine on the creative community in his *Wired*.[2] Producer Julia Phillips emphasizes the rampant sexism, unbelievable incompetence, and chronic insecurities in Beverly Hills in her sensational autobiography, *You'll Never Eat Lunch in this Town Again*.[3]

Yet the most thorough assessment of the troubles in Hollywood can be found in Steven Bach's *Final Cut,* a chronicle of "dreams and disaster" in the production of director Michael Cimino's gargantuan failure *Heaven's Gate*.[4] Bach does present one hero, a Fortinbras to Cimino's Hamlet, director Martin Scorsese. As Cimino's *Heaven's Gate* spun its way toward doom, Bach recalls, Scorsese's *Raging Bull* was also being considered for production, though the studio, United Artists, felt the boxing project was "so violent we doubted it could ever be made" (Bach, 90). Money was gushing into *Heaven's Gate,* the decade's most spectacular failure, while *Raging Bull,* which would eventually become the most widely praised film of the 1980s, languished in preproduction limbo.

Bach then describes a meeting between studio representatives David Field and himself, would-be producer Irwin Winkler, and would-be filmmakers Martin Scorsese and Robert De Niro. Executive Field hammered at the "tremendous obscenity problem" (Bach, 164) decrying planned close-ups of Jake La Motta's erect penis as he pours ice water on it prior to a boxing match, and lamenting the focus on a protagonist as likable and moral as a cockroach. Scorsese and De Niro listened carefully and within six months resubmitted a less incendiary script, one with a more fully rounded and sympathetic characterization of La Motta. United Artists quickly agreed to proceed.

As Bach recalls the revised text, he notes, "The script was unaccompanied by a request for writer payment, and no credit arbitration was ever requested. . . . But the title page that covered the draft of *Raging Bull* that made Jake La Motta a human said, in small type tucked modestly in the lower right hand corner, RdN. MS didn't even claim that" (Bach, 166). Bach's anecdote reveals Scorsese's dilemma as a director. Scorsese wants to explore the dark side of the human soul, doubts and despair, psychotic violence and rage, guilt and the quest for expiation and salvation. Yet he wants to be a mainstream Hollywood filmmaker, working on well-financed projects aimed at the mass audience. The record of his life thus chronicles America's most idiosyncratic, personal artist struggling to work in the nation's most cliché-ridden, genre-dominated popular art.

Scorsese remains the New Yorker displaced in Hollywood, the Italian American Catholic in a land of WASPs, the urban street boy in a nation of accountants and yuppies, "God's lonely man" seeking an audience for his last testament.

Any consideration of Scorsese's films brings one back to the great tradition of cinema. The child of an immigrant ghetto, Scorsese shared all outsiders' love for the nickelodeon and the movie palace. As a small boy, he sauntered past the buildings where D. W. Griffith created the language of film in Biograph shorts to reach the Commodore Theater and the Academy of Music in New York, often sitting with his father, Charles, or his mother, Catherine, in the same majestic orchestra where they had courted each other. In these old movie houses, Scorsese confronted the myths of the Western, the animated fantasies of Disney, and the somber melodrama of film noir. A sickly child, Scorsese also immersed himself in television's "Million Dollar Movie," watching every repeated film until he'd ingested every image. Then Scorsese was off to film school as part of a film generation weaned on Europe's New Wave. At New York University Scorsese also mingled with political-activist, underground independent filmmakers; ran Lincoln Center's Films in the Parks; and labored on *Woodstock* with Michael Wadleigh.

In the 1970s Scorsese was off to Hollywood to work with Roger Corman on exploitation films, to edit more music documentaries, and finally to jump into studio productions with major stars, big budgets, and elaborate production facilities. On the West Coast he mingled with the "Movie Brats," including George Lucas and Steven Spielberg, only to be caught in the whole music/groupie/drug/celebrity scene. The 1980s saw his attempt to rebuild his career in smaller, more personal projects, including *The Last Temptation of Christ,* arguably Hollywood's most controversial film. In the 1990s, Scorsese has expanded his forays into producing and acting, as he continues to direct major features at a furious pace.

Throughout his career, Scorsese has maintained his personal integrity and vision while confronting the realities of a transformed, tempest-tossed, conglomerate-dominated Hollywood. He now ranks as America's most accomplished and most interesting filmmaker, clearly the artist who will lead the American film into the new century.

ACKNOWLEDGMENTS

Father Gene D. Phillips encouraged me to prepare this volume on Martin Scorsese, and to him I owe a large debt of gratitude for his many kindnesses, for his friendship, and for his inspiration as a mentor. His many notable contributions to Twayne's Filmmakers Series have enriched film literature immensely. Most of all, however, it is just grand fun to discuss movies with Gene. His knowledge is immense, his judgments unerring, and his wit unrivaled.

Janice Baio most generously facilitated the research for this volume, and Maria Leo provided easy access to Scorsese's student films and other materials.

As always, Charles Silver and his staff at the Film Study Center of the Museum of Modern Art demonstrated what an invaluable resource this much-heralded institution continues to be. Similarly, Mary Corliss and her staff at the Film Still Archives of the Museum of Modern Art most graciously located all the stills for this volume. All the publicity stills in this text are from the Museum of Modern Art/Film Stills Archives.

The staff at the Lincoln Center Library for the Performing Arts also aided in the research for this volume. Despite substantial budget cuts and reduced operating hours, the research center at Lincoln Center remains a most usable and pleasant facility, thanks to the heroic dedication of its overworked staff.

To Barbara, my wife, and Catherine, my daughter, I owe more than words can say. This volume would not exist without their love and support.

CHRONOLOGY

1942   Martin Scorsese born in Astoria, Queens, New York, on 17 November to Charles and Catherine Scorsese.

1950   Transfers from public school to St. Patrick's Elementary School in New York's Little Italy, where his parents have moved because of financial problems.

1956   Enters Cathedral College, the seminary of the Archdiocese of New York, on Manhattan's Upper West Side.

1957   Transfers to Cardinal Hayes High School in the Bronx.

1960   Enters New York University and meets Halg Manoogian, the professor who inspires him to be a filmmaker. Student film, *What's a Nice Girl like You Doing in a Place like This?,* receives critical acclaim.

1964   *It's Not Just You, Murray!* is hailed as the finest student film ever made; it is shown at the New York Film Festival two years later and has a brief commercial release. Scorsese receives his degree from New York University.

1966–1968   Attends graduate school at New York University and teaches film courses.

1968   Short film, *The Big Shave,* screened at the Sixth New York Film Festival.

1969   Supervises the editing of *Woodstock* and serves as assistant director. *Who's That Knocking At My Door?*

1970   *Street Scenes 1970* featured at the Eighth New York Film Festival.

1972   *Boxcar Bertha.*

1973   *Mean Streets* premieres at the Eleventh New York Film Festival.

1974   *Italianamerican* premieres at the Twelfth New York Film Festival.

1975   Ellen Burstyn receives an Oscar for Best Actress in *Alice Doesn't Live Here Anymore* (1974).

1976   *Taxi Driver.*

1977   *New York, New York* premieres at the Fifteenth New York Film Festival.

1978   *The Last Waltz. American Boy: A Profile of Stephen Prince* screened at the Sixteenth New York Film Festival.

1979   *Martin Scorsese: Movies Are My Life* has its American premiere at the Seventeenth New York Film Festival.

1980   *Raging Bull.*

1982   *The King of Comedy.*

1985   *After Hours.*

1986   *The Color of Money.*

1988   *The Last Temptation of Christ* generates a storm of controversy worldwide.

1989   "Life Lessons" in *New York Stories.*

1990   *GoodFellas.*

1991   *Cape Fear.*

1993   *The Age Of Innocence.*

I

From Little Italy to Seminary to New York University: Scorsese's Trinity

On 3 October 1974, in an auditorium filled to capacity with urban sophisticates and film mavens, Catherine Scorsese, an elderly Italian garmentworker, shared her family's secrets with the world. The final credits of her son Martin's film *Italianamerican* carefully recorded the recipe for Mama's spaghetti "gravy" and for her preternaturally light meatballs. Catherine Scorsese's instructions may have lacked Julia Child's panache, with her peasant directness ("Throw the meat in"), her common-sense judgments ("When it's brown, take it out"), and her pedestrian technique ("Mix it with your hands"), yet the audience knew this was an authentic heirloom recipe, as real as the Scorsese family's obvious love for one another and as rich as the Sicilian tradition they had transplanted to New York's Little Italy.

Italianamerican, Martin Scorsese's personal favorite among all his works, began as the brainchild of Saul Rubin, who garnered a bicentennial grant from the National Endowment for the Humanities to produce a series of television programs under the title "A Storm of Strangers" for the Public Broadcasting System, with each segment illustrating the impact of one nation's immigration on the American melting pot. Scorsese, whose early career had established his credentials as an ethnic director, a *paisan,* seemed a perfect choice, but when approached, he quickly turned the project down. He wanted nothing to do with a mundane, stereotypical account of Italians pouring off ocean liners, encountering Ellis Island, then crowding into Lower Manhattan. Scorsese, a hot young talent busy shooting his first big-budget Hollywood feature, *Alice Doesn't Live Here Anymore,* thought a routine documentary assignment was out of the question.

Later, however, Scorsese envisioned his own way of exploring Italian immigrant culture: he would bring the camera home with him for the weekend dinner he routinely shared with his parents. Rubin was willing to take a chance, though the grant demanded that Larry Cohen outline the project and that Scorsese's longtime buddy Mardik Martin prepare questions for the Scorseses. All the while, though, Scorsese trusted his judgment; he flew back from Cannes for the project, relying on his parents to provide the spice the film needed.

And spicy *Italianamerican* is. The film resembles a home movie gone mad. Cinematographer Alex Hirschfield's bright color footage of the Scorseses's overstuffed, three-room apartment emphasizes the red of the plastic-covered sofas; the clutter of the dining table, and the claustrophobia of Catherine's overdecorated kitchen. Everyone is bumping into everyone else; privacy is impossible, so banter becomes a necessity. Neither Charles nor Catherine Scorsese knows whether to ignore the camera or to play to it. Eventually, this long-married couple give up on performance and decorum; they speak intimately instead to each other and to Marty. At one point they both drop what they're doing to badger their son about how bad his "short" tooth makes him look. Even Martin Scorsese finds it hard to be a dispassionate, professional director under such a torrid assault. He is clearly embarrassed.

Catherine Scorsese, on the other hand, seems apprehensive. This Italian mother constantly looks over her shoulder, scrutinizing the area just off screen, checking that her sauce doesn't burn, worrying that the furniture Marty's crew moved isn't damaged, and watching out that her neighbors don't see a film crew working in her apartment. Charles Scorsese, meanwhile, complains that his wife is hamming it up. He's concerned that the truth be told and that everything be natural.

Italianamerican was shot in only six hours, though Scorsese claims he got more than 90 minutes of usable footage. Half that footage is contained in this 45-minute short, and the director swears there's enough good material left for a sequel. Revelation does follow revelation in the reveries. Charles Scorsese eloquently remembers making extra money lighting the stoves for his Jewish immigrant neighbors on the Sabbath; rhapsodizes about the pleasures of listening to the brand-new Atwater Kent radio they bought; and laughs nostalgically about Irish bars. Catherine Scorsese, embarrassed by his candor, offers her own vignettes about winemaking; about her mother's love for her father, a young cavalryman; and about a miraculous fig tree blighted by the curse of human hatred.

Charles and Catherine begin the film wondering what they can say after 40 years of marriage; by the end of the film, their mix of folk wisdom, apocryphal stories, platitudes, and premonitions sums up their love completely. Sensing that her son's camera has seen enough, Catherine queries her husband, "Is he still taking this?" and warns her son, "I'll murder you. You won't get out of this house alive."

Martin Scorsese did get out of his home alive and with exceptionally vivid footage. The material in *Italianamerican* constitutes the bedrock of Scorsese's art. The director's roots go deep in the Sicilian section of Little Italy; to understand his art, one must consider the culture of Elizabeth and Mulberry streets. His life embodies the dilemma of the Italian immigrant in America so skillfully limned in Richard Gambino's autobiographically moving and sociologically sound study, *Blood of My Blood.*[1]

Gambino forcefully documents the rigid hierarchy of Italian immigrant values, beginning with the primacy of family. In the New World especially, Italian peasants, the *contadini,* must observe *l'ordine della famiglia,* loyalty to their family, for this code alone preserves all the "blood of my blood." Next comes allegiance to the extended family of Italian compatriots; villagers must behave honorably toward other villagers. Non-Italians, under this morality, are mere outsiders, strangers who deserve no respect. Thus, unlike other immigrants, Italians from the Mezzogiorno who prospered in New York didn't assimilate. Instead, they either remained in small ethnic enclaves, such as Little Italy or Bensonhurst, or migrated en masse with relatives and neighbors to settlements on Staten Island and in Queens. When Catherine and Charles Scorsese tried to escape the confines of the Bowery in Manhattan, they moved in with relatives in Corona, Queens, where Martin Scorsese was born on 17 November 1942. In Queens, Scorsese remembers, the family home had a spacious backyard with a beautiful tree he considered all his own. As a toddler he developed respiratory problems, and at age four he underwent a tonsillectomy, the rationale for which the anxious child never understood, becoming convinced that the whole horrific episode was a trick played on him by his mother.

This operation left Scorsese plagued by asthma; all his life he has been struggling for breath, the smothering atmosphere of his urban scenes, as well as the neck wound so central to many of his plots, can be traced to his childhood trauma.

Scorsese's youthful anguish intensified when, for reasons never spoken about in the family but clearly centering on financial distress and his father's business problems, his parents abruptly left Queens and moved back to 253 Elizabeth Street, a few doors from his grand-mother's home and several steps from the all-important Sicilian Social Club. Scorsese lived here from 1950 until 1966, about two blocks away from Mulberry Street, the center of Neapolitan social life, and within walking distance of Greenwich Village and New York University, environs that were psychologically and socially so alien that Scorsese admits the only time he visited the Village before his college days was one brief sojourn to a friend's ninth birthday party.

Scorsese's early youth and adolescence are best characterized by his neighborhood nickname. In the macho land of Little Italy, with its emphasis on toughness and athletics, Martin Scorsese, the sickly boy who couldn't splash under the fire hydrant, who couldn't roughhouse with his peers, and who hated sports, was "Marty Pills." Even Marty Pills, however, couldn't escape the violence of ghetto life; it was a "hit or be hit" environment, with survival guaranteed only to the fittest or most wily. Scorsese never could compete, so as he told David Ansen, he had to pay heavy dues on the street: "The only way I was able to defend myself was to be able to take punishment. Then I got a lot of respect. They said, 'Oh, he's okay, he can take it. Don't hit him.' The guys were pretty big, and I had asthma."[2] Scorsese's adult fixation with punishment and redemption, with suffering and acceptance, and with salvation through physical sacrifice, so manifest in *Raging Bull, Taxi Driver,* and *The Last Temptation of Christ,* has its roots in his own rites of passage in an urban jungle. One of his childhood friends summed up Little Italy's code for film reviewer J. Hoberman of the *Village Voice*: "If you weren't able to give a beating, you had to take one," and as the friend noted, Marty was "always the littlest guy, the weakest, but he fought."[3] The necessity of that fight, the anger of the loser and the loner, and the dignity of struggle against overwhelming adversity—these became director Scorsese's major themes.

Scorsese's coming-of-age in Little Italy was further complicated by continuing economic problems. *Italianamerican* is larded with recollections of *la miseria* (poverty) and *sfruttamento* (exploitation of laborers), especially in the poignant tales of immigrant ancestors in ludicrously overcrowded apartments, experiencing endless labor and intolerable deprivations. Charles and Catherine Scorsese didn't have life much better.

To Marty the child and the young man, the economic squeeze meant his parents were rarely home. Discussing his troubled youth with Guy Flatley of the *New York Times,* a meditative Scorsese confessed that his loneliness as a child played a critical role in shaping his later films: "I look for thematic ideas running through my movies and I see that's the outsider struggling for recognition. . . . It hit me about two nights ago, remembering how lonely I was as a kid. My parents worked, and I came home from school at 3 and sat at my kitchen table making up stories on my drawing board, or watching television, or escaping to the movies."[4] Scorsese's heightened introspective powers reflect his agonizing years in analysis; he even went so far as to thank his therapist in the credits for *Mean Streets.*

The mental anguish of a sensitive, frail boy isolated in a harsh, threatening environment haunts Scorsese's autobiographical musings. Like Travis Bickle of *Taxi Driver,* Scorsese envisions himself as "God's lonely man." Speaking to Paul Attanasio of the *Washington Post* about "Film, Faith, and Fire" in 1985, the director was still possessed by the violent phantoms of his childhood: "I grew up a block away from the Bowery. Right around the corner. Turn the corner, and go to school in the morning with my little books and bags, and these bums are fighting with broken bottles, putting out each others' eyes, blood flowing in the street. When you're six years old, that's gonna make an impression."[5] Scorsese was actually eight before his family moved anywhere near the Bowery, and his hyperbole of gouged-out eyes and torrents of blood suggest how impressionistic his memories are; to this sickly schoolboy, however, the dangers were real enough.

Young Scorsese's principal survival strategy came in a flight from danger—a physical flight from the Bowery and from streetcorner society and an imaginative flight into the world of movies. Charles Scorsese recognized that Martin would never find fulfillment with the gang on the corner. So he began taking his son regularly to the Academy of Music, the very theater where he'd courted Catherine Scorsese years before.

The movies set Martin Scorsese free, affording him so many "guilty pleasures" that he couldn't limit himself to the dozen favorite movies *Film Comment* requested he list for its readers. His loves were far too numerous and too passionate. In a provocative dialogue with his alter ego, screenwriter-collaborator Paul Schrader, published in *Cahiers du Cinema,*[6] Scorsese freely admitted that his most erotic experiences as a child and as an adolescent occurred in a darkened movie theater. Scorsese felt, for example, an almost-uncontrollable sexual love for Wendy in *Peter Pan.* He first experienced sexual rapture at 10 over a poster for *I Shot Jesse James* with Barbara Britton, only to fall madly in love at 13 with Elizabeth Taylor in *Giant* and with Jean Simmons in *Great Expectations.*

Scorsese embraced Westerns as his favorite genre. Like J. R. in *Who's That Knocking at My Door?* Scorsese believed that everyone must love the Hollywood West, the idealized world of John Wayne and Trigger, shootouts and desperate cavalry charges, helpless women and noble, self-sacrificing men. Scorsese was so moved by *A Duel in the Sun,* a film he saw with his mother, that he had to cover his eyes. Later, one of the milestones in his life was his first encounter with John Ford's *The Searchers,* a film he saw at the Commodore with his most frequent neighborhood companion, film aficionado Joey Morale.

Scorsese was far from a passive observer of films. After he saw a film, Scorsese would come home and draw primitive storyboards, planning his own productions. When three-dimensional movies were the rage, he actually started cutting out figures to place them in a set, but this project proved short-lived. Scorsese's cutouts seemed too much like paper dolls, and such pursuits were too embarrassing for a teenage boy in an Italian home.

Clearly, these many hours laboriously re-creating film frames and film sequences by hand at his kitchen table shaped Scorsese's later ideas about narrative structure and visual composition. These time-consuming, almost obsessive childhood productions taught him also about film editing, aspect ratios, and various film genres.

Scorsese also tried to re-create films by acting them out for his friends, but this effort too was squelched by social pressure. Among his abandoned projects *Vesuvius VII* affords a fine insight into Scorsese's juvenile inventiveness. *Vesuvius VII* was Scorsese's homage to the popular contemporary television show "Surfside Seven." He managed to convince several friends to dress up in togas and cavort on a Lower East Side rooftop. Unfortunately, an attempt at special effects destroyed a coffee table, so the project was never completed. Scorsese had planned to use "Does Your Chewing Gum Lose Its Flavor on the Bedpost Overnight?" to counterpoint his images; thus, even this primitive project reveals both his familiarity with television and media and his willingness to embrace new musical forms and employ them in a strikingly novel fashion.

The hallmark of all his later films would be this unique conjunction of contemporary popular music and film narrative; often the lyrics of his favorite rock-and-roll tunes comment most tellingly on his characters' dreams and aspirations, yet at other times the lyrics function ironically, pinpointing the popular delusions that warp personalities. Frequently his operatic and symphonic selections confer greater solemnity to the ritual of everyday life or they suggest mock-heroically how stunted his characters have become. Of all his contemporaries, Scorsese has ranged the most freely and widely between the worlds of popular music and the Hollywood film.

If the film world and pop music stood as Scorsese's chosen "City of Man," the Roman Catholic church proved his introduction to the "City of God," and like Augustine, he would be torn between the two. While Italian immigrants were largely Roman Catholics, their creed was, in the words of sociologists "an amalgam of Christian doctrines, magic, and pagan beliefs" (Gambino, 15–16). Martin, the son sent to St. Patrick's School on Mulberry Street, was acutely aware of the distinction between his ancestors' faith and the Catholicism promulgated by his school's Irish clergy and nuns. Scorsese is most explicit on this dichotomy in a complex interview he did with Richard Corliss after the release of *The Last Temptation of Christ*. Scorsese obviously knew he had a sympathetic and knowledgeable listener in Corliss, a writer who began his career with an infamous article analyzing the Catholic church's Legion of Decency, so the director plumbs this intricate question most candidly. Survival was such a problem for most Italian immigrants and for his parents, Scorsese argues, that "I don't think the church figured into their life that much." They were in essence, he maintains, "pagans" who put the church in "a certain perspective," never allowing it to affect their personal lives on issues like birth control. For them, he continues, and for his grandmother, the church had more to do with icons and rituals, with statues and sacramentals, with feast days and festivals: "My grandmother was the one who had the portrait of the Sacred Heart. Also the niche with the statue of the Virgin Mary grinding the snake under her foot. Also, the beautiful, gigantic crucifix over the bed, with Jesus in brass and the palms from Palm Sunday draped over the crossbar."[7] Scorsese's sensuous recollections of these pious artifacts suggests his own involvement with them, even as it confirms Gambino's observation that the "Old World *contadini* regarded religious observances, churchgoing, and other sacred habits as *cose femminile,* women's things" (Gambino, 232). Although many critics have commented on Scorsese's preoccupation with the visible signs of sanctity and worship, the

most original assessment of the impact of the external paraphernalia
and liturgy of Catholicism on his art remains Scorsese's own off-the-
cuff observation to Diane Jacobs: "I've never gotten over the ritual of
Catholicism, but I guess it's the same type of feeling some might get
from taking an acid trip."[8]

Scorsese's flashbacks to Catholic imagery focus acutely on the Irish
version of Catholicism hammered home at parochial school. In one
of those ironies so common in New York City's history, the Irish had
no sooner built their church and schoolhouse on Mott and Mulberry
streets than the Civil War intervened, and a new wave of immigration
followed, leaving a student body that was primarily Italian. The
church was slow to respond to the change, so year after year nuns
from Ireland arrived at St. Patrick's school to tutor Italian children.
Describing this mixup, Scorsese jokingly observed, "You had a little
enclave of Irish mafia religious thinking in the school which conflicted
with the home lives of the Italian kids."[9]

Still another conflict was brewing with the Puerto Ricans who were
beginning to attend St. Patrick's school. The mantle of the church did
little to quiet the ethnic combat between the old Italian immigrants
and the new Latin immigrants. Scorsese recalls seeing a street fight
where a Puerto Rican kissed his knife, and this image recurs in many
transformations in his films.

Scorsese attended St. Patrick's in the 1950s, and the nuns' apocalyptic visions of hell and nuclear holocaust, of damnation and the Com-
munist threat shaped his nightmares. In a 1987 interview with James
Truman, Scorsese recalls the terrors of Cold War air-raid drills:
"They'd take us all out of the classroom and lead us to the catacombs
under the church, and we'd have to pray the rosary under the church,
echoing among the graves. That was very grim. We were told that
this was what the fire of Hell would be like."[10] These hours in hell,
Scorsese realizes, helped shape both his temperament and his visual
style. As he recognizes now, he was so sensitive then that he has never
"been able to get past a lot of that stuff" and freely admits the aftermath of his early indoctrination: "Images from then are always coming back to me. The camera movement in a lot of my films certainly
comes from creeping around those catacombs, with the sound effects
of the echoing rosary" (Truman, 79–81).

Despite all its strict sanctions and stern commandments, Catholicism did offer Scorsese a vision of eventual salvation and heavenly
bliss, a community of fellow worshipers, and the drama of august

rituals. In an essay assessing religion's impact on his art, Scorsese assigns much importance to the serenity and beauty he found in church: "And the nuns liked me. I needed to be accepted somewhere. I couldn't do it in the streets—the kids were really rough . . . so I guess the acceptance I went for was in the church. I started going to Mass, and those Masses were kind of theatrical. The church itself, St. Patrick's Old Church, was enormous to an eight-year-old—and it still is, it's quite a beautiful church. As a result of all that, I began to take it much more seriously than anybody in the family did" ("Streets", 91–92). Years later, Scorsese would convince his friend Francis Ford Coppola to use St. Patrick's Old Church as the setting for the baptism scene in *The Godfather*. The youthful Scorsese avoided meat on Fridays, fasted during Lent, observed his Easter obligation, and followed the Stations of the Cross frequently. The only chink in his sacerdotal armor was his inability to give up his "guilty pleasures" for Lent; he never allowed his churchgoing to get in the way of his moviegoing or to limit his obsession with the "Million Dollar Movie" on New York Television.

Scorsese became the altar boy whose specialty was the 10:30 A.M. funeral mass on Saturday. As an altar boy of 11 or 12, Scorsese idealized a young parish priest, who shared the boy's penchant for movies. The mentoring relationship proved so important that Scorsese decided he had a calling to be a parish priest himself. Recalling these years in a *Newsday* interview in 1987, the filmmaker hypothesizes that the vocation was his attempt to find joy in a dreary world: "I guess being that young and having experienced some traumatic things . . . I maybe was looking for some peace or an answer of some sort, an idea of how one achieves any kind of happiness. And I started to say 'Well, at least with a religious vocation, a priest or a nun might have more of an inside line to heaven.'"[11] Two critical concerns expressed here, the problem of "how one achieves any kind of happiness" and the concept of "an inside line to heaven," could both be subtitles for virtually all Scorsese films. The angel-headed hipsters of *Mean Streets* and *Taxi Driver*; the entertainers in *New York, New York, The King of Comedy*, and *The Last Waltz*; the athletes of *Raging Bull* and *The Color of Money*; and the Messiah of *The Last Temptation of Christ*—all seek the solace of "any kind of happiness" and the security of "an inside line to heaven." The deeply personal nature of Scorsese's cinema has its wellsprings in his own endless quest for the joy of Christian agape and the wonder of the Parousia.

Charles and Catherine Scorsese frowned on the idea of their son as a priest, mirroring an attitude common in Sicilian culture. As sociologists Nathan Glazer and Patrick Moynihan have observed, immigrant mores dictated that "a man is supposed to be a man, and celibacy has always been something of a problem for the South Italian culture, which tends to see sexual needs as imperative and almost incapable of suppression or moderation."[12] Nevertheless, in September 1956 young Scorsese enrolled at Cathedral College, the seminary for the New York archdiocese, and began preparations for the priesthood. The journey from Little Italy to the Bronx, from city streets to secluded seminary, proved trying for this conscientious adolescent, and his doubts and fears intensified daily. Scorsese movingly described his spiritual angst to Gene Siskel in 1988: "I took the Gospel very seriously. I wondered then and I still wonder whether I should quit everything and help the poor. But I wasn't, and I'm still not, strong enough."[13] Scorsese's ministry and witness bound him to outcasts and the despairing, just as his cinematic vision embraces exiles and misfits, the lost and the damned. If Scorsese left behind the Roman collar, he has never lost his fiercely Christian vision, or his feelings of inadequacy and guilt for not being "strong enough." Diane Jacobs recalls that when she asked Scorsese about the "strongest legacy" of his Catholic upbringing, he replied most "unequivocally" that his inheritance was "a major helping of guilt, like a lot of garlic."[14]

Some of the guilt may have been generated by Scorsese's expulsion from the seminary. Various reasons have been offered for his sudden departure including tales of his roughhousing and brandishing fake guns and of monsignors screaming at this strutting Italian pseudo-toughguy that he wouldn't learn anything until his head was hit on a brick wall. The most realistic assessment might be Scorsese's own admission, "I discovered girls and started dreaming and I let out the energy by becoming a class clown."[15] The erotic energy of the would-be-celibate-priest Scorsese could be neither contained by cold showers and devotional readings nor sublimated in the guilty pleasures of cinema. Like the adolescent Catholic protagonist of his film scenario "Jerusalem, Jerusalem," an as-yet-unrealized section of the *Mean Streets* film cycle, Scorsese agonized over his habitual masturbation, a mortal sin in Irish Catholic rubrics, enough to damn a boy to everlasting flames. The muddle in his mind was torturous, director Scorsese explained to writer Maureen Orth, because his obsession with women and their bodies overwhelmed his good intentions. His solitary attempts at religious meditation quickly gave way to unwelcome "images of women's ankles" which inevitably led him to sinful acts. His moral scrupulosity compounded the problem. Developing these ideas, Scorsese offered Orth a catch-22-like vision of his moral universe: "It's the old concept of mortal sin: you're in the wrong if you're tempted. And if you give in, it is a mortal sin. That's what they taught us, right?"[16] While Catholic ethicists might answer no and attempt to refine Scorsese's statement of canon law, his interpretation of temptation and guilt provides a backdrop for his *The Last Temptation of Christ*. Like Jesus in that film, Scorsese the seminarian was beset by voices, overcome by urges, and bedeviled by desires. Dreams of bliss in a woman's arms made it impossible for Scorsese himself to accept the cross of celibacy.

Upbeat, sensual secular music was also drowning out the Gregorian chant of the seminary for Scorsese. Scorsese could blame it all—his alienation from traditional Italian culture, his constant distraction from studies, and even his crisis of faith—on rock-and-roll, on Elvis, Fats Domino, Bill Haley, and Little Richard. Scorsese listened to the radio constantly and bought all the latest records. His collection became so extensive that frequently he used his own records in his films because he "couldn't find new copies."[17] Rock-and-roll rhythms would merge with Scorsese's movie memories as he pioneered the movement to merge popular music, avante-garde film techniques, political revolution, and personal liberation in a new youth culture. The music was driving him out of the seminary and into the streets in his black leather jacket.

Poor grades at Cathedral sealed Scorsese's fate, so he soon made the arduous journey from Little Italy to a different Catholic institution in the Bronx, Cardinal Hayes High School, training ground for the Catholic laity. Scorsese loathed the doctrinaire, regimented education here, but he struggled to erase his academic shortcomings to qualify for college. Clinging to his ethnicity and his faith, Scorsese hoped to attend the mecca of upwardly mobile Italian immigrants: Fordham University, a Catholic school whose student body was almost 50 percent Italian. At Fordham he planned to study theology and merit another chance at the priesthood.

But Fordham would not have him. The only college open to Scorsese was the university right around the corner from Little Italy, New York University, where he enrolled in 1960, majoring in literature. Scorsese's fortuitous entry into this Greenwich Village–based university at the dawning of the Age of Aquarius and the following turbulent decade he spent at New York University's School of the Arts—studying, pursuing a graduate degree, scrambling for work in film, and teaching—would eventually transform American cinema. At New York University and in beatnik coffeehouses in the Village, Scorsese would discover filmmaking as his vocation. He would also meet both a cadre of talented beginners and an established fellowship of experienced independent filmmakers—people who eventually enriched his life and his art, among them writer Mardik Martin, philosophy-student-turned-film-editor Thelma Schoonmaker, director-producers Brian DePalma and Michael Wadleigh, iconoclastic mentor John Cassavetes, and actors Jon Voight, Harvey Keitel, and Robert De Niro.

No one individual would have a greater influence on Scorsese's art, however, than Haig Manoogian, an unassuming professor of film at New York University who shaped the philosophy of the whole 1960s generation of that university's film school students. In a field where all the emphasis was on technique and the latest equipment, where putatively the best schools were those fabled training grounds for Hollywood pitched in the West—the University of Southern California and the University of California at Los Angeles—Manoogian's philosophy proved as irresistible to Scorsese as the clamoring of John the Baptist in the wilderness. Ensconced in New York, Manoogian argued that "individuality and artistry" would be the real "life blood" of American movies, proclaiming forcefully in his classic textbook *The Filmmaker's Art* that technical skills are worthless unless the filmmaker concerns himself "about his own development, his maturity, his power to see, to think, and to feel."[18] Scorsese, mesmerized by this new gospel of personal filmmaking, faithfully attended Manoogian's lectures. Scorsese realized that his Italian heritage, his Catholic faith, his rock-and-roll music, and his inner turmoil could all be synthesized on screen; cinema could make him whole. Manoogian's vision of filmmaking shaped Scorsese's new calling. Scorsese thought, he later wrote, that all his religious passion could be the wellspring for his films: "But once [Manoogian] started talking about film, I realized that I could put that passion into making movies, and then I realized that the Catholic vocation was, in a sense, through the screen for me" ("Streets" 93). Years later Scorsese would dedicate *Raging Bull* to Manoogian. A measure of how deeply Scorsese had been influenced by Manoogian's theory of filmmaking and how much of his religious passion Scorsese was able to release into film can be found in Pauline Kael's poetically negative appraisal of *Raging Bull,* which charges that Scorsese has "got moviemaking and the church mixed up together; he's trying to be the saint of cinema."[19] Martin Scorsese, the son of Little Italy, the altar boy from St. Patrick's church, and the graduate of New York University, does indeed struggle mightily to be "the saint of cinema," and more often than not he succeeds.

2

The *Mean Streets* Trilogy (1963–1973)

When Martin Scorsese entered film school, an upheaval was taking place, one that critic Stanley Kaufman would label "the most cheering circumstance in contemporary American art"—the emergence of a "film generation" whose members saw cinema as art, adulated European filmmakers, and flooded film schools to make personal statements.[1] Excitement filled the air, spurred by heightened political consciousness, the dawn of personal freedoms, and an emerging cinematic aesthetic. In those early days, Scorsese remembers the convergence of a global film consciousness and a dynamic New York tradition: "Every day a new film was opening from around the world that was totally unique. The beauty of it was that you had John Cassavetes making *Shadows,* which really made us believe if he could do that—pick up a camera and go out in the street—so could we."[2] The film director was, in contemporary parlance, a superstar, and a third of American undergraduates declared they aspired to the job.[3]

In the scramble for self-expression, Scorsese proved himself the ultimate street fighter, overcoming fierce competition, limited budgets, dreary surroundings, outmoded equipment, and institutional bureaucracy. Although NYU offered this poor boy, living on student loans and parental largesse, a chance, his own drive enabled him to complete four short films as an undergraduate and a feature film as a graduate student and instructor. Scorsese's appraisal of NYU emphasizes his struggle: "It was very hard to make a film at school because the script had to be approved and that sort of thing—we just kept fighting and making films."[4]

Inesita—The Art of Flamenco, Scorsese's first student project, was directed by Robert Siegal, with Scorsese as cinematographer and prop man. A routine exercise, *Inesita* did establish a clear link between musical composition and visual form. It also helped Scorsese discover the rhythms of film and the dynamics of shaping sequences. Years later Scorsese would confide to Mary Pat Kelly that while *Inesita* is only nine minutes long and quite amateurish, it inspired much of his technique in both *New York, New York* and *The Last Waltz*: "[A]nd in a funny way, the dancing is covered almost like I covered the scenes in *New York, New York*. The dance is broken up, and the music is broken up. The MGM studio sequences in *The Last Waltz* are covered in a similar way"[5] Litterateur-turned-cineast Scorsese was beginning his transition from NYU's bookish liberal arts undergraduate curriculum to the performance-oriented milieu of NYU's professional training center, the Tisch School of the Arts.

Scorsese's next student film, *What's a Nice Girl like You Doing in a Place like This?*, was inspired by his reading Algernon Blackwood, an English mystic and prolific horror-story writer. Much about Blackwood appealed to 1960s undergraduates, including his romantic cosmology and his heavy dependence on popular psychological concepts. Blackwood's fiction often depends on a doppelgänger, or double, developed in strictest Freudian terms. Scorsese's reliance on mirrors, fascination with paired characters, explorations of alter egos, and his juxtaposition of divergent points of view—all these elements can be traced to his early initiation into the Gothic, violent, and surrealistic fictions of necromancer Blackwood.

While Scorsese does not credit a specific Blackwood story as the inspiration for *What's a Nice Girl like You Doing in a Place like This?*, he does name his protagonist Algernon. Algernon, a writer, buys an ordinary picture of a boat on a lake, and the picture mesmerizes him completely. Although "the picture is nothing to look at," the writer cannot escape his fascination. His marriage and honeymoon provide only temporary distraction; soon he's drawn back to the picture and finally disappears into it. The overt lesson drawn is his psychiatrist's mysterious dictum that "life is fraught with peril."

This short film maintains its comic tone and rich irony most strikingly through a clear dislocation between hypnotic images and deadpan dialogue. This disharmony is accentuated by Scorsese's use of New Wave cinematic techniques: jump cuts, oblique compositions, associational editing, and freeze frames. *What's a Nice Girl like You Doing in a Place like This?* pays homage to Scorsese's favorite directors; it combines the pyrotechnics of Godard with the humanity and surrealism of Fellini in a mélange leavened by the dark comic genius of Mel Brooks.

In his first short, Scorsese convinced himself, "You no longer had to shoot a film in the traditional manner, which required a master shot, medium shot and close-up, with the camera tracking or panning to follow a character." (*Scorsese* 1989, 14). Scorsese and his contemporaries were reinventing film grammar, stretching the limits of narrative embracing contrapuntal structures, and having fun. If movies were giving meaning to Scorsese's life, he was bringing a new vitality and sensuousness to film.

What's a Nice Girl like You Doing in a Place like This? quickly garnered an impressive string of accolades. But his next short, *It's Not Just You, Murray!* (1964), catapulted him to the forefront of student filmmakers. *Murray* represents Scorsese's first full-fledged attempt to recall his childhood in Little Italy and to balance the values of family, church, and tradition against the materialism, deception, and violence of the Mafia.

Murray chronicles the exploits of a shallow gunman, whose adventures in crime from 1922 to 1964 are cataloged in the style of Hollywood gangster classics like Raoul Walsh's *The Roaring Twenties* featuring a glittering universe of fast cars, fancy guns, champagne bubbles, and dancing girls. Murray, a dim-witted gunsel, celebrates his lifelong friendship with his partner, Sam, as the visuals ruthlessly reveal that Sam has cheated Murray at every turn: setting Murray up for a term in prison, double-crossing Murray in the division of illicit profits, even sleeping with Murray's wife. Murray, however, blinded by his small share of the loot, remains fervently convinced that he is one of the "happy people" who have "everything" they want in "this sweet life."

The irony in *Murray* has been wedded to Scorsese's larger theme: that the glamorous gangsters of Hollywood fictions are blind to the desolation crime has wrought in their lives. Sam, a vampire in stylish silks, has devoured Murray's soul, leaving him only a fancy car. Crime may pay, but its coin is tinkling brass in Scorsese's vision. *Murray* foreshadows Scorsese's later ruminations on mob life, success, and lost integrity in *GoodFellas*.

For all its thematic density, however, *Murray* remains joyous. Scorsese cherishes the gangsters he debunks; Murray remains so close to the director's heart that Murray uses the director's father's—Charles Scorsese's—favorite introduction for his tales: "Now, I'm going back ten, twenty years . . ." Much of *Murray* was filmed in the Scorseses' apartment, and all the incidents are based on family stories about his uncles and their Sicilian *compari*. Scorsese's mother, Catherine Scorsese, plays the mother in *Murray*, offering a large plate of spaghetti, only to be constantly rejected by her son, who favors Sam's blandishments over her pasta. Ironically, when Catherine Scorsese recalls Martin's days at NYU she speaks of forcing food on her overworked son: "There were a lot of times when he was working at NYU when I used to get into a cab and bring him some food and then wait to make sure he ate it. I used to say to him, 'Look, Marty, don't worry. It'll all come out in the wash'."[6]

For *It's Not Just You, Murray!*, what came "out in the wash" ensured that the young director would have more opportunities to make films. *Murray* proved such a success that the Fourth New York Film Festival featured it on 13 September 1966, and Don Rugoff played it commercially at his Cinema One theaters after having the 16 mm print blown up to 35 mm. The Hollywood Producers' Guild honored *It's Not Just You, Murray!* as the best student film of 1964, so the starstruck Scorsese flew to the West Coast and found himself seated at the podium with Alfred Hitchcock, who was receiving a Milestone Award. Scorsese and Hitchcock, directors linked by their Catholicism and their mutual interest in the dark side of humanity, in violence, guilt, and psychological terror, never spoke, yet their presence together mirrors the transition between young and old, the transition from the studio system to a new, freewheeling, deal-oriented Hollywood.

Back in New York, the cocky Scorsese wanted to move into feature production and to work in the professional gauge, 35 mm. He had seen 24-year-old Italian director Bernardo Bertolucci's *Before the Revolution* receive a dazzling acceptance at the New York Film Festival, and Scorsese was afraid the world was passing him by. If Bertolucci could captivate American critics with his complex vision of a young man torn between revolutionary impulses and conformist drives, between his passionate love for his aunt and his prudent engagement with a more established maiden, Scorsese felt sure he could garner attention for his images of young men in America facing similar dilemmas in love, religion, and politics. Looking back on these years, Scorsese admits, "I guess I got a bit of a swelled head."[7] Scorsese and his regular cinematographer, Richard Coll, who also wanted to work in 35 mm, hustled enough film stock to prepare *Bring on the Dancing Girls*. In the course of their production, which Scorsese maintains is the first 35 mm student film shot on the East Coast, he and Coll discovered that the larger format meant larger problems. The bigger equipment meant, Scorsese confessed, that "we couldn't move the camera and get the angles that we wanted," and as a result the film was best only "when nothing was going on" and the Italian boys were "just sitting or driving around" (*Scorsese* 1989, 25). Scorsese had faith in these offbeat moments, a faith that would sustain him in the equally adventuresome improvisations in *Mean Streets*.

Bring on the Dancing Girls eventually was recut and edited with new 16 mm footage to become *I Call First*. As is the case in many of his later projects, Scorsese continued reworking his material, and by 1970 he had a new film with added footage entitled *Who's That Knocking at My Door?* Yet even the embryonic feature *Bring on the Dancing Girls* boldly announces director Scorsese's newest fixation—college coeds. Like many Italian men, he was trying to distinguish "nice girls" from "dancing girls" in a not-so-subtle variant of the madonna-whore complex.

All accounts of Scorsese's youth agree on one particular: he was not popular with local girls, because he was short, sickly, shy, and devoted to the church. For all his feverish nights in the seminary, Scorsese had little real experience with women. At NYU Scorsese found dating much easier and began forays into obsessive love. Scorsese's whole life evidences his initial frenzied involvement with his lovers and his eventual disenchantment and boredom.

At NYU Scorsese acted out a variant of *Love Story* and *Goodbye Columbus,* the perennial American Cinderella story of love between a vibrant but poor ethnic and a gorgeous, wealthy heir to the upper-class throne. Years later the thunderstruck suitor could rhapsodize to journalist Guy Flatley about the awakening of love he experienced: "When I went to the university, I met girls who were blond. As a kid, I had literally only known dark-haired girls. But the girls of N.Y.U. were blonde, sweet-looking, intelligent, wore pleated skirts, and spoke proper English. And they were very rich" (Flatley, 1976, 34–35). The key elements of this narrative—the sheltered, introspective, inexperienced Italian boy meeting the cultured, experienced blond girl in pleated skirts—form the plot of *Who's That Knocking at My Door?,* Scorsese's first feature, and a blond in pleated skirts provides the focus of Travis's romance in *Taxi Driver.* More than any other American film director, Scorsese shapes his emotional difficulties and confusions into complex cinematic dramas. His films unabashedly mirror his soul.

An example of the transfiguration of personal dilemmas into the material of art can be found in Scorsese's torturous analysis of his first marriage. In a revealing albeit mean-spirited magazine article, John Lombardi goaded Joey Morale, Scorsese's boyhood chum and the model for Tony in *Mean Streets,* to detail the director's love life.[8] Joey reminisced about Scorsese's four-year "steady" relationship with a Sicilian girl from the neighborhood, Phyllis, who remains a close friend of Scorsese's parents. Everyone assumed a marriage was in the offing until Scorsese brought home a cultured Irish-Jewish girl from NYU, Laraine Marie Brennan, whose voluptuous beauty inspired the character Teresa in *Mean Streets.* Everyone, including Morale, felt that Scorsese hadn't "played straight" with Phyllis, holding on to her until he was sure of Laraine's affections. One local ruffian named Chick, Morale reports, was so outraged that he began a "vendetta" against Scorsese, and Morale was forced to intervene: "I tell [Chick] anything happens I'm gonna break his balls off and feed 'em to him for breakfast." Nevertheless, Scorsese was forced to "lie low for a while," an action that reminded Morale, a film buff, of Johnny Boy's own desperate attempt to escape the vendetta in *Mean Streets.*

Scorsese has been reticent about discussing his marriage to Laraine Brennan; it led him to face crises in his life, raising questions about religion, about career versus domesticity, and about severing connections to his past. When Scorsese does mention Laraine, it's in the context of rebellion against his parents' values, against church teachings on sexuality, and against the war in Vietnam. Yet Laraine Brennan and her virgin bridegroom Martin Scorsese were married in the most traditional of ceremonies in New York's august cathedral, St. Patrick's, soon after his graduation. They then moved to Jersey City, where on 7 December 1965 their first child, Catherine—named for her paternal grandmother—was born.

Scorsese seemed, on the surface, to be living out the immigrant's dream of assimilating into mainstream America. His first marriage, however, proved no social coup. The strain of sustaining a relationship was intensified by the meanness of life in New Jersey; by the endless hustling for money to continue his education, to make films, and to support his family; and by his own awakening to social realities in America. Scorsese soon found himself drifting away from Laraine and his daughter. The acclaim he received as an undergraduate filmmaker did little to ease his way into a career. For a while Scorsese worked for the Maysles Brothers, but eventually he settled on a position Haig Manoogian offered him as a teaching assistant at NYU.

Scorsese frequently refers to his days teaching film as his years doing Johnny Carson monologues, a curious link to his analysis of Rupert Pupkin in *The King of Comedy*.

Scorsese's colleague as teaching assistant, Mardik Martin, was born in Iran but raised in Iraq and had worked at MGM's distribution office in Baghdad. Martin and Scorsese proved kindred spirits, so they collaborated on all of Scorsese's early scripts. Underpaid and overworked, they were searching for an angle into the big time; meanwhile, their wives pressured them to be practical.

Things became so bleak in both their marriages that the two erstwhile movie moguls often found themselves "free" only in their cars, much like the street boys in Scorsese's early films. They developed a project called *This Film Could Save Your Marriage*, a parody of skin-flicks that often offered this tagline as a justification for close-ups of copulation; the Scorsese-Martin project offered humorous close-ups of actions designed to wreck even the most solid relationship. Shivering in their Valiant, dodging their wives, Scorsese and Martin also outlined volumes of autobiographical material rife with religious, sexual, and political themes. Writing filmscripts was their therapy and their marriage counseling.

Mardik Martin's friendship, however, was not destined to save Scorsese's first marriage; Scorsese was enduring a bitter lesson in the conflict between career and marriage, a theme that would be central to *Alice Doesn't Live Here Anymore* and *New York, New York*. For all his distress, Scorsese managed to do a massive amount of scripting with Martin. *Mean Streets* was one project prepared in 1966. Scorsese sketched the outline, Martin fleshed out the structure, and the first draft, under the title *Season of the Witch*, also credits contributions by another NYU student, Ethan Edwards. *Season of the Witch* can best be described as a diamond in the rough; all the main elements of *Mean Streets* are there in a cruder, more didactic form. The strident tone of the writing is suggested by the song that was meant to be superimposed like a news bulletin on the screen at the beginning of the film: Bob Dylan's "Subterranean Homesick Blues."

Mardik Martin and Martin Scorsese, schoolboys for many more than 20 years, vented all their spleen in *Season of the Witch*. Whereas the finished *Mean Streets,* which premiered at the New York Film Festival in 1973, develops ideas by indirection and implication, *Season of the Witch* hammers home its points, emphasizing particularly religious criticism and sociological insight. Martin and Scorsese envisioned

Season of the Witch as part of a messianic trilogy, beginning with *Jerusalem, Jerusalem,* continuing with *Who's That Knocking at My Door?,* and concluding in *Season of the Witch.* The concept of this religious trilogy preoccupied them; their vision was epic and tragic, and they wanted to make a theological cinematic masterpiece, in the mode of Eisenstein's political trilogy *Ivan the Terrible* or Marcel Pagnol's humanist French trilogy, *Marius, Fanny,* and *Cesar.*

The treatment for the trilogy's first installment, *Jerusalem, Jerusalem,* was completed on 29 March 1966, though Scorsese did not copyright it until 1979, and spoke of making it as a television film as late as 1981. *Jerusalem, Jerusalem,* an unabashedly candid confession, represents a transparent roman à clef, with Scorsese as J.R., a young boy tortured by guilt over his habit of masturbation, trying to regain his spirituality in a three-day retreat at a Jesuit monastery. The retreat master, Father McMahon, offers little solace for J.R., dismissing him at the retreat's end with an injunction to see a good Catholic psychiatrist. In the three days, however, J.R., whose readings include *The Lives of the Saints* and *The Screwtape Letters,* participates in an outdoor procession through the Stations of the Cross as he fantasizes about a contemporary crucifixion in New York City, hears a hellfire-and-brimstone sermon on the evils of premarital sex, and experiences his own religious vision.

Scorsese made an identical retreat to a Jesuit seminary as a teenager, where his retreat master also suggested psychoanalysis, a recommendation that launched Scorsese into his first therapy, which extended over seven years. The highlight of Scorsese's retreat followed a sex sermon that centered on Christ's suffering as recorded in the Shroud of Turin. The terrified youth experienced a disorienting epiphany: "I was also a city boy, so anything in the country, a noise, seemed scary. It became like an auditory hallucination where I heard crickets that got louder and louder and louder until they made me feel like I was going to burst. And then I saw the smudges on the window become like the face on the Shroud. That happened about three times during the night. I walked around the halls trying to get out of it" ("Streets," 98). Scorsese remains so obsessed with the sermon, his vision, and the concept of premarital sex as a damning offense that *Mean Streets* still includes a key scene where his friends mock Charlie for believing a retreat master's parable about illicit lovers trapped in a burning car.

One element of *Jerusalem, Jerusalem* deserves special comment. The dramatic intercutting of J.R.'s journey through the Stations of the

Cross and his vision of an urban crucifixion foreshadows Scorsese's frequent use of scenes from the Passion and references to the crucifixion in his films, as well as suggesting the wellspring for his project *The Last Temptation of Christ*. There is a connection between J.R.'s guilty prayers and the suffering of the urban Christ figure: the key concept of the atonement as construed in Catholic dogma. For Catholics, the crucifixion is more than a historic martyrdom; expiation and atonement constitute eternal processes, so the nails are always being driven in by sin, yesterday, today, and tomorrow. For Scorsese's tortured protagonists, the suffering on Golgotha exists as their past, their present, and their future. *Jerusalem, Jerusalem* provides the eternal perspective against which the rest of the *Mean Streets* narrative functions. The headnote for *Jerusalem, Jerusalem,* which Scorsese borrowed from Robert Bresson's film *Diary of a Country Priest,* could serve as an introduction to all three film projects: "God is not a torturer. . . . He only wants us to be merciful with ourselves."

The tender mercy that propelled Scorsese's career forward was Haig Manoogian's continuing interest in his protégé, friend, and teaching assistant. Manoogian had always felt guilty about the failure of *Bring on the Dancing Girls* and remained interested in its insightful treatment of streetcorner life. So when wealthy attorney Joseph Weill entered the graduate film program at NYU, hoping to better understand the business of the affluent show business clients his prosperous firm represented, Manoogian saw an opportunity to resurrect Scorsese's stalled project. Investing his own meager savings and his wife's pin money, Manoogian formed a partnership with Weill and Scorsese to develop the feature film *I Call First*; even Charles Scorsese contributed funds diverted from one of Martin's student loans.

I Call First premiered at the Chicago Film Festival in November 1967, and Roger Ebert of the Chicago *Sun-Times* greeted the roughly constructed feature with the review every tyro film director dreams of. Ebert gushed enthusiastically about a great moment in American film, the advent of an instant classic that fused the disparate worlds of American cinema by combining the technical proficiency of traditional Hollywood films like *On the Waterfront* with the fresh, spontaneous insights of experimental underground films like *The Connection* and *Shadows*. Scorsese and his cohorts celebrated their triumph, and when journalist Ebert and artist Scorsese met to discuss the film, Ebert opined that Scorsese could be "the American Fellini in ten years." Scorsese quickly asked, "Gee, do you think it will take that long?" (Hoberman 1983, 38).

Then nothing happened, nothing at all. No distributor picked up *I Call First,* and no studio recruited Scorsese. Thrown back on his own wits to survive, Scorsese struck out in a hundred directions at once. He worked for CBS editing news footage, developed filmscripts, joined the Humphrey campaign for one day, and prepared a short for the U.S. Information Agency, a film so odd, he recalls, that the agency immediately destroyed it. Scorsese even did one week's preproduction work on a directing assignment, *The Honeymoon Killers.* The producers asked Scorsese to make a black-and-white film, while he wanted to shoot in color; as a compromise he agreed to "a kind of tabloid *National Enquirer*–type style."[9] Conflict came when Scorsese refused to do retakes and alternate angles. As a graduate of film school, Scorsese felt that "a director who really knows what he's doing does it in one take" ("Confessions," 134–35). His more sober producers knew that their $150,000 budget would never cover the overly long, epic, stylized film that would result from exercising this self-indulgent fancy on a 175-page-long script. Scorsese discovered there was room for experimentation and error in film school but not in the world of B-movies. He was fired. Only when Scorsese could balance artistic inspiration and Hollywood economics would he prosper as an American filmmaker.

Disheartened, Scorsese turned to Europe as an answer to his problems, making commercials in England and Holland. Then Scorsese applied for a grant offered in conjunction with the Jacques Ledoux Fourth International Film Festival in Belgium. He won enough color film stock for *The Big Shave,* his bloody parable about a young man entering a small bathroom, preparing to shave, and then gradually destroying himself, cutting his throat with the razor. Scorsese told attendees at an American Film Institute seminar that the bathroom where this short was shot was so small that the crew couldn't move about; the resulting footage accentuates the claustrophobic mood, while the editing style is "all clips like a television commercial" (*Dialogue* 2), ironically counterpointed by the big-band sound of Bunny Berigan's rendition of "I Can't Get Started." The music heightens the central irony, for, as critic Michael Bliss notes, the orchestration reinforces the message that the real issue is not the failure to get started but instead "that he simply cannot stop."[10] Obsessive behavior and the darkness of violent impulses are linked to the bathroom spectacle by one of Scorsese's allusions, a credit for "Whiteness by Herman Melville." Scorsese had intended to intercut live action footage from Vietnam but contented himself with a final title card, "Viet 67." Scorsese planned the film as part of a week-long antiwar rally in New York City but postproduction took too long, so *The Big Shave* eventually screened at the 1968 New York Film Festival.

The Big Shave clearly symbolized the self-destructive urges behind the Nixon-Kissinger excursions in the Far East, yet it also revealed Scorsese's own demons, the ambition, self-hatred, and loathing consuming him. Scorsese recognised that *The Big Shave* dealt with "something else . . . going on inside me, I think, which really had nothing to do with the war. It was just a very bad period, a very bad period" (Kelly 1980, 19). Scorsese's artistic career seemed on hold, his marriage was crumbling, and even his teaching seemed to be falling apart.

A dramatic picture of Scorsese at this time was provided by one of his undergraduate students, who described the night Scorsese showed his class *The Big Shave* as follows: "So we watched this guy slice up his face, the gore escalating until he slit his own throat. But to tell the truth, even then Marty didn't fool us. War in Viet-nam, well sever my eyeball, what was happening on that screen didn't have anything to do with no forty klicks past the Da Lang Bridge. Marty's battle was closer to home. It'd be more than a bit melodramatic to say our class of *cineastes* adopted skinny, wheezing Marty that night, but, for sure, it wasn't a performance you forgot too soon."[11]

Haig Manoogian hadn't forgotten Scorsese or *I Call First*. At one of the screenings he arranged for potential distributors, Manoogian happened to meet an army pal who had served in his platoon, Joseph Brenner. Brenner, a power in the exploitation market, agreed to distribute the film if nude scenes could be added. Manoogian struck the deal, and the footage was shot by Scorsese in Amsterdam. Harvey Keitel flew to Amsterdam for the shooting, and flustered Scorsese nervously filmed the nude sequence in an artist's loft. Coincidentally, the actress in the key scene where J.R. sprays her naked body with playing cards, Anne Collete, had appeared in Godard's *All the Boys are Named Patrick,* a befitting homage to Scorsese's New Wave idol. Scorsese, late of the seminary, smuggled the raw footage through customs in the pockets of his raincoat when he returned to New York City.

Who's That Knocking at My Door? then had a major New York release. Scorsese saw his cinematic diary transformed into a theatrical feature. Despite the limitations in continuity and technique resulting from the prolonged genesis; the mixture of student 35 mm footage, later 16 mm footage, and the 16 mm nude inserts; the total shift in casts and production personnel, including a new cinematographer, Michael Wadleigh; and all the compromises necessitated by irregular to nonexistent funding *Who's That Knocking?* constituted a major statement by an important new filmmaker.

Scorsese intended his Little Italy trilogy to be unprecedentedly realistic, unrelentingly factual, and painfully true. All the episodes in *Who's That Knocking?* actually occurred; most constitute thinly disguised autobiography. Keitel, who got the lead role by answering an ad for performers in an NYU student film in 1965 and who kept faith with both the project and Scorsese for several lean years, functions as a Scorsese surrogate in his portrayal of J.R., a psychologically stunted Italian man, torn by his desires to remain true to his culture and faithful to his church, yet irresistibly drawn to a cool, intellectual blond called only "the girl" in the credits. Those familiar with Scorsese's life recognize this tale immediately as a musing on his first marriage, a liaison that was disintegrating the whole time the director reworked his film.

The crisis in *Who's That Knocking?* concerns sex, specifically the loss of the girl's virginity years earlier as the result of date rape. In J.R.'s universe there are only virgins and whores; a girl is either *una buona femmina* (a good girl) or a *disgraziata* (a disgrace). Most of J.R.'s "love talk" with the girl really amounts to an indoctrination in sexual repression. This beautiful blond, whose hair is backlighted and spotlighted to give her a Madonna-like halo, moves sensuously through J.R.'s apartment, all soft shoulders, shy smiles, and tender kisses.

J.R., the ex–bank teller, on the other hand, gropes frantically for a justification for his reticence, offering disjointed, half-articulated phrases, such as "I love you, but . . . I feel silly saying this. . . . Just not now. . . . Call it anything you want—old fashioned, what . . . If you love me, you'll understand what I mean." Later when he finally structures his ideas enough to rationalize his bizarre behavior, he muses as he daydreams about his romps with prostitutes that "There are girls and there broads. A broad isn't exactly a virgin. You play around with a broad. You don't marry a broad."

The girl, incredulous, answers, "You don't mean that." She finds out how much he does mean it when she recounts her rape, only to hear him reject her and her "story" in bitter disbelief: "I can't understand it. If anyone else hears a story like that, how can they believe it? How can I believe you? It just doesn't make sense." Scorsese punctuates the dialogue here with one of his favorite devices: he repeats the sound of a door slamming three times, hammering home the sense of closure. Scorsese had noted Truffaut's use of a triple cut between three close-ups in several films, and he adopted this triple repetition of image or sound as his own. Similar triple cuts, visual and aural, haunt key moments of Scorsese films. In *Who's That Knocking?* Scorsese out-Ibsens Ibsen: his slamming door echoes the conclusion of *A Doll's House*.

J.R. flees his confrontation with adult reality by dashing back to the boys at the Eighth Ward Pleasure Club. But the boys cannot insulate him. The film reflects his consciousness as it drunkenly flashes back on the girl's struggle and eventual humiliation and rape. Others may be content to harass and fondle bimbos like Suzie and Rosie from the Bronx, but J.R. cannot erase the image of his girl with her angelic blond hair and her gentle loving ways. For a while it looks as if he can break free, for he goes to her apartment to declare, "You know I love you." Like Ibsen's Helmer, however, Scorsese's J.R. has no conception of a real relationship between equals, and he clumsily proposes marriage in the most demeaning of terms: "I understand and forgive you. . . . I'm gonna marry you anyway." The girl sharply rebukes J.R., declaring, "You can't marry me anyway!" Their potential reconciliation degenerates into a savage shouting match, with J.R. finally dismissing her as a "whore" and the girl insisting that he "Go home, go home."

After three unsuccessful but dramatic pushes on the down elevator button, J.R. symbolically tumbles down the steps, and the film cuts to him in church, limning a dramatic collage of terrifying religious icons. Santa Lucia, Sicily's most important female saint, looms large in this sequence, complete with her goblet and severed eyes. Italians idolized her for gouging out her eyes rather than marrying; the counterpoint to J.R.'s plight reinforces Scorsese's theme, as does his last shot of J.R. kissing the feet of the crucified Christ only to find his mouth filled with blood. The taste of blood at the foot of the crucifix, together with the disjunction between the life of the flesh with women and the call to a celibate Golgotha, haunts Scorsese, J.R., and the Messiah of *The Last Temptation of Christ*.

Several critics have tried to complicate the sexual theme in *Who's That Knocking* by arguing that there was no rape, that the girl was lying. Thus, Lesley Robinson in *Film* argues that "When she tells J.R. her story of being raped in a car, although we see a flashback of what she says happened, neither we the audience nor J.R. the listener are really convinced by it. It could be a ploy to make him think he's the first man she really wanted, and the camera accentuates this duplicity by making this flashback sequence grayer and more disjointed than the rest, as if the girl were making it up as she went along."[12]

Other variants on this theory spin elaborate webs of duplicity, but all seem beside the point. The fact of the rape looms less important in the narrative than its psychological impact on J.R. And the best explanation of the variation in style in this sequence is provided by the plot summary circulated by Joseph Brenner at the film's opening: "the scene is subjectively handled, and the loss of virginity being based on rape is more a condition of J.R.'s imagination, as his mind plummets forward to justify the situation and feels that he has been betrayed."[13] An adequate appreciation of *Who's That Knocking* requires more emphasis on the source of the cracks in J.R.'s consciousness than on the cause of the tear in the girl's hymen.

J.R.'s real love affair centers on the guys in the streets, the preening male corner gang so prominent in Italian American immigrant life. Scorsese's camera loves the boyish antics, the exaggerated gestures, and the overblown macho display. Scorsese so adulates his *vitelloni* and the rhetoric of their ritual insults, the so-called *passatella,* that he undercuts the hetereosexual romantic interest. J.R. and Scorsese cannot divorce themselves from this male exhibitionism, and they revel in the overt display of sexual potency. Scorsese's most orgiastic camerawork treats not J.R. and the girl as they wrestle in bed but instead J.R. and his friends as they jostle and fight over guns, girls, booze, and debts.

The film reviewer for *Time* saw this obsession with the "street and its milieu" as a failing and damned *Who's That Knocking* because Scorsese "overindulges in scenes with J.R. and his buddies that are of peripheral importance."[14] Shift perspectives and one can see that the buddy and male-bonding aspects of the film constitute its main strengths and prepare the way for *Mean Streets*.

Many critics have commented on the tensions between the values of J.R.'s male friends and the love he feels for "the girl." For example, Holly McLennan has observed that Scorsese's males are alienated from heterosexual love: "For all their commitment to notions of good girls and bad girls, they are really only capable of loving each other. Only from each other can they get the support and tenderness each of us needs and, in the end, the tragedy is that theirs is a world without women."[15] But it's not just that the girl and J.R.'s cronies war inside his head for his affection; in his worldview they are also warring over his immortal soul. His "salvation" lies in his allegiance to church and family, not in his love for a blond or in his pleasure with his male friends. Each element in J.R.'s bizarre trinity excludes the other; he cannot integrate girl, friends, and God in one life. His choices are limiting rather than liberating, self-destructive rather than nurturing. Yet J.R.'s dilemma obviously parallels the choices Scorsese himself was facing between the world of movies, his love for his first wife, his roots in Little Italy, and his Catholic faith.

Some critics, such as Michael Bliss, identify the church as the villain in *Who's That Knocking,* arguing melodramatically that the film centers on Scorsese's repudiation of J.R.'s doctrinaire faith. In Bliss's view there is a clear answer to the question the title, borrowed from a rock song, poses: "It is the Catholic-corrupted, Catholic-appropriated Jesus, the God of pain and destruction . . . who is knocking at the door; it is the God of morbidity who demands entrance" (Bliss, 47). Bliss's argument in its hyperbole mistakes Scorsese's reservations for rejection. Undoubtedly, J.R. suffers from the guilt his faith generates and longs for a purification that never comes, but *Who's That Knocking?* also suggests the security and nurturing to be found in the bosom of the church and the eucharist of Italian family life.

The film opens in a flashback to J.R.'s youth, and we see him as a boy with four other siblings receiving, the Brenner summary expostulates, "the warmth and love of his mother and the heavy influence of the uncompromising teachings of the Roman Catholic Faith" (Brenner, 2). The love of his mother is embodied in the bread she feeds her son, an especially potent symbol for Italians, for, as Richard Gambino explains in *Blood of My Blood,* where Americans say "as good as gold," the Italian simile is *"buono come il pane*—as good as bread." (Gambino, 17). Scorsese accentuates the family ties in *Who's That Knocking* by casting his own mother as the bread giver and by returning compulsively to J.R.'s rejection of the bread of Italian life.

Similarly, Scorsese underscores the tangible symbols of Catholicism by loading his frame with crucifixes, holy-water fonts, plaster-of-paris statues, and votive candles. Many reviewers lambasted the panoply of Roman Catholic symbols surrounding Harvey Keitel as directorial overkill, but Scorsese actually shot the key scenes of J.R.'s religious indoctrination in his family's apartment, specifically in his mother's bedroom using her statues and sacramentals. In the film J.R. sternly warns his girl as she examines the statue, "Anything happen to that and my mother will pass out." The line between art and life is frequently stretched thin in Scorsese's films, but it is even thinner than usual here in *Who's That Knocking?*

No one who knew Scorsese's earlier films could ever ignore the autobiographical elements in *Who's That Knocking?*; nor could they ignore the emergence of a particular Scorsese look and sound. The film is plagued by technical glitches, including lighting mismatches and microphones visible in many interiors, yet daring close-up visuals convert statues into medieval gargoyles and transform plastic sacramentals into overpowering religious presences. The nude scenes are powerfully erotic; the fragmentation of bodies, as well as some rapid editing and 360-degree crane shots, highlight the libidinal tension.

All the Scorsese "signatures" are in *Who's That Knocking?*, including the emblematic neck wound, which climaxes the romp with Suzie and Rosie; the endless car rides down glistening city streets; the absurdist macho banter; the constantly repeated triple cuts; the extended allusions to Western movies; and the relentless rock-and-roll music. The soundtrack for *Who's That Knocking* was intended, Scorsese admits, to be "a grenade" (*Scorsese* 1989, 28), playing off visuals against contradictory pop-rock lyrics and setting off the whole empty life of the streets against the intense rhythms of jukebox standards. Scorsese's grenade was meant to fragment his audience around the question, Do you want to dance?

Soon after the release of *Who's That Knocking*, Joseph Brenner Associates announced a long-term commitment to Scorsese projects, specifying that the next film would be *Battle Queen*, written by Mardik Martin and starring Harvey Keitel and Zina Bethune in what Scorsese, the proposed director, termed "the story of five World War II veterans who have a reunion every year to discuss the war," a story that "reveals their characters through their efforts to prove their manhood in killing."[16] Scorsese would make a number of films in which his protagonists prove their manhood in killing, but *Battle Queen* wasn't one of them. Unhappily, Scorsese found himself back at square one, hustling in New York in a troubled period he poignantly described to filmmakers at the American Film Institute: "I was killing myself in New York. Death. Pure death in New York. . . . I mean, guys I knew are dead now. Really."[17]

Death may well have been on Scorsese's mind because the grandfather he was named for died in the summer of 1969, and the grieving Scorsese felt that an era was coming to an end. Luckily, Scorsese's prodigious skills as a film editor were being highly touted among New York filmmakers, as were his growing commitment to leftist political causes and his love for contemporary music. All these traits endeared him to another NYU filmmaker, Michael Wadleigh, who helped Scorsese make his next big career move. Wadleigh had important music and film contacts, and soon he and Scorsese were on their way to Max Yasgur's farm to record the Woodstock Music and Art Fair, an Aquarian exposition that promised in its ads "three days of peace and music."

The promoters of Woodstock—Michael Lang, Artie Korfeld, Joel Rosenman, and John Roberts—had no idea of the turmoil they would cause until hundreds of thousands of concertgoers, hippies, political activists, and dropouts clogged all the roads to Bethel. What followed were three incredible days of mud, fellowship, and music, with Scorsese, Wadleigh, and scores of others documenting it in 16 mm, 8 mm, and any other format they could lay their hands on. Scorsese spent the whole time—15–17 August 1969—on stage, caught up in the music and the filming: Scorsese arrived in Woodstock formally attired, wearing expensive cufflinks. In the first few hours he lost his cufflinks, and by the end of the festival he was wearing jeans. Throughout his life he would be torn between his love for fancy fashions and tailored silk suits by Armani and his obsession with the dreams of outsiders and the music of iconoclasts and rebels.

Film producer Fred Weintraub hired a helicopter to drop a certified check onto the stage at Woodstock to secure the rights to the film and then goaded Warner Brothers into distributing the amalgam of this diverse concert footage, *Woodstock,* which eventually won the Academy Award for Best Documentary feature in 1970 for its putative director, Wadleigh, and for its putative assistant directors, Scorsese and Thelma Schoonmaker. Accurate credits for films have always been a tricky issue, but in the case of *Woodstock* the matter is especially tangled. Schoonmaker was also mentioned as a candidate for an editing Oscar for *Woodstock,* yet most participants agree that Scorsese played an equal role in editing the literally hundreds of hours of footage shot during the concert.

Back at New York University, Scorsese marshaled his editing talents to salvage another project. Politically active students from the university working together with a radical group of independent documentary filmmakers called the New York Cinetracts Collective had been filming the May 1970 student demonstrations on Wall Street.

During the ongoing confrontations—which were intensified by nationwide student strikes; secret military incursions in Cambodia; and the killings at Kent State—NYU film equipment was lost, destroyed, or pilfered; consequently, the scuttlebutt around the university held that if a film couldn't be salvaged from this economic loss, heads would roll, notably Scorsese's. Instructor Scorsese had so embroiled himself in diverse political film projects that his house had become an impromptu commune for the dissidents and radicals. Meanwhile more footage was exposed as the National Student Strike brought its demands to the White House in an emotionally charged antiwar rally.

Scorsese mustered his troops in the overutilized, underfunded editing rooms at NYU, supervising a gifted group of editors, including Schoonmaker, as they evaluated the uneven pieces of amateur 16 mm footage, trimmed them into sequences, intercut the narrative elements, added a soundtrack consisting of diverse reactions to the war and to student protests, and molded them into an accomplished documentary entitled *Street Scenes 1970,* which became one of the most widely discussed short films screened at the New York Film Festival that fall. Schoonmaker later told Terence Rafferty that her joy in working on these political films convinced her to keep working with Scorsese, even though almost a decade of problems with the editors' union kept her from receiving any credit for helping to shape his films. Describing the rough-and-tumble days of *Street Scenes,* when small crews worked in the most primitive conditions, hauling film canisters around town and mounting their camera and camera operator in a wheelchair for tracking and dolly shots, Schoonmaker proclaimed that "I was working with a group of people who were so committed to not just the best in film work but to their own personal visions. . . . [W]orking with people who cared as deeply as someone like Marty did about their films is very seductive—you never want to work any other way."[18]

Scorsese had been deeply moved by the slaughter at Kent State and told interviewers, "From that point on, I was sick. I asked myself, 'what can we do instead of closing things down? Why don't we open things up?'"[19] Scorsese was searching for original answers, not tired rhetoric, political cant, and hackneyed propaganda. Scorsese employs a heated informal debate among journalists, filmmakers, and friends to conclude his film. Their freewheeling discussion concerns the responsibility of filmmakers to truth and social change, frequently pitting Scorsese's students and the members of the collective, who espouse an activist role, against Scorsese's friend Jay Cocks of *Time* magazine, who constantly calls for "reason."

Scorsese's editing in this last sequence, the only part of the film he shot himself, suggests an end to any age of reason. As presented, neither radicals nor more restrained analysts have the answer. Life has become so complex and multifaceted that there appear to be nothing but confusion, chaos, and ambiguity. As Scorsese later explained to Bella Taylor, "I used footage that showed nobody knew what to do, neither radicals nor conservatives. Everybody was yelling at everybody and the picture ends in the middle of an argument because that was when the film literally ran out. I just left it that way. I thought 'Perfect, it was God sent.'"[20]

Such random, seemingly inexplicable final scenes occur frequently in Scorsese's canon. *Alice Doesn't Live Here Anymore,* for example, ends with a shot of a Monterey sign shown entirely by accident, yet the impact of this symbol reverberates long after the credits. For Scorsese, conclusions and resolutions seem artificial. He prefers open-ended, dense structures where ambiguity and complexity abound. Either player may win the final match in *The Color of Money*; the street boys of *Mean Streets* may or may not change or survive; Alice may or may not live here or there again; the "Raging Bull" may be a broken-down entertainer or a reborn philosopher; the "Taxi Driver" may be an apocalyptic saint or a mad assassin; the "King of Comedy" may be an emperor or a court jester. Scorsese puts little trust in a rational universe progressing in orderly ways to a preordained goal. His fictional universe frequently lacks causality and structure, and his characters depend more on the final mercy of God than on any day-to-day evidence of divine Providence. In Scorsese's world everyone is unwittingly destined to fulfill God's plan.

Scorsese's own sense of destiny told him that his future did not lie in university teaching, with its meager pay, or in editing antiwar movies. Thus, when Fred Weintraub, who loved Scorsese's work on *Woodstock,* invited him to Hollywood to edit *Medicine Ball Caravan,* Scorsese heeded the call to go West. As he embarked for California, he also finalized his divorce. Martin settled in California in an apartment with Harvey Keitel, the J.R. of *Who's That Knocking* and the Charlie of *Mean Streets.* Neither of these New Yorkers felt comfortable in their new home, however, and they half-feared, half-fantasized that their fellow tenants included a weird assortment of perverts, drug addicts, and dangerously violent types.

Scorsese was no more comfortable with his new project. *Medicine Ball Caravan* purported to document the tour of a large troupe of performing artists busing from Los Angeles to Washington, D.C., in the summer of 1970 to foster peace, spread love, and celebrate music. In rough cut, however, the disjointed collection of 8 mm, 16 mm, and 35 mm Techniscope footage ran nine hours, with little sense of purpose. Scorsese later complained that he "had to re-direct the whole picture," since it had "no concept at all."[21] The young filmmaker labored under great pressure. Fred Weintraub was his friend, and this was Scorsese's debut on the West Coast. In addition, Scorsese was already romantically interested in Weintraub's daughter, Sandy, who would become his lover and helpmate, serving as unofficial coproducer, coeditor, coscriptwriter on his projects and nursing him back to health when the workload overwhelmed his frail constitution.

Hollywood professionals respected the job the fledgling editor had done on *Medicine Ball Caravan* and Scorsese was soon supervising the montage for another musical documentary, *Elvis on Tour*. Seeking to avoid a permanent niche in editing rooms and a life working on documentaries, Scorsese threw himself into the Hollywood scene. As he explained to interviewer James Truman, making it in the movie business involves hustle: "I moved to LA and hustled and hustled and hustled. I went to every party, I went to every person's office, I read everything and I went to every movie" (Truman, 79). One contact Scorsese made was Roger Corman, the producer of low-budget adventures for American International Pictures. Corman's eye for talent established him as a legend; his apotheosis was complete when downhome critic Joe Bob Briggs crowned Corman the "King of the Drive In," ruling monarch of "the three kinds of drive-in movies: Blood, Breasts, and Beasts."[22] Corman had seen *J.R.* (the retitled version of *Who's That Knocking?*) and promised Scorsese he could direct the sequel to *Bloody Mama*. Ever wary about Hollywood hype, Scorsese viewed Corman's offer as little more than a casual remark, so he continued his frenzied quest for a Hollywood contract.

Soon thereafter Scorsese met one of the feature players in *Bloody Mama*, Robert De Niro, at a Christmas party given by actress Verna Bloom. The two displaced youths from Little Italy had known each other casually as teenagers, when De Niro ran with a street gang called the Forty Thieves and was known as "Bobby Milk" or "Bobby Irish." They reminisced about De Niro's exploits around Kenmare Street, and De Niro suggested that they make a "film about that neighborhood" (Truman, 77). Within a year they would team up on *Mean Streets.*

But first came the promised but still-unexpected call from Roger Corman in which he told Scorsese, "Here's a couple of thousand dollars. I want you to direct a picture. Every fifteen pages it has to have nudity, a little violence here and a little action there, otherwise you can do what you want with it" (Carducci, 12).

The dumbfounded Scorsese went to Arkansas at the helm of *Boxcar Bertha,* a foray into a new depression-era, crime-spree genre modeled on the contemporary hit *Bonnie and Clyde.* Little that he had learned at NYU prepared Scorsese for Corman's no-nonsense, shoot-and-run, profit-oriented operation. In 24 days of shooting, Scorsese received an unofficial diploma from Corman's academy of practical filmmaking. One important lesson Scorsese learned involved trimming scripts. *Boxcar Bertha* had a literate shooting script by Joyce H. Carrington and John William Carrington, loosely based on Boxcar Bertha Thompson's autobiography, *Sister of the Road.* Scorsese shaped that script to suit his own interests and to manifest his personal vision, as he abided by the demands of the action genre, delivering the bullets and the sex.

On location Scorsese learned to use insert shots and extra coverage to ease editing problems. Frequently Scorsese was tempted to make the same errors he did on *The Honeymoon Killers,* shooting all long master shots without any short shots, reaction shots, or inserts. His experienced cinematographer balked, however, and implored him to do more close-up work, more short shots, and more transitional footage.

Corman's production crew showed Scorsese the transcendent importance of the bottom line; personal expression must fit the Corman projected budget. Scorsese profited from still another critical Corman mandate. Corman, as director Jonathan Demme observes, always aims at the audience: "Keeping your audience—that's the thing that Roger teaches you."[23]

Boxcar Bertha never ignores its audience and never overestimates the drive-in crowd. The sex-and-violence quotient remains high, even though the overall narrative stresses social consciousness, proletarian rage, and rabid unionism. In the American International Pictures universe of *Boxcar Bertha,* the comely heroine, played by Barbara Hershey, gets opportunities to seduce not only her man but eastern con men, railroad cops, and clients at the local bordello.

The torrid erotic pace of *Boxcar Bertha* is matched by the ceaseless violence. The contemporary reviewer for *Variety* complained that the whole enterprise was "not much more than an excuse to slaughter a lot of people."[24] With mind-numbing regularity there are plane crashes, stickups, fistfights, episodes of torture, and finally the film's pièce de résistance, a crucifixion so daring in its execution and so horrible in its effect that Jeffrey Lyons, writing for *Rock,* declared it "should have been cut."[25] On the other hand, Archer Winston, writing for the *New York Post,* saw the final crucifixion as proof of Scorsese's "ability to stage certain episodes without squeamishness," arguing further that Scorsese is "so very strong with the crucifixion you feel this is part of a better, bigger picture. . . . [T]he picture you were thinking was in shorthand expands to the heroic dimensions of tragedy."[26] This dichotomy in critical reactions foreshadows the great debates about violence in *Taxi Driver* and *Raging Bull*; some viewers always feel Scorsese overdoes the blood-and-gore, while others see the physical violence as part of a grander vision.

Interestingly, the crucifixion in *Boxcar Bertha* came from the original script, but the stylish presentation of it is pure Scorsese. Scorsese considered this sequence the "most important" element in *Boxcar Bertha* and "figured I might as well get it out of my system once." (Kelly 1980, 20). Driven by his belief that the inclusion of a crucifixion scene in his first Hollywood project was "a sign from God," Scorsese worked full throttle on this scene and was pleased with the results: "I like the way we shot it, the angles we used, and in particular the way you saw the nails coming through the wood, though they were never seen piercing flesh" (*Scorsese* 1989, 36).

Crucifixions and purgation through violence never drop out of Scorsese's system, and on the set of *Boxcar Bertha* Hershey, when she discovered Scorsese's Catholic fixation on atonement, gave the young director a book she thought he might like, Nikos Kazantzakis's *The Last Temptation of Christ,* requesting that if Scorsese every filmed the novel, she be cast as Mary Magdalene. *The Last Temptation of Christ* became Scorsese's albatross; he constantly declared that filming the Kazantzakis novel was his ultimate objective.

Scorsese's immediate prospects proved less enthralling. Corman coupled *Boxcar Bertha* on the theater circuit with *1000 Convicts and a Woman,* and offered Scorsese, who had joined the Directors Guild of America, his choice of two exploitation projects: *The Arena,* a female gladiator film, or *I Escaped from Devil's Island,* a *Papillon* clone. Luck-

David Carradine as the crucified Bill Shelley in *Boxcar Bertha* (1972). American International Pictures. The Museum of Modern Art/Film Stills Archive.

ily, Scorsese was poised to make his own escape. He had worked on *Minnie and Moskowitz* with his idol John Cassavetes, fine-tuning the soundmix; Cassavetes had carried the young filmmaker financially when his fortunes were low.

So as soon as Scorsese had his rough cut of *Boxcar Bertha,* which ran about two and one-half hours, he invited Cassavetes to take a look. There have been many public discussions, accusations, denials, and apologies concerning exactly what transpired that night. Scorsese's most detailed account credits Cassavetes with giving him "the best piece of advice" he received in this period, for after seeing the rough cut of *Boxcar Bertha,* Cassavetes "turned to me and said, 'Do you realize you just spent a year of your life making shit? Any director in Hollywood could have made that, and you're better than them, you have something honest to say'" (Truman, 79). Cassavetes advised Scorsese to work on his own scripts.

Wounded, Scorsese rewrote *The Season of the Witch,* transforming it into *Mean Streets.* His lover Sandy Weintraub had an enormous input in the rewriting. When they reread the old script, Sandy suggested that Martin put in more stories of Little Italy, and he responded by adding the "mook" scene and the firecrackers episode, as he cut away at the allusive religious dialogue. The idea that guided him, Scorsese told Chris Holdenfield, was to open up emotionally, to make the project less cerebral and more personal: "*Mean Streets* comes from feelings, from myself, my own life in a sense."[27]

Personal expression proved a hard sell for Scorsese. At various stages in its development the script was turned down by the American Film Institute's program for feature films by new filmmakers; by Joseph Brenner, and by Roger Corman. Scorsese, eager for work, was editing *Unholy Rollers* for American International, an action-packed sexploitation project centered on roller-derby women, when he approached Corman with *Mean Streets.* The ever-practical producer did see one angle to make *Mean Streets* a viable project—shoot it as a black gangster film, changing the Italian decor to the more marketable urban ghetto of blaxploitation films. Scorsese wanted to make *Mean Streets* so much that he actually considered Corman's suggestion seriously for a few days, but then he rejected it.

As Scorsese's revised script made the rounds, two students in Jon Voight's acting class, Richard Romanus and David Proval—who eventually played key roles in the film—interested their mentor Voight in the project; and it seemed he would be able to package a deal. Meanwhile, however, Scorsese had a casual dinner engagement with rock impresario Jonathan T. Taplin arranged by their mutual friends, Jay Cocks and Verna Bloom. As an undergraduate at Princeton, Taplin managed to supervise the arrangements on the road for Bob Dylan, the Band, Judy Collins, and others; he was such a renowned master of detail that George Harrison personally requested him to supervise the Concert for Bangladesh. Taplin and Scorsese had been at Woodstock, and now Taplin wanted to try the film business. Scorsese showed Taplin his script for *Mean Streets* and took him to a private screening of *Boxcar Bertha*. Taplin was impressed, so he convinced a boyhood friend, E. Lee Perry, to invest his recent inheritance in the film.

The rest of the funding came in the form of a deferment from the Canadian Film Institute Laboratory, which rated scripts and offered various forms of delayed payment based on the project's merit. *Mean Streets* scored high in the program's initial evaluation, so the film received generous terms. Nevertheless, the puny budget for *Mean Streets* forced Scorsese to make compromises. He depended heavily on Roger Corman's seasoned professionals, especially Paul Rapp, whom Scorsese credits with showing him how to "make a movie in 21 days," a movie named *Mean Streets*.[28] Rapp convinced Scorsese to use the crew from *Boxcar Bertha* on *Mean Streets*; to shoot only exteriors in New York City, doing so as quickly as possible; and to shoot the bulk of the film in Los Angeles, where filming was less expensive. Reluctantly, Scorsese agreed that if his vision of Little Italy was ever to get to the screen, much of it would have to be shot on the West Coast. Thus, as Marion Weiss reports, only six days of shooting for *Mean Streets* were done in New York City, all by a nonunion crew composed mostly of students, under the guise that *Mean Streets* was a "thesis film" and not a theatrical production. The round-the-clock New York City shooting was plagued, Weiss observes, by "problems with wireless microphones, a truck that caught fire, and a vehicle that ran over an electrical distribution box" and by "cold, wet weather."[29] The rest of *Mean Streets* was shot in Los Angeles.

To fool audiences into thinking they were always in New York, Scorsese scoured the Los Angeles area for gritty locations.[30] The mailbox, for example, that Johnny Boy blows up was really in San Pedro, California, not on Mott Street. The restaurant Charlie hopes to manage was not a Manhattan bistro but the Green Hotel in Pasadena. And the nude scene with Teresa is shot not in a New York hotel but at the Biltmore in Los Angeles. Even the climactic sequence and car crash in

Crucifixion as a motif in *Mean Streets* (1973). Warner Brothers. The Museum of Modern Art/Film Stills Archive.

Brooklyn were actually filmed in the Wall Street section of Los Angeles. Scorsese's substitutes work so well, however, that virtually every major reviewer declared, as did Vincent Canby in the *New York Times,* that *Mean Streets* was "shot entirely on its New York locations."[31]

Reviewers also universally commented on what Canby labeled the "furious drive" of the film: its boundless, almost-frenetic energy, manifest in its restless camerawork, bold visual compositions, and often-jarring editing. Discussing *Mean Streets,* Scorsese jokingly dismissed those who find its visual style a distinctive signature of the director: "I made *Mean Streets* on a 27 day schedule, a lot of handheld shots, not because they were supposed to be handheld, but because we didn't have time to lay down tracks—and they all talk about nervous camera technique! . . . I think my style is evident in the way people relate to each other in my movies, not in my camera movements."[32]

The real energy of *Mean Streets* resides in its consummate portrait of its protagonist, Charlie Cappa, Jr., played by Harvey Keitel but rooted in Scorsese's psyche. *Mean Streets* transmutes Scorsese's autobiographical confessions into high art as it carries audiences deep behind the mask Charles wears in Little Italy and into a universe of cosmic retribution. On the surface Charlie lives the dream existence J.R. aspires to in *Who's That Knocking,* secure in his well-organized neighborhood, revered by his pals, protected by his mob connections, loved by his mistress, and anchored by his Catholic faith. But Charlie's interior monologues, frequently done as voiceovers by an uncredited Scorsese, reveal a tortured soul, as self-deceived as Browning's monk in a Spanish cloister.

Charlie wants to strike his own bargain with God, and his opening lines define the terms of his covenant: "You don't make up for your sins in church. You do it in the streets. You do it at home. The rest is bullshit and you know it." *Mean Streets* records Charlie's dialogue with the Lord as he tries to work out his redemption. Charlie learns "You don't fuck around with the Infinite." All his stratagems cannot avoid the final bloodletting. Charlie's one of the damned, about to discover that he plays by God's rules, not his own.

In his published comments on Charlie, Scorsese emphasizes his role as "another false saint" (Jacobs 1976, 89) who fails to save himself as he fails to save the two people he purportedly loves, Johnny Boy and Teresa. For all his mumbled prayers, biblical allusions, altar-boy jokes, and lighting candles in church, Charlie fails to realize Catholic ideals in his life. Haunted by rituals and sacramentals, Charlie can never find grace, experience agape, or practice real charity. He wants a mechanical religion with him deciding the rewards and punishments. He will hold his hand to the fire occasionally, but he never confronts the real issue of living the good life in an evil world. By the end of the film, Charlie must lament his own shortcomings: "I guess you could say things aren't going so well tonight, but I am trying. I am trying." Charlie sees his failure, so he can only revert to the sentimental, hopeful prayer with which Scorsese began *Jerusalem, Jerusalem*: "God is not a torturer. . . . He only wants us to be merciful with ourselves."

While critics have seen the ending of *Mean Streets* as an apocalyptic and despairing vision of God's terrible wrath, Scorsese intended a more hopeful lesson. In his vision Charlie's wound, a shot in the hand, is his "stigmata," Johnny Boy's neck wound is not fatal, and Teresa survives—for, as Scorsese envisions the narrative, "they all learn something at the end of *Mean Streets,* only they have to get it from, again, the hand of God."[33] Scorsese's major films are grounded in

Charlie (Harvey Keitel) contemplates the pain of hell's flames in *Mean Streets* (1973).
Warner Brothers. The Museum of Modern Art/Film Stills Archive.

Catholic teleology; the assassin's bullet can convey the judgment of
God, a taxi driver can unleash divine retribution, and a boxer can bear
witness to Christ's suffering.

The immediate inspiration for the conclusion of *Mean Streets* was a
hair-raising incident in Scorsese's life. He and Joey Morale were cruis-
ing the neighborhood in the backseat of a teenage friend's red convertible but then decided to go home to Elizabeth Street early. Exactly
three minutes after they left the car, there was a shootout, and the
driver of the red convertible was shot in the eye. This bizarre episode
took on even larger import for Scorsese, since the night's senseless
violence foreshadowed, he felt, another assassination two months
later when John Kennedy was killed. Scorsese worried that he personally was being tested by the violence in the nation and in his
neighborhood.

In *Mean Streets* the test of Charlie's faith, his ability to accept
Christ's burden, centers on his willingness to love his neighbor. The
second Johnny Boy floats into the bar with his porkpie hat and check-
ered pants, Charlie moans his recognition of God's appointed trial:

"All right, Lord. Thank you for opening my eyes. We talk about penance and you send this through the door. We play by your rules, don't we?" *Mean Streets* chronicles Charlie's inability to shield Johnny Boy from the consequences of his actions. Johnny Boy has borrowed money from Michael, Charlie has vouched for him, and the debt will finally be paid in blood.

Johnny Boy, like most of *Mean Streets,* was based on Scorsese's vivid memories of Little Italy. The inspiration for Johnny Boy was Salvatore Aricola, a neighborhood legend nicknamed Sally Gaga, revered for his zany exploits, his success with women, and his independence. Salvatore's brother Robert, a performer in *Mean Streets* and in Scorsese's student shorts, recognized Johnny Boy's similarity to Sally Gaga, observing that like Johnny Boy, "Sally didn't live by any kind of code as far as I could tell. He was always screwing you—with money, with women, whatever—but he at least did it in style."[34] The style in the portrayal of Johnny Boy in *Mean Streets* is Robert De Niro's main contribution to the film. Originally De Niro had wanted to play Charlie, the lead, but as the project evolved, he transformed his role as Johnny Boy into the more dynamic characterization.

De Niro swaggers through the film, trailing girls behind him, setting off fireworks everywhere he goes, insulting friends and enemies alike, drinking, lying, improvising, and shooting bullets from ghetto rooftops across graveyards to the Empire State Building. In the rooftop sequences Scorsese was heavily influenced by *On the Waterfront* (1954). Like Brando's Terry Malloy, De Niro's Johnny Boy is a small-time hustler who seems much bigger than life, an off-balance madman with nowhere to go and nowhere to hide. His transgressions mirror Charlie's own inhibitions, and as Pauline Kael acutely notes, his "careless, contemptuous explosions seem a direct response to Charlie's trying to keep the lid on everything—it's as if Charlie's id were throwing bombs and laughing at him."[35] Johnny Boy is the friend Charlie cannot introduce to his uncle, an aristocratic Mafioso and the cousin of Teresa, Charlie's secret lover. The coauthor of *Mean Streets,* Mardik Martin, further develops the idea of a split personality, with Charlie as superego and Johnny Boy as id, when he hypothesizes that the two characters actually reflect the warring inclinations in the film's director, "both sides of the Scorsese coin": "One is the guilt ridden nice guy who's basically a coward. The other is a crazy doer who doesn't care how he destroys himself" (Holdenfield 1977, 37).

Scorsese's rewritten *Mean Streets* omits any straightforward explanation of the bond between Charlie and Johnny Boy, but a key exchange between the two obliquely hints that earlier Johnny Boy had taken a severe beating protecting Charlie. Yet Charlie can never own up to his responsibilities. Cautioned by his uncle that "honorable men" associate only with "honorable men," Charlie feigns indifference to his friend's plight.

Charlie also disguises his relationship with Teresa Ronchali. Teresa is *"cumpari"* with Giovanni, Charlie's uncle, but he cautions Charlie about her desires to leave the neighborhood, desires he interprets as a sign of disrespect for her parents. In addition, Teresa's epilepsy makes her an outcast. Pushed to elaborate on the autobiographical nature of Charlie's affair with an epileptic, Scorsese warily shifted the focus to the symbolic nature of her affliction: "Well, the epileptic thing is interesting, but it's more of an abstract idea than anything else. The Harvey Keitel character didn't see himself as someone who was capable of relating to a complete woman; so he had to have a woman who was scarred in some way" (Jacobs 1976, 89). When Teresa has a seizure after an emotionally charged encounter with a spiteful Johnny Boy, Charlie abandons her to the ministrations of a neighborhood woman, played by Catherine Scorsese.

Teresa's unclothed body may rivet Charlie's attention and unleash his libido, but his dreams of her are wrought with darker symbolism. In *Season of the Witch,* Scorsese included a scene where Teresa and Charlie were nude on the bed, and he ejaculated blood, not sperm, over her. In *Mean Streets* the dream is reduced to a few lines of dialogue, but the imagery of a sex-related bloodbath remains. Charlie's nightmare links his orgasm with violent death and foreshadows the symbolic wounds he, Johnny Boy, and Teresa suffer. These overtones of violence and loathing manifest themselves when Charlie declares, "With you I can't get involved. You're a cunt," only to retract his insult with a weak rejoinder, "only joking." The bitterness in his pronouncements is reinforced by a gesture imitating the action of pulling a trigger of a gun, which is accompanied on the soundtrack by the noise of a real gunshot. Obviously, Eros and Thanatos are confused in Charlie's troubled conscience.

The confusion in Charlie's mind mirrors, as critic Jon Landau notes, the polarities Charlie can "neither integrate nor choose between": "the cross versus the gun, the sensuous surface of a church statue versus the sensuous surface of a black bar dancer bathed in rhinestones, Giovanni's picture of the Kennedys and Mussolini resting along side of the pope; and even Charlie's choice of favorite people, St. Francis of Assisi and John Wayne."[36] Charlie craves material success and eternal salvation, any way he can manage it, inside or outside the law and morality, on earth and in heaven, and he wants it without commitment or sacrifice. Charlie and his hoodlum buddies have, in Scorsese's opinion, been snared by a delusional American promise of gold-lined streets and easy success. As the director explains, "*Mean Streets* dealt with the American dream, according to which everybody thinks they can get rich quick, and if they can't do it by legal means, then they'll do it by illegal ones" (*Scorsese* 1989, 47).

Charlie wants to reign in both the confessional and the bar, but his conscience reminds him that the American dream does not parallel God's plan. In a scintillating analysis of Scorsese's religious dimension, "The Sacraments of Genre: Coppola, De Palma, and Scorsese," Leo Braudy demonstrates how the gap between Catholic visions of salvation and capitalism's images of success defines these Italian American directors' content and technique. Braudy notes that these three directors evidence a "guilty conscience" over the sense of "the gap between secular metaphors of ritual, sainthood, authority, and their religious counterparts" and that guilty conscience "generates so much of the aesthetic and ideological richness of their films."[37] Braudy concludes his exegesis by asserting that the same guilty conscience haunts the young directors in their "assertion of style" because of "the usurpation of divine or parental authority it implies" (L. Braudy, 28).

Scorsese is clearly the stylistic usurper in *Mean Streets*; his masterpiece undermines all the old movie conventions, slicing the eyeball of traditional Hollywood narrative structure and pounding the eardrums with an insistent and incessant soundtrack unlike the mood music customarily employed in commercial films. In postproduction Scorsese remained convinced that *Mean Streets* would never be released, that it would instead sit on the studio's dusty shelves as an artifact of Italian urban culture and film school excesses. Indeed, the many negative reviews of *Mean Streets* underscore the challenges Scorsese was posing for those accustomed to Hollywood's "invisible" editing, seamless plots, and polished dialogue.

Rex Reed, of the New York *Daily News,* lacerated *Mean Streets* as "a baffling exercise in excessive self-indulgence about four moronic hoods that takes some kind of prize for total confusion and chaos. . . .

The result is all style in the form of nervous collapse and no content."[38] Clearly, Reed was nervous over the many sequences in *Mean Streets* where Scorsese uses jump cuts, associational editing, and other modernist techniques. *Mean Streets* refuses to fit its diverse elements into an unambiguous pattern; there is no pat, final, decisive "happy ending." Instead, there are vague musings about the red light, assassins kissing guns, symbolic neck wounds, the closing of a street fair, minor gangsters watching film noir movies on television at home, fireplugs spouting, Johnny wandering in the alley, Charlie kneeling in the street, Teresa sprawled in the car, and shades closing on tenement windows. *Mean Streets* shows a few days in an environment; at film's end the environment endures, as Charlie's home movie rambles to its end.

Scorsese admits that he had trouble editing the last sequence of *Mean Streets* and got some advice from Sid Levin, who receives credit on screen for shaping the whole film. Scorsese maintains, however, that the rest of the film is his work as an editor: "Sid didn't cut it; I cut it. Sid came in and showed me and made an initial cut in the last section where they're singing 'O Marienello' at the end, which is the traditional song that ends all the Italian festivals. . . . At that point, I couldn't cut it. It was five months editing and I was really freaked. The rest of it I cut. Brian De Palma came in and Sandy Weintraub helped me" (*Dialogue*, 8).

Scorsese's narrative in *Mean Streets* has a clear structure that depends on the audience sensing two separate realities: (a) Little Italy and its "mean streets" as geographic entities and (b) a different but no less real Little Italy as experienced by Charlie and his friends. As he did in *Murray* and *Who's That Knocking?* Scorsese counterpoints the two elements of an actual place and a psychological space, trusting that his audience will recognize the gaps between the two, and in the recognition learn much more about the protagonists and their stunted lives. Phillip Kolker discusses this gap between consciousness and reality in his *Cinema of Loneliness,* observing that "the New York of *Mean Streets* . . . is reflective of the energy of the characters. . . . Through composition, lighting, camera movement, and cutting [Scorsese] provides the viewer a primary perceptual pattern, a point of view, which is then joined with another point of view created within the narrative, that of the central character. . . . Scorsese represents states of mind and guides viewer response to them with great care and through a complex organization of visual and cultural elements."[39] The fragmentation in point of view in *Mean Streets* begins in the opening sequences, when real home movies of the Scorsese family gradually open up to the larger movie of Charlie's current life. Then Charlie goes to the mirror to assess his own reflection, only to stumble back (in a triple cut) to his own bed. Within minutes complex narrative issues have been raised: What is real and what is dream? Which side of the mirror will this film focus on? How do these home movies relate to the commercial film at hand? And why is reality being restructured and by whom? The opening of *Mean Streets* announces Scorsese's fixation with point of view, distorted psychological states, mythical posturing, self-discovery, and delusion. By film's end the director of this auto-biographical excursion casts himself as the assassin coming to fulfill God's will and destroy his alter ego, Charlie. Critic Janet Maslin remarked on the multiple ironies here, noting that Scorsese's small acting role has complex overtones: "[W]hat an unsettling cameo that is, since Charlie is very much an autobiographical character for him."[40]

By the time he completed this act of self-immolation, Scorsese was turning 30 and had his first ulcers. *Mean Streets* premiered at the eleventh New York Film Festival where Scorsese was heard to sigh, "Now it's over. That film is an exorcism for me" (Gardner, 31).

3

Alice Doesn't Live Here Anymore (1974)

Mean Streets brought Scorsese fame but little fortune. Music royalties as well as payments to the San Gennaro Street Fair swallowed up the profits. *Mean Streets* would not make Scorsese the rich man he ardently longed to be, but it did put him in the catbird seat among young directors.

Scorsese received more than two dozen scripts within one month of the film festival. From *Mean Streets* on, his life would catapult through the fast lane, his phone would never be silent, and he would be constantly enmeshed in too many good deals, all being made simultaneously and all overdue yesterday. His appetite for money, women, and fame; his need to create films and exorcise the old devils of self-doubt and despair; and his conviction that personal salvation through art lies just around the next corner—all these things would combine to make Scorsese one of the most accomplished American film directors ever but also the most driven, and insecure.

Like the lionized bohemian of his "Life Lessons," Lionel Dobie, Scorsese lives at the edge: his marriages are always crumbling, his health is always failing, and each project is always his last chance to redeem himself. Scorsese the urban poet is inspired by New York's architecture yet terrorized by the city's denizens, immersed in the tabloid reality of contemporary life yet haunted by spiritual reveries, buoyed by unbridled freedom, widespread adulation, and immense wealth yet constrained by his devotion to craft and to tradition.

Scorsese knew when he made *Mean Streets* that there was one more hill to climb, *The Last Temptation of Christ*. He did not know that it would be more than a decade until he could ascend Golgotha. The first script Scorsese assayed after *Mean Streets* was a sequel describing

Charlie and Johnny Boy five years later on Staten Island trapped in unhappy marriages and dead-end jobs. Mardik Martin developed Scorsese's ideas for the plot as a cinematic autobiography: "Charlie will have married an Irish Catholic girl—it's just the sort of inept act of rebellion he's capable of. . . . Most of the movie will revolve around Charlie's family—his parents and grandfather—and it will be filled with ghost stories. . . . Johnny Boy will be deemphasized. He'll wind up in an asylum cell, naked, and when Charlie visits him, he'll think it's another loan shark come to collect" (Haun, 1).

Scorsese's affinity for urban misfits and for stark portraits of deprivation in the midst of wealth also attracted him to a script by Ken Friedman, a work called *Booster,* about New York shoplifters. Scorsese had a vision for this black comedy: "[*Booster*] is the story of a guy who's coming apart. He's the best and the worst of New York crazies."[1] Meanwhile, however, other forces were in motion that would deflect Scorsese from both Staten Island and his crazies.

A script called *Alice Doesn't Live Here Anymore* had been making the rounds of the studios, and because it was owned by David Susskind and had been linked to Anne Bancroft, Barbra Streisand, and Diana Ross, it was garnering attention. Eventually Ellen Burstyn, whose career had been given a lift by *The Exorcist,* took an interest in this story of a widowed homemaker who dreams of being a film actress, and Burstyn began putting a package together for Warner Brothers. Burstyn scheduled a dinner with Francis Ford Coppola to ask him to suggest a director suitable for the project who wouldn't be too proud to be involved in this star vehicle. Burstyn wanted an Oscar, and she wasn't ashamed to admit it. Coppola suggested Scorsese, but Burstyn was hesitant to engage a chronicler of macho dilemmas for what she conceived of as a film by, for, and about women.

Burstyn agreed to screen *Mean Streets* and what she saw surprised her. She recognized that "It was a movie with a life and reality of its own" (Gardner, 36). Burstyn wanted to use her Actors' Studio friends in *Alice*; the project was to showcase her and the Strasberg Method. Burstyn fretted that the Doris Day formula in the script might damage the film's prospects; it had scared other talented people away. With Scorsese, she knew she would get a contemporary look, innovative camerawork and editing, and an original soundtrack.

Most important, however, was the urgent, vibrant, cinema verité–like quality in *Mean Streets,* for Burstyn feared that Robert Getchell's script for *Alice,* his maiden effort, was too glib, facile, and polished.

Scorsese, she recognized, would rough up the edges and provide gritty, ambiguous, disarming realism. Like a jazz musician, he would find new riffs in an old score, improvise harmonies and cross-rhythms, and expand and explore new ideas, all within the structure of an old-fashioned "woman's picture."

Burstyn dispatched a script to Scorsese, using John Calley, head of production at Warner Brothers, as her intermediary. As chance would have it, Scorsese's live-in collaborator, Sandy Weintraub, read the text first and recommended it to Scorsese, applauding its attention to women's concerns. Scorsese decided, "it would be good to try and make a woman's film as honest as possible especially since a lot of people thought *Mean Streets* showed I couldn't direct women" ("Confessions," 137). Calley reinforced Scorsese's resolve. *Alice,* Calley reminded his young protégé, would show Hollywood that he could make a commercial film, written by someone else, starring established talents, involving a large budget and complicated production, and starring a woman.

Scorsese's six-hour interview with Burstyn about the *Alice* project went smoothly. As Burstyn remembers her hiring of Scorsese, she "asked Marty if he thought he knew anything about women. He said no, that it would be a learning experience. I thought that was a smashing answer."[2] So the director of masculine tragedies on overcrowded city streets found himself, like Alice, traveling cross-country in search of recognition as an artist, making several stops in the sun-drenched open plains of the Southwest to confront his sexual hangups and changing social realities.

As the force behind *Alice,* Burstyn, insisted it be "the story of a woman today with our consciousness as it is now" (Gardner, 36). She and Scorsese surrounded themselves with powerful women in major production roles, including Audrey Maas and Sandra Weintraub as producers, Toby Rafelson (director Bob Rafelson's wife) as production designer, and Marcia Lucas (director George Lucas's wife) as editor. Scorsese was collaborating with forceful, articulate, committed women. The director whom French critics describe as "*ce spécialiste des amours difficiles*" in his private life was preparing a public statement about women in contemporary America.[3]

Alice, like the "women's films" it emulates, centers on the travails of its protagonist, a 35-year-old widow with a 12-year-old son, lots of dreams and insecurities, and little money. Like all soap operas, it demands that a handkerchief be poised ready to dab a tear or two; its laughs are bittersweet, since the mood is tinged with desperation. Alice may be strong, resilient, and defiant, but her path is long, wearying, and confusing. Her yellow brick road is crowded with cowardly bullies, heartless club managers, and drab motel rooms. The men in her life function as milestones in her development, starting with her cloddish husband, progressing through her demented male chauvinist lover and her rebellious son to her sensitive suitor-fiancé. For all its contemporary allusions, *Alice* finally takes its structure from the old Doris Day films as a picaresque adventure highlighting Alice's dreams and the sacrifices she makes for her men.

Alice Doesn't Live Here Anymore amounts to an Ellen Burstyn tour de force, directed by Martin Scorsese. Burstyn was on a roll, winning both the Oscar for *Alice* and the Tony for *Same Time, Next Year,* an unprecedented sweep for a female performer. Within a few years Burstyn would become the first woman president of Actors Equity and the codirector of the Actors' Studio. Hers was the dominant role both in shaping the deal for *Alice* and in mounting the production. Scorsese was at best second fiddle.

Scorsese managed, however, to put his mark on *Alice*. Screenwriter Robert Getchell marvelled at how Scorsese managed to get the upper hand: "[*Alice*] didn't turn out the way I'd planned. Though meant to be first for the actress, second for me, and third for the director, Martin certainly came in somewhere in the top one-and-a-half of three, and all to the good of the picture."[4] The price of ascendancy for Scorsese was labor and frustration, sweat and unhappiness.

Alice proved a difficult time for Scorsese, though he later tried to frame a more positive image of the experience, declaring that the whole film became "a kind of therapy for me" (Carducci, 10). Therapy or torment, *Alice,* includes many lines of dialogue culled from heated discussions of male-female prerogatives that marked a turning point in the lives of Sandra Weintraub and Martin Scorsese. Soon afterward they went their own separate ways.

Scorsese did everything he could to avoid the label "feminist film" for *Alice*. In interviews about the project, he stressed its *human* issues. To Diane Jacobs he even expressed surprise that everyone saw *Alice* as a women's lib statement: "To tell you the truth, the reviews that praise *Alice* as a feminist picture couldn't have surprised me more. I don't like to think of it as a woman's picture, but as a human picture—if that doesn't sound too corny" (Jacobs 1976, 89). Unfortunately, it sounds disingenuous and corny; Scorsese's denials only emphasize the feminist slant. Audiences knew *Alice* was a political bombshell. NBC in its special "Women and Men" pointedly juxtaposed footage from *Alice* with the similarly plotted Doris Day vehicle *My Dream Is Yours,* and the National Organization for Women organized a one-day work boycott with the motto *"Alice Doesn't"* blazoned on their banners.

Indeed, the main flaw in *Alice* concerns its simplistic approach to men. No male character proves as complex or as sympathetic as the female roles. *Alice* seems a Lewis Carroll version of *Mean Streets,* a *Mean Streets* pushed through the looking glass. The film begins, for example, with a fantasy of Alice dreaming of fame as she sings an Alice Faye song, only to have an iris shot propel the audience through space and time into what could be a set from *The Incredible Shrinking Woman,* with a mature Alice entrapped as indentured slave to her brattish child and handmaiden to her crude husband, an ill-kempt Coca-Cola deliveryman whose vocabulary is mainly grunts, whose sexual overtures look like wrestling moves, and whose interest in Alice seems buried under comic books, racing forms, and an obsession with television sitcoms. This opening domestic sequence makes similar scenes in *The Diary of a Mad Housewife* appear blissful; any sane person would agree with Alice's curses about her environment. There can be no doubt, as she shouts out her back window, that "Socorro sucks!"

Scorsese apologized about the injustice he had done in *Alice* to Billy Green Bush, who plays Donald, the buffoonish husband. Scorsese planned a more "Ozzie and Harriet" look and shot a lengthy sequence elaborating Donald's personality that landed on the cutting-room floor when preview audiences seemed bored. In test screenings, *Alice* didn't garner audience enthusiasm until Alice and her son were careening down the American road. Eliminating the Socorro footage violated Scorsese's conception of the project; he had wanted Socorro to be at least a third of the film.

This problem of editing long, ambiguous, dense narratives down to the Hollywood norm of an action-packed, easily comprehensible story with a happy ending becomes a hallmark of Scorsese's entire career. He frequently laments that his best ideas were left on the cutting-room floor. In projects like *New York, New York,* each new resurrection of the film reveals more complexities. For *Alice* Scorsese screened an early version more than an hour longer, but the studio prevailed and major sequences were eliminated. Scorsese's capitulations to studio pressures have prompted James Monaco to proclaim, "There's no better example of a contemporary director seriously crippled by trying to accommodate himself to the system of commercial film production than Martin Scorsese."[5]

That *Alice* was compromised by deletions cannot be denied. Eliminating footage of Alice's marriage undercuts the film's structure and makes Alice's character less intriguing. As Molly Haskell complains in "Character in Search of an Author," her bitter pan of the film, the truncated beginning makes a mishmash of what follows. There are too many unanswered questions about the mature Alice, her husband, her son, and their motivations. Audiences are left wondering, as Haskell does, "What is a woman with the sultry sophistication and tart tongue of Ellen Burstyn . . . doing with a primeval brute like this? Where did this smart-ass kid come from? They are like different feathers and different species, and scenes that should set the tone of the movie and the terms of Alice's 'oppression' are merely baffling."[6] In his novel *Alice Doesn't Live Here Anymore,* writer Robert Getchell pays attention to the terms of Alice's courtship and marriage and expends great effort defining her special relationship with her son, Tommy, a relationship Getchell presents as a substitute romance and a oedipal dilemma. Getchell's portrait of life in Ponca City, Oklahoma, finds few echoes, however, in Scorsese's rendering of Socorro, New Mexico.

Further complicating issues is the sudden happenstance of Alice's widowhood. Without a treatment of her home life, one of Scorsese's key themes is obscured. The material in *Alice* interested him because Alice was not a woman whose consciousness of her predicament was gradually raised. As Scorsese saw it, Alice would never have left home were it not for the accident. Her liberation was not a feminist's dream come true but a simple twist of fate. Alice was literally bumped onto the road of life by her husband's fatal accident. Alice never would have left her husband or found herself, Scorsese maintains, had it not been for Divine intervention: "It's a very important point. . . . She would not have moved unless the hand of God came down and said, 'Bang. This is it. Make your decision. What are you going to do?' . . ." (*Dialogue,* 22). The brevity of the footage in Socorro muted both Scorsese's feelings about Providence and feminist interest in consciousness-raising. The rush to the road allows time only to sketch slapstick, wisecracking characters; audiences hardly know mother and son before the two pals sail down the interstate in a bizarre permutation of a buddy movie. No wonder Scorsese argued that the film should be titled *Alice Steps Out.*

Despite the abbreviated introductory scenes, feminists have much to rejoice about when Alice stops to find work singing in Phoenix, Arizona. Though the geography of the film seems tangled, and Alice takes a circuitous route to Monterey, California, the Emerald City of her dreams, the women's liberation slant does take firm hold here. Everywhere she turns, good old boys humiliate Alice. In a key confrontation a leering bar owner asks the would-be singer to turn around so he can see her, and she explodes, "I don't sing with my ass," a line not in the original script, but improvised on set, and based on Burstyn's experiences in show business. In a land of male chauvinists, Alice gets her job when she breaks down in tears, disarming a bar owner who takes a chance on her; feminists could chuckle at the message that tears are as important as talent and that men will be kind to women so long as they're willing to admit weakness and dependency. Alice strikes a fair bargain, paying for her piano and taking a cut of beverage sales, but her entrée was a few tears and a forlorn confession that she was down on her luck.

Alice's gig goes well enough though it's achingly obvious that her crooning will never lift her far from a saloon and a plateful of tips. Meanwhile her son, Tommy, is going stir-crazy in a motel room, driven bonkers by the drivel on afternoon television. Scorsese films Burstyn's songs—at home, in audition, and at the bar—with a relentlessly moving camera, craning, panning, and gliding from one perspective to another, switching filters, exposures, and lighting effects to heighten involvement. But the visual pyrotechnics highlight the truth that Alice is a mediocre singer, though her competent arrangements cover her flaws. Alice's stint in show business wears her down. The bloom has left her tired rose, and she's preoccupied with fatigue, body aches, and small wounds when she's seduced by a fan, a young dude named Ben Eberhardt who won't take no for an answer.

Ben, played by Harvey Keitel, reignites Alice's sexual spark, and they are soon feverishly bedding down for unrestrained bliss. Alice savors Ben's energy and relishes his physical prowess. Her independence has made her more responsive sexually, so it's only when Ben's terrified and pregnant wife comes visiting that Alice begins to understand what a victim she and all women are. Ben embodies every feminist's nightmare, a certifiably psychotic male chauvinist pig. He violently attacks both women. Within seconds Ben has smashed in the door, beaten his wife, abused Alice, and threatened Tommy.

Scorsese considers Ben the "most accurately delineated" character in *Alice* and worked hard with Harvey Keitel to make Ben both "funnier" and "crazier" (Carducci, 14). The two buddies recognized many of their prejudices in this vagabond; accordingly, they used the character to understand their own experience. Scorsese admitted that *Alice* became "a very draining process because of the personal involvement in it" and isolated the sequences with Ben as especially cathartic: "It's my own relationship with people I'm in love with, relationship with my friends. Harvey—what he represents of me in that film, what he represents to himself. Everybody's playing this like a documentary part of themselves really in the picture, and so am I" (Macklin, 35).

The most effective scene in *Alice* treats Ben's explosion. Because the players were working in a confined space, every action had been rehearsed beforehand to ensure that no one would be hurt. Nevertheless, there was an air of danger on the set, and Keitel used it to his advantage. When the sequence began, Keitel made demonic gestures and paced about with an intensity that unsettled everyone. He appeared out of control, swallowed up by Ben's violent streak, and Scorsese was thoroughly shaken. As the director remembers the scene, "He terrified me. That rarely happens between professionals on a set, but it happened then."[7] The resultant footage, shot with a handheld camera, stands as one of modern cinema's most intensely horrific moments and foreshadows De Niro's "over the top" outbursts in *Cape Fear*.

In this sequence Keitel added several improvisations that enrich the film immensely. The whole exchange about his scorpion medallion— "See this? You bother it, and it'll kill you. So don't mess with it"— flowed from his aroused anger and not from the printed page. Keitel also improvised the line "That bitch is messing with me" during the take. Scorsese saw how well these lines fit the scene and went with Keitel's inspiration.[8] Interestingly, Scorsese, whose astrological sign is Scorpio, became enamored of Keitel's totemic scorpion and borrowed it to wear on set for the rest of the film. A few conferences with his analyst helped Scorsese to admit later that wearing the scorpion revealed the anger he was suppressing during the film, as his macho fantasies of violence and dominance were threatened by the new feminist consciousness informing the project. Scorsese's passage from the machismo of Little Italy to the enlightened sexual attitudes of modern feminism would never quite be complete. This child of an urban ghetto never loses his fascination with the athletic guys congregating

Ellen Burstyn would garner an Oscar for her portrayal of Alice in *Alice Doesn't Live Here Anymore* (1974). Warner Brothers. The Museum of Modern Art/Film Stills Archive.

on streetcorners, with the gangsters, the hustlers, the con men, and the divinely mad, despite his quest for an age of innocence.

The new feminist ideal of masculinity enters *Alice* after the frightened singer flees Phoenix with Tommy and drives to the outskirts of Tucson, Arizona. Unable to find work as a singer, Alice reluctantly accepts a job as a waitress in Mel's Diner, a run-down greasy spoon whose employees seem close to the end of their ropes. Alice's disgust with her co-workers and herself melts, as she discovers the hearts of gold that hide behind foul mouths, neurotic behavior, and sexual badinage. The agent for Alice's ultimate redemption, David, a divorced rancher with a craggy face, gravelly voice, and down-home charm teaches her about integrity, personal responsibility, and mature relationships. David also projects his own authoritarian stance, however, boldly announcing that there are rules in his house. In the major crisis of the film, David strikes Tommy after the foul-mouthed adolescent has provoked him, and Alice, abashed at his violence, runs away. David's no sadist, but he's no marshmallow either; to remain with him,

Alice will have to accept his anger, embrace his imperfections, and treat him as an equal, as a flawed but lovable human being. At first she hides from this truth, but some soul-searching conversations with Flo, another waitress, convince Alice to compromise and accept a future that includes David, Tommy, and her dreams of Monterey.

In its attempts to define this relationship among equals, *Alice Doesn't Live Here Anymore* falters agonizingly; none of the collaborators on this project could frame an adequate definition of the new truths of Alice's life or establish the new foundations of her romance with David. There are many "Please's," "I understand's," and "I'll back you up's," but an equal number of silences, anxious expressions, and hesitancies remain. Obviously, no one—not the writer, the director, or the cast—could find a clear resolution for the film's dilemmas or a solution for Alice's quandaries; thus, no one is entirely satisfied with the film's rather forced reconciliation between Alice and David. Compromise haunts their last few moments together. After creating an acute feminist consciousness, the film still employs a Prince Charming as a deus ex machina to awaken Sleeping Beauty and lead her into a muted happily-ever-after. For Alice, there's always that Monterey sign beckoning in the distance despite the *place* she seems to have found here and not there.

All the principals in *Alice* have complaints about the film's treatment of Alice's romance with David and justifications for its obvious compromises. The final scenes between Alice and David were constantly being revised. In the earliest conception, a script Scorsese never saw, the tone was different, and Tommy committed suicide. As the novice screenwriter reworked his plot, ex-professor Getchell explored more literary devices, with Tommy running away to Monterey and Alice failing at her dream of singing when she follows him there. In another Getchell's working script the movie ended, Burstyn recalls, with "an on-screen marriage, your basic rainbow fadeout, happily every after in Tucson, with Alice singing her heart out."[9] Burstyn suggested a militant ending with Alice saying maybe to David's proposal, then charging on to Monterey with Tommy. This ending left everyone on set lamenting the emotional void in Alice's life.

Then one day during rehearsals, Kris Kristofferson improvised some new lines. Burstyn remembers the incident clearly: "Then, the day before shooting started, when she said she was going to Monterey, Kris improvised and said 'O.K., come on, I'll take you to Monterey.' And my heart stopped" (Barthel, 3). Kristofferson's inspiration provided an ambiguous truce in which Alice gets David and his assurance he'll support her in her quest for a career in singing. No one was ecstatic about this uneasy resolution, yet everyone accepted it because it reflected the accommodations they made in their lives between a career and domestic life.

Scorsese returns compulsively to this topic in his later films. Haunted by his inability to sustain marriages as he fulfills his career aspirations, Scorsese rarely shows his protagonists achieving even the uneasy peace he captures for a brief moment in *Alice*. Further down the road come the disillusionment of *New York, New York*, where marriage and music clearly don't go well together; the hellish despair of *Raging Bull*, where brutality creeps from the ring to the home; the cruel, competitive universe of *The Color of Money*, where women and pool don't mix; and the theological agony of *The Last Temptation of Christ*, where domesticity is presented as the devil's final weapon against the divinely inspired. On small canvases and large, Scorsese constantly reiterates his plaint that the real artist cannot go home anymore. Like Lionel in "Life Lessons," Scorsese's heroes draw inspiration from love but not sustenance.

Scorsese urged his own ending for *Alice* wherein Alice would continue down the road, alone, independent, and enlightened, an ending like the conclusion of Paul Mazursky's *An Unmarried Woman*. But he was convinced by his cast and crew that such a powerful ending would paradoxically be misinterpreted as feminist propaganda. So Scorsese worked hard to develop some rich resonances in the last romantic encounter in *Alice*. He liked the silences, the body language, the understated but intense emotions, and tangled motivations in the showdown. Scorsese recommended that viewers study the "part right before he turns around and says, 'Please,' when he says, 'Gee I think I understand you. There's got to be another way.' She's so touched she can't even answer; she sort of nods her head and that's the whole picture" (Macklin, 26).

Scorsese is fascinated with silent language; his key moments depend on an actor's ability to convey powerful themes in quiet gestures. He's most comfortable working with an introspective and intense player like Ellen Burstyn or Robert De Niro. Often his whole picture depends on one gesture, on one intensely realized instant. For all the violence, visual pyrotechnics, blaring music, and visceral language of his art, Scorsese cherishes the privileged moment, the epiphany that mirrors a character's encounter with the transcendent, the instant when a character asks, "You talking to me?" of an unseen presence.

Few critics saw Alice's nod as the crux of Scorsese's film, and his admittedly poorly realized scene of Alice accepting David's entreaties, accompanied by the applause of all the regular customers and denizens of Mel's Diner, drew unmitigated wrath from reviewers. John Simon, the doyen of vituperation, told his readers the film "has a heart conceivably bigger than a bread box, but a brain surely smaller than a bread crumb."[10] Molly Haskell saw the conclusion as no less flawed than the truncated beginning: "[W]here she is going will never be understood" (Haskell, 38). And Pauline Kael, the materfamilias of criticism, saw the film as *A Doll's House* mangled in its trip down the American road to Hollywood: "If Ibsen had written *A Doll's House* for the movies, Nora would have taken her children and moved them right into the warm, permissive home of a rich, liberal suitor who was waiting in the wings. Alice gets a double helping of pie-in-the-sky: she gets a warm-and-sexy good provider, and she can pursue her idiot dream of becoming an Alice Faye."[11]

Kael's allusion to *A Doll's House* is instructive. In Ibsen's drama Nora must choose between children and her freedom. In *Alice* our widow embraces her child as a sign of her independence and freedom; the triangle in *Alice* pits her troubled son against her admiring suitor. This added dimension attracted Scorsese and Burstyn to the project. She used the filming to deepen her own understanding of her relationship with her son, Jefferson, a 13-year-old who lived on location with her and played her neighbor's child in the film. Scorsese explored his own relationship with his aging mother, Catherine Scorsese, as he filmed *Alice* and pondered the real importance of the women in his life.

Both Scorsese's parents were much on his mind during the production of *Alice*. Their escalating problems with money and health reminded him most acutely that no one lives forever, so he began to make his own oral and visual history of the elder Scorseses in *Italianamerican,* a documentary he prepared and edited as he was putting the final touches on *Alice*. Scorsese's intimate friends observed that "the oddly fraternal give and take" between the irascible Catherine Scorsese and her precocious son Martin "resembles the on-screen relationship between Alice and her son."[12] Once again Scorsese was using the main characters of his narrative to explore facets of himself. Clearly,

Scorsese could identify with Alice, a woman trapped in a dead-end marriage and oppressed by a society that made her dreams of a career in art seem unreachable. Alice's prison mirrored both his own plight and his parents' reality, as he explained to Diane Jacobs: "Well, she'd been trapped—just the way I was trapped. I mean, I was married as soon as I got out of college. Although Alice wasn't Italian, she came from the same society with the same strictures. You get married and then what do you do? You have a kid. . . . But then people like Alice and the Italians of my parents' generation are held together by the sacred notion of The Family. That's why the pasta sauce is so sacred to an Italian family" (Jacobs 1976, 88).

Alice details Scorsese's attempt to fathom what holds modern life together and to discover the sauce of his existence as he explores the psyche of sons and lovers, mothers and would-be artists, homebodies and vagabonds. For all its attention to women's concerns, Scorsese felt compelled to explore his life in *Alice*. Through Alice and Tommy he hoped to come to terms with Catherine and Martin and savor the full measure of her famed pasta sauce.

Alfred Lutter, who plays Scorsese's Tommy, had never acted professionally, so the director elicited a nuanced performance from a gifted amateur. In two weeks of rehearsals and eight weeks of shooting, Lutter experienced, Scorsese suggested, "a whole life in terms of the movie and his feelings toward Ellen and me and everything"; as a result, Lutter's performance had, in Scorsese's view, "a very organic quality because his feelings were all flow" (Howard, 23). For the first third of the movie, Tommy seems incapable of doing anything but looking back. Using denial as a strategy—denial of his father's death, his mother's abilities, and his own worth—Tommy wisecracks endlessly as he denigrates Alice's plans. The next third of the film finds him disoriented by the "weirdness" of Tucson, the rivalry with David for his mother's affections, and his budding romance with the raffishly androgynous Audrey (Jodie Foster). After David hits him and his mother banishes him, Tommy has his own dark night of the soul, landing in jail drunk after a criminal escapade with Audrey. When he awakens the next morning, he is sober and sane, with his eyes on the future. The film finds its denouement as Alice and Tommy walk across the horizon, happy with their accomplishments, matured by their errors, and fortified to face the future. Scorsese was worked frantically to capture a special look for their walk. As he told Paul Gardner, "the walk represents their future. I wanted it to look diffuse, disjointed, and uncertain" (Gardner, 36). For Scorsese, the accommodation Alice reaches with David is dubious; he has hinted they would have problems in the future and go their separate ways. The climax for the film is the understanding Tommy and Alice reach that they are mutually dependent yet free, that life is a bridge linking past and present, that Tucson is a "place" for them to live and grow. One can almost hear Judy Garland clicking her heels, murmuring "There's no place like home," in the background.

As Scorsese was shooting his conclusion, cameraman Kent Wakeford told him that his frame would include on the horizon a large MONTEREY sign, an advertisement for a nearby shopping center. Dazzled by the irony that Alice would always be surrounded by images of Monterey, Scorsese told Wakeford not to crop the shot to exclude the ad, arguing that "if it came into the frame that way, it must be a sign. Leave it" (Macklin, 21–22). A sign it was, though semiologists could spend weeks determining if it was iconic, symbolic, or totemic, and much ink would be spilled debating its thematic import.

Working on *Alice* immersed Scorsese in the world of the Actors' Studio and forced him to rethink the nature of performance, the interpretation of scripts, and the role of the director in a collaborative art form. Scorsese had never studied acting formally; nor had he received organized training in working with actors. The months of labor on *Alice* provided him with a thorough indoctrination in the theories and practices of Strasberg's disciples.

Working with the Actors' Studio personnel on *Alice*, Scorsese developed a preproduction technique that has served him well on later projects. For two weeks he, Sandy Weintraub, Ellen Burstyn, and other principals rehearsed at his suite at the Hotel St. Regis, developing monologues, exploring emotions, and extemporizing lines. Scorsese would videotape these sessions, discuss them with the players, then ask Robert Getchell to incorporate material into a reworked script that provided a framework for more improvisations on location.

The infamous "outhouse" scene, for example, where Alice and Flo get down to the nitty-gritty of life and love, was inspired by an episode in Sandy Weintraub's life when she collapsed at a New Year's Eve party only to be confronted by her hostess in her bathroom. And the marvelous shot of the waitresses sunbathing behind the diner was a last-minute inspiration on Scorsese and Diane Ladd's part. Looking for a suitable location, they shuffled some chairs around only to discover how striking the sunbathing would look. Diane Ladd brought a cross made of safety pins to summarize Flo's essential strengths. In the film Flo uses that cross dramatically when she declares, "You know what this is? This is what holds me together." Writer Robert Getchell was happy to include these discoveries in his script; the resulting text merited him an Academy Award nomination and led to a lucrative television series based on his characters.

Scorsese, in turn, drew much of his finest work on *Alice* from the original material Getchell provided. The more Scorsese read the first draft of *Alice,* the more he saw that what Getchell excelled at was "like '30s stuff, with all that snappy dialogue and all" (Carducci, 14). Inspired by this "30's stuff" Scorsese decided on some radical experiments in a prelude to the modern story, set in the never-never land of Hollywood spectaculars, of Oz and William Cameron-Menzies. The opening minutes of *Alice*—which cost more than $85,000 to film, a sum greater than the total budgets of some of Scorsese's earlier films— were Scorsese's first footage shot on a real studio set, and he was as happy as a kid turned loose in a candy store. In one of Hollywood's ironic accidents, this footage proved to be the last film shot on these Columbia soundstages. Scorsese tried to jam every movie allusion he could into this sequence, borrowing from an eclectic mix of his own special memories of *Duel in the Sun, Gone with the Wind, The Wizard of Oz, Invaders from Mars,* and *Tobacco Road.* Wistfully seeking to rediscover the source of those cinematic illusions which had shaped his youth, Scorsese rationalized this opening sequence as a reflection of not only his dreams but Alice's: "It's a flashback, written in the original script to Monterey, California, in 1948. I wanted to find a new way of looking back. I mean, how did Alice relate to her past psychologically? In her mind, Monterey is fantasy, pure illusion. So I shot a flashback as if it were a Hollywood movie being made on a sound stage. Unreal. Because that's where Alice is at" (Gardner, 36).

Scorsese couldn't resist playing with all the toys of his craft in this overblown introduction. As would later be the case with *New York, New York,* the appeals of the set itself overwhelmed the director's control over his narrative. Scorsese recalls the filming of this opening scene for *Alice* with raffish delight: "I got a little crazy with the site and the redness and all that stuff. I had fun with the fog. You know, you've got fog machines, use a fog machine, see what happens. Got a crane—use a crane. It's fun. Also I figured it's a strange opening for a picture so what the hell" (*Dialogue,* 6). Scorsese sustained this craziness throughout the sequence, liberating his revisionist commentary on Hollywood confections. Amid this rosy dream, Alice orders her mother to "Blow it out your ass!" As always, Scorsese stretches the limits of the dream, explores both its pros and its cons, and relishes the balance between worship and blasphemy, insanity and inspiration.

In *Alice* Scorsese's experiments boldly in visual style. Given the generous budget for the project, Scorsese decided he could freely explore the use of camera movements as a means of conveying meaning. Every shot in *Alice,* he felt, could reflect the character's psychology. Since Alice was on the move, Scorsese decided that his own camera should reflect her inner confusion: "Really, push it to the limit, I thought, by moving the camera all the time . . . to reflect her own state of mind. Constant turmoil. The camera is always sliding around, shifting around, saying, 'Wait a second, I feel this way. But I don't feel that way. I want to go back here. No I shouldn't'" (Macklin, 28).

On the set of *Alice,* Scorsese was still in school: rediscovering visual logic and the principles of cinematography. In Mel's Diner, a cramped space, Scorsese avoided close-ups because he felt the close-up had been overused and looked better in television and other small-screen formats; on the big screen, he hypothesized, "they should be used sparingly" (Gardner, 36). Similarly, to maintain the intimate look of *Alice,* a psychological drama, Scorsese avoided using a telephoto lens until the very last scene, the vision of their future. The one place Scorsese repeated shots, always using a 360-degree tracking pan, was in the treatment of Alice's performances. Scorsese knew critics would deplore this repetition, but he balanced his thematic concerns against such fears.

Critics mercilessly attacked Scorsese's visual style in *Alice.* Academic reviewers like William Pechter lamented the "excessively lunging, thrusting visual style."[13] Pundits like Judith Christ deplored "the handheld pursuit of the image, lending an exhausting freneticism to what is melodramatic on its own," arguing that the "camera show" gave *Alice* "a dizzying feeling of puffery and makes this small drama so consciously small that it ultimately becomes patronizing."[14] As usual, the most negative criticism came from *Esquire*'s John Simon, who rhapsodized about a director "trying too hard and delivering too little," about a visual stylist "as stereotypical as all our good old Hollywood hacks" (Simon 1975, 38). Simon concedes that Scorsese has learned the classic syntax of movies and often "uses it demonstratively" as Simon reluctantly lauds the music sequences: "Give him a . . . piano with Alice seated at it, and he will track semicircularly from right to left, then from left to right, sometimes even full circle, intercutting this with close-ups of the heroine, and making sure that, if Alice is performing at the center of a circular bar, there should be plenty of blurry customers' backs temporarily blocking the camera's vision. He also knows how to pull back his camera from Alice at her home piano, dolly out through the window across a hedge, then change to a lateral motion and track along with Tommy" (Simon 1975, 40–41). Simon's dutiful if sardonic recognition of Scorsese's mastery of the grammar of the Hollywood film mirrored the gossip on the grapevine in Hollywood. *Alice Doesn't Live Here Anymore* had been prepared "Academy all the way"; it was an Oscar-bound, prestigious product, one announcing the arrival of a new superstar, Martin Scorsese. He was now "bankable" and the dealmakers were alerted. Even before *Alice* was released, Scorsese would be in preproduction on several major projects, including a big-budget, "old-fashioned" musical, *New York, New York,* and an urban psychological thriller, *Taxi Driver.*

One intriguing deal didn't come to fruition, however. During the shooting of *Alice* in Tucson, the godfather of American cinema, its most accomplished and ornery actor, Marlon Brando, approached Scorsese about the possibility of directing his Wounded Knee film, a drama largely concerned with the plight and suffering of American Indians. In Tucson Brando began his courting of Scorsese with praise for *Mean Streets* and for Scorsese's contribution to the recognition of Italian Americans in the United States. Scorsese, who worshiped Brando's achievements, was delighted by Brando's comments. As he told critic Chris Holdenfield, "It was the highest compliment: [Brando] understood [*Mean Streets*], he understood the picture" (Holdenfield 1977, 38).

Brando's project was an offer Scorsese couldn't refuse, and the two of them worked on the screenplay. Scorsese visited Indian reservations, and driven by his conscience, he worked long nights with Brando on a storyboard. Meanwhile *Alice* had to be promoted, the screening of *Italianamerican* at the New York Film Festival beckoned, Academy Awards were at hand, *Taxi Driver* was being structured, and the deal for *New York, New York* had to be finalized. And there were the Indians to be dealt with; several had already harassed Sandy Weintraub sexually. If *Alice* had engaged feminist interest and pressure, the Wounded Knee project would be another political cauldron.

Scorsese was being torn apart by the freedom of the new Hollywood: there were too many details and deals, proposals and negotiations. Something had to give, and eventually it did; Scorsese's frail constitution wasn't up to the challenge. So after one particularly arduous all-night session with Brando, Scorsese found himself temporarily in the hospital. Then Ellen Burstyn won her Oscar and implored Scorsese, who accepted it on her behalf, to give himself much of the credit. Scorsese demurred, but all of Hollywood knew he had made her success possible. From *Alice Doesn't Live Here Anymore* on, the stakes for Scorsese would be even higher. No longer a boy genius capturing film school sensibilities with a 16 mm camera, Scorsese had made the shift to the West Coast, taken a house on Mulholland Drive, and perched himself in the dreamy hills of Hollywood.

4

Taxi Driver (1976)

Scorsese didn't spend all his time relishing the mountain air in Hollywood; his weekends involved treks to Malibu beach. As a confirmed nonswimmer, he went not to enjoy the surf, sun, and bikinis but to wheel-and-deal at the estate of Michael and Julia Phillips, the producers of the Academy Award–winning smash *The Sting,* who hosted a literary salon, which included such luminaries as John Gregory Dunne, Joan Didion, Gloria and Willard Huyck, and the talk of the town, tyro screenwriter Paul Schrader, who had sold Warner Brothers his script *The Yakuza* for $350,000. Crowding other beach blankets at the Phillipses' hacienda were would-be stars Al Pacino, Robert De Niro, and Jill Clayburgh and erstwhile filmmakers Steven Spielberg, John Milius, and Brian De Palma. Didion would eventually complain, "There was too much ambition in one room for a Sunday afternoon"; amplifying her idea, the abrasive Schrader opined, "There was enough frustration to light a small American city."[1]

Schrader had few friends in Hollywood, but a legion of acquaintances eager to exploit his writing skill. Ironically, this superhot screenwriting talent had not seen a single film until his late teens. His youth had been spent in the austere bosom of the Christian Reformed church, a dour Calvinist sect that frowned on alcohol, dance, movies, and art as worldly distractions. Schrader enrolled in Calvin College, a seminary for the pious faithful in Grand Rapids, Michigan, but went AWOL to enroll in film courses at Columbia University in New York City. There, at an Upper West Side bar, the apostate Schrader quaffed beers with film critic Robert Warshow's son Paul, who, in sodden bonhomie, introduced the wayward backslider to his mentor, Pauline Kael. Kael recognized Schrader's abilities and used her influence to have him admitted to UCLA's film program.

Schrader distinguished himself at UCLA working as film critic for the Los Angeles *Free Press* and preparing his thesis for publication by the University of California Press under the title *Transcendental Style in Film: Ozu, Bresson, Dreyer.* The American Film Institute selected Schrader for its advanced film study program at Greystone, but he resigned in protest over budget cuts. Schrader then began to peddle his writing skills in the shark-infested waters of Hollywood.

Schrader met Scorsese on Thanksgiving 1972, and they spent the afternoon with their mutual friend, Brian De Palma, discussing Jacques Tourneur's *Out of the Past* and other film noir classics. Thereafter Scorsese pleaded with Schrader to prepare an adaptation of Dostoyevski's *The Gambler,* but Schrader demurred, citing obligations to other projects, such as his outline for *Close Encounters of the Third Kind* and his collaboration with De Palma on *Obsession.* Schrader did, however, proffer one screenplay he thought would be right for the creator of *Mean Streets,* a script he had written earlier, entirely on speculation: *Taxi Driver.*

Taxi Driver arose out of a bad period in Schrader's life when his marriage to designer Jeannine Oppelwall had collapsed and his mistress had walked out. Beset on all sides, Schrader turned to drinking and found himself wandering the streets at night, recuperating in all-night porno theaters. Then Schrader's stomach gave out, and he was rushed to a hospital for ulceritis. All these problems—the rejection by two women, the drinking, the aimless drifting, the alien urban environment, the porno and the stomach pains—would be incorporated in Travis Bickle, the protagonist of *Taxi Driver,* who proclaims himself "God's lonely man."

Michael and Julia Phillips optioned *Taxi Driver* and held the script for several years, putting together one package after another. At one point it appeared that Robert Mulligan would direct Jeff Bridges in *Taxi Driver,* but a distraught Paul Schrader insisted that the producers first see Martin Scorsese's *Mean Streets.* That screening convinced everyone that there was one natural triumvirate of talents for *Taxi Driver*: Schrader, Scorsese, and De Niro.

Scorsese's success with *Alice,* De Niro's fame for *The Godfather, Part Two,* and Schrader's hot hand in selling scripts complicated this small project immensely. For a while prospects for *Taxi Driver* looked so bleak that Scorsese considered making it in black-and-white on videotape. The young director was caught in a juggling act, trying to hold *New York, New York* and *Taxi Driver* together, as De Niro mulled other assignments and Schrader fielded requests for screenplays from every major director in Hollywood.

Things came to such an ugly pass that lawyers began to circle *Taxi Driver*. Instead of litigating, everyone agreed to take a huge salary cut and forgo profit participation, so David Begelmann of Columbia Pictures had a deal he couldn't refuse: De Niro, Schrader, and Scorsese for a puny $1.3 million. At that price Columbia didn't care that the principals, including Scorsese, were convinced that *Taxi Driver* wouldn't mean big box office.

In July and August 1975 Columbia Pictures's maverick project *Taxi Driver* hit the streets of New York City for filming, with a group of principals who had art and personal expression on their minds. This dark picture of a lonely cabbie had none of the glitzy, high-tech, swashbuckling charm that reaped more than $300 million in American rentals for George Lucas's *Star Wars* and *The Empire Strikes Back,* none of the alien invaders that brought more than $200 million to Steven Spielberg and his *Jaws* and *Close Encounters of the Third Kind,* and none of the nostalgia, gloss, and mythology that amassed more than $100 million in domestic rentals for Francis Ford Coppola's *Godfather* saga. Yet because it was a small-budget production, there was no need to compromise. As Schrader explained, "We figured if we're going to compromise on money, we're certainly not going to compromise on anything else. There's nothing in the film that was put there at the studio's insistence."[2] While Scorsese may not have had the clout that big-budget projects bring, he did have a freedom that few Hollywood directors ever achieve.

For all their commitment, New York City shooting in the summer of 1975 almost proved too much for the *Taxi Driver* company. July 1975 in New York resembled storm season in a tropical rain forest—steamy heat, then torrential downpours. The potholes in the streets became so bad that the camera mounted on Travis Bickle's "dependable taxi" frequently jarred loose, ruining shots and fraying tempers. Rex Reed, who visited the set, reported a confrontation between Scorsese and his mother, Catherine, who in her zeal to keep everyone supplied with Italian pastries walked into camera range during a difficult sequence, ruining the take.[3]

Everyone was suffering from the bad vibes in Gotham City that summer: the apocalyptic feeling that fiscal collapse was at hand, that the political system had failed, and that racial war was around the corner. New York seemed to have missed out on the American economic boom. Within one year a popular Republican president and his message for the Big Apple were laconically summarized by the New York *Daily News* in the most famous headline of the decade: "Ford to City: 'Drop Dead.'" Even New York City boosters like Scorsese had to admit: "That summer was a down point for New York, and it shows in that film, in the mood of it. It was so hot you could see the violence shimmering in the air, taste it in your mouth, and there we were in the middle of it."[4]

To cope with the problems Julia Phillips the producer outlined as "Big pressure, short schedule, and short money. New York in the summer. Night shooting," the cast and crew of *Taxi Driver* turned to cocaine; as a result, Phillips, a heavy drug user, recognized the project as "a cokey movie" (Phillips, 211–12). Her one visit to the set further convinced her "they all were doing blow" (Phillips, 212). Scorsese's coke indulgence would eventually be cited in acrimonious divorce proceedings. Schrader's consumption of dope became legendary in Hollywood, and De Niro was with John Belushi the night he died "wired," a victim of Hollywood's blizzard of show.

Several violent incidents unnerved the production crew during the July 1975 shoot. When they were scouting locations around Lincoln Center, they saw a big man walk over to an old woman waiting for a bus and punch her in the mouth for no apparent reason. Another day on location, when the ensemble was filming Travis Bickle's murder of a stickup man in a bodega, a real murder occurred right around the corner at Eighty-Sixth Street and Columbus Avenue. Soon the movie's players and the aftermath of a real crime became intertwined. As Scorsese explained to Carmie Amata, "We didn't know which cops were for us and which were for the real killing around the corner. Everything got mixed together and we really couldn't tell, so we just shot whatever was happening around us."[5] Scorsese intended *Taxi Driver* to have the surrealistic aura of a New York out of control, chaotic and threatening, a New York that reflected Travis Bickle's tortured psyche.

When Columbia representatives, disturbed by the numerous delays thunderstorms were causing for location shooting, suggested that some sequences be moved indoors, Scorsese shut the production down. Months later he told a group of film students inquiring about the difficulties of working with Hollywood studios that he had warned his associates, "That's it. If they don't like the way I'm gonna make the picture, then I won't make the picture." The lesson Scorsese urged on his pupils was "that you really have to love something enough to kill it" (Holdenfield 1989, 48). Columbia Pictures loved its low-budget package too much to see it die, so Scorsese got the assurances he needed and the production slogged on.

Scorsese threw so much of himself into *Taxi Driver* that the production dragged on weeks over schedule, and finally Columbia Pictures insisted the shooting stop and the editing begin. Tempers flared again; Scorsese's health flagged; but finally he capitulated. The editing process for *Taxi Driver* proved another nightmare. As Scorsese confided to *After Dark*'s Norman Stoop, "I had to edit the picture to get a rough cut in four weeks—like a Roger Corman movie."[6]

Scorsese had come far, however, from his *Boxcar Bertha* days, and despite all the tensions complicating his location shooting, all the exigencies of shooting a studio film on a tight budget, and all the intricacies of collaborating with talents like the short-fused Schrader and the intense De Niro, the young director had managed to create a personal masterpiece, a riveting exploration of loneliness, sexual repression, and self-destructive violence. Scorsese took Schrader's intellectual script, De Niro's superhuman energy, and his sensual imagistic vision and fused them into a memorable incursion into the dark side of human consciousness; into a netherworld of hookers, pimps, shysters, and opportunists pursuing dreams of unobtainable success; and into an America eviscerated by the war in Vietnam, by a polarization between haves and have-nots, insiders and outsiders, white and black, and by its own fixation on guns, violence, and vigilantism, all in the name of law and order.

Taxi Driver revolves around one enigmatic figure, Travis Bickle, the embodiment of twentieth-century America's "lonely crowd," a pathetic, one-dimensional man alienated from society, crippled by fear and loathing, and held hostage by the culture of narcissism. Travis, who communicates little to others, is capable of remarkable insights into his cursed life. In his diary he records his fate quite perspicaciously: "Loneliness has followed me all my life. The life of loneliness pursues me wherever I go: in bars, cars, coffee shops, theaters, stores, and sidewalks. There is no escape. I am God's lonely man." Travis's description of himself provides a sly allusion to Thomas Wolfe's "God's Lonely Man," a portion of which Paul Schrader cites as his epigraph to his original script.

Immediately before drafting *Taxi Driver,* Schrader had reread Sartre's *Nausea,* and the screenwriter took a philosophical, existential, and literary tack in delineating Travis's Sisyphean suffering. Asked to explain his literary antecedents, Schrader concentrated on the European intellectual tradition: "The intention of writing that script was to take a hero from European fiction and film—the man from the underground, the stranger, Roquentin from *Nausea,* the character from *Pickpocket.* To take that character whose essential dilemma is 'Should I exist' and put him in an American street context."[7] While Scorsese and De Niro would provide the green card for this stranger and make Travis a natural rather than a naturalized American, the existential dimension was never eliminated from the film. In fact, one of the few scenes written for *Taxi Driver* during its production provides the most heavy-handed example of European existentialism in the film. As it happened, Peter Boyle, the ex–Christian Brother who plays Wizard, an elder statesman cab driver whom Travis turns to for advice, had been part of the rat pack at the Phillipses' salon. One afternoon he mesmerized the sandal set with an improvisation as Jesus Christ, the standup comedian in a tawdry Las Vegas piano bar. Schrader and Scorsese, two altar boys at heart, never forgot this semiblasphemous display and wanted Boyle to work on *Taxi Driver.* Boyle chaffed at Wizard's limited lines, however, so Schrader wrote a new shtick especially for Boyle, a cut-rate philosophical rap positing that existence precedes essence.

In these new lines the semiarticulate Wizard assures Travis that "You do a thing and that's what you are" and that taxi driving finally becomes you as "you become the job." This complex explanation of the title for the film takes on mock-heroic grandeur as Wizard continues to translate Sartre and Camus into New Yorkese. Wisdom comes when we "get drunk" or "get laid," the Wizard pontificates, since "We're all fucked. More or less." Travis dismisses this sermonizing as the craziest stuff he's ever heard, but Schrader and Scorsese have the double edge of irony on their side. Wizard may mangle existentialism in this parody, but the larger theme remains. Peripatetic Travis is stuck in an absurdist world, and his problems provide overheated permutations of existential dilemmas. Wordsmith Pauline Kael was right on target when she characterized *Taxi Driver* as "a movie in heat, a raw, tabloid version of *Notes from the Underground.*"[8] In Schrader's angst-ridden, autobiographical portrait of Travis Bickle, Scorsese got the Dostoyevski adaptation he'd always wanted.

Travis's first voiceover plainly defines his existential quest: "I don't believe that one should devote one's life to morbid self-absorption. I believe someone should become a person like other people." The agonizing search for identity proves perilous for this cabbie lost in the steam clouds, thunderstorms, neon lights, and dark streets of New York 24 hours a day. The film's most daring visual—a dizzying plunge into the effervescent turmoil of Travis's glass of Alka Seltzer, inspired by a similar descent into a coffee cup in Godard's *Two or Three Things I Know about Her*—was intended, Scorsese indicated, to show that "Travis is lost in his private universe."[9] Travis's stunted development and inability to find his place in a modern city propel him into his yellow cab. He can't sleep nights, and he finds little to occupy his days, he tells his prospective employer, so he might as well get paid for his haphazard wanderings. That way, his therapy would all be on the meter.

Scorsese's approach to Travis Bickle's loneliness concentrated on emotions. Scorsese's first inspiration for a sequence for *Taxi Driver* eschewed violence, urban blight, and literary overtones; the first footage he conceived for *Taxi Driver* was a prolonged shot of Travis on the phone with Betsy as the camera tracked away from him down a long hallway to a desolate corridor with more phones and nobody there. This scene was the last setup Scorsese filmed for *Taxi Driver*, and it remains his favorite.

Talking with Rex Reed during the shooting, Scorsese emphasized Travis's personal problems. The Travis Scorsese described to Reed echoes the themes of his two earlier Hollywood features. Scorsese told Reed that *Taxi Driver* was "about a guy who desperately needs to be recognized for *something*, but he has nothing he can do to gain himself the recognition. He has something to say, but he's not sure what, so finally, out of frustration, he turns to violence as a means of expressing himself. It's a kind of an exorcism for me. That's why I have to make this movie. It'll be more like *Mean Streets* than *Alice*" (Rex Reed, 5). Travis clearly contains elements of a guilt-ridden Italian boy fantasizing home movies on elaborate storyboards. If Schrader looked to art to define his cabbie, Scorsese looked inward to understand his torment.

Another element in *Taxi Driver*'s treatment of loneliness and alienation came from Schrader's chance encounter with Harry Chapin's song "Taxi." Chapin's lachrymal ballad helped focus Schrader's attention on the cultural artifacts that contribute to Travis's sense of estrangement. Travis, for example, feels threatened by "American Bandstand" and its celebration of teenage sexuality. In one of the film's most chillingly funny sequences, Travis aims his gun at the gyrating dancers on his television screen, only to have everything fall out of balance as his set crashes to the floor and explodes. This theme of popular culture as the great leveler and consequently the dangerously powerful arbiter of acceptable behavior receives humorous reinforcement as Scorsese juxtaposes events on a make-believe television soap opera and the bizarre episodes in Travis's life.

Media confections and Travis's world remain as out of touch as Senator Palantine, the would-be presidential candidate in *Taxi Driver,* is with his potential supporters. Palantine, played by erudite critic Leonard Harris, cites Walt Whitman as the inspiration for his populist slogan, "We are the people," an eerie precursor to Jerry Brown's "We the people." Yer Palantine seems congenitally incapable of approaching the populace. His courtly manners and princely mien awe Travis. As a passenger in Travis's cab, Palantine asks the tongue-tied cabbie what he thinks the next president should do; Travis can frame no coherent answer. In an interior monologue, however, Travis echoes the plea Kurtz makes in *Heart of Darkness* to "exterminate the brutes": "He should clean up this city. It's full of filth and scum. It's like an open sewer. . . . We need a President that would clean up the whole mess. Flush it right down the fucking toilet."

Travis's isolation arises from both society's overwhelming demands and his stunted nature. Scorsese felt Travis was "emotionally arrested at the age of 13" (Rex Reed, 5). Nevertheless, De Niro spent months trying to get a handle on the emotional complexities of the role. A fanatic when it comes to preparing for an assignment, De Niro obtained a New York taxi license and drove around 12 hours a day to get the feel of the hack's life. De Niro also practiced for days with various handguns to get a sense of Travis's weapons fetish. Then he had two dozen midwesterners read the script into a tape recorder so he could get the nasal twang down perfectly. In the week before shooting, De Niro lost 15 pounds to enhance the haggard, strung-out look of his Travis Bickle. Pressed by interviewers to define his concept of Travis, De Niro stressed his use of animal imagery to conceptualize his taxi driver. All his preparations, he half-jested and half-explained, made him see Travis as a crab. Developing this metaphor, De Niro explained: "I just had that image of him. You know how a crab sort of walks sideways and has a gawky, awkward movement. . . . Crabs are very straightforward, but straightforward to them is going to the left, and to the right. They turn sideways; that's the way they're built."[10]

Travis was also built from a psychological profile Scorsese had developed by a former Green Beret officer. The Scorsese of *Street Scenes* and *The Big Shave* used Travis Bickle as one more opportunity to bring the war home. Bickle's violent behavior symbolized the heritage of Vietnam that Lyndon Johnson, Henry Kissinger, and Richard Nixon struggled to deny. My Lai was millions of miles away, the politicians asserted; the drug use, prostitution, black marketing, and other crimes so rampant in Southeast Asia, they suggested, could never make it home from the war zone. Travis afforded proof that all these assurances were lies. One look at his marine battle jacket with its "King Kong Brigade" patches; one glance of his Mohawk haircut, the style favored by Special Forces units on search-and-destroy missions; and one glimpse of the horrible K-bar knife he straps to his combat boots—these belied all the political doublespeak. Travis Bickle may have won his honorable discharge, but the war would always be with him. He had swallowed totally the marines' message that "might makes right." He knew, as did the gung-ho military leaders in Vietnam, that sometimes you had to destroy people to save them, that winning hearts and minds was often a matter of napalm, antipersonnel devices, and saturation bombing. Travis upheld the tradition of *semper fidelis,* for he would always be faithful to the values he learned in Vietnam.

Scorsese bragged, in fact, about the fan mail he received for *Taxi Driver* from women who thanked him for finally making a feminist film. They had seen, Scorsese acknowledged, the central theme in his film: "this picture just takes the idea of macho and takes it to its logical insane conclusion, graphically, pornographically, insane" (Kilday, 32). Travis's years in Vietnam had reinforced the madonna-whore complex so common among American males; he could not reconcile motherhood or sanctity with sexuality. He wanted his women virginal and pure, even as he compulsively frequented pornographic movies.

The nexus in *Taxi Driver* between Travis's repressed sexuality and his cathartic violence provides the dramatic energy; each failed romance loads another cartridge into Travis's weapons. Travis suggests the connection between sex and violence with his first description of the routine of cab driving: "Every night when I return the car to the garage, I have to clean the come off the back seat. Some nights I clean off the blood." All his confreres at the Bellmore Cafeteria exchange anecdotes that veer from sexy tales of passengers changing pantyhose in the middle of a ride to horror stories of cabbies battered by knife-wielding crazies cutting off ears. And the movie marquees that flash hypnotically through his windshield balance *Secret Ecstasy* with *The Seven Blows of the Dragon*. Travis's urban island drifts between the pleasure principle and the death urge with no parking places in between.

Travis's first fare in *Taxi Driver*, a loquacious businessman fondling a black prostitute in a long blond wig, foreshadows Travis's attempt to pick up the black candy-counter salesgirl at the Show and Tell tri-ple-X-rated movie theater. Although the distracted girl—played by Diahnne Abbott, De Niro's real-life girlfriend, whom he married soon after the film was finished—is immersed in her romance magazine and its fascinating exposé on "How Your Money Effects [*sic*] Your Sexual Life," Travis continues his banter until she summons the manager. Travis then mutters a request for candy and soda and takes his seat in the spartan auditorium, slumping, eyes glazed, as a daisy chain of nude bodies performs on the screen.

As a sad outsider, Travis garners the audience's sympathy, an effect Scorsese intended. Scorsese viewed Travis, he told interviewers as "a sympathetic figure" with real affinities to himself: "There's certainly a lot of Travis in me, some of the same emotions. There are deep, dark things in all of us and they come out in different ways. I've dealt with mine through analysis; a lot of people release them sexually, but Travis can't even do that" (B. Taylor, 15). Screenwriter Schrader also felt these affinities and allowed De Niro to play Travis dressed entirely in Schrader's favorite clothes: his dungarees, boots, belts, shirts, and jacket. Even Schrader admitted, however, that "It was spooky to see him in my clothes."[11]

Travis's second rejection, the cold shoulder from his dream girl Betsy, moves him closer to armed violence. This motif of sexual re-jection leading to physical violence receives reinforcement from Ber-nard Herrmann's musical score. On the set Herrmann labored to explain to his colleagues the progression in musical and psychological motifs. Scorsese recalls that one day he noticed that "whenever you see a woman you hear da-da-da-da, but at the end of the slaughter it's DA-DA-Da-DADA-DUM-M-M-M!" and he asked Herrmann to ex-plain. Patiently, Herrmann expostulated on his pattern, revealing that "the reason he did it that way was to show that this was where Travis' fantasies about women led him. His illusions, his self-perpetuating way of dealing with women had finally brought him to a bloody, violent outburst" (Amata, 17). Herrmann died as he was completing *Taxi Driver*, and the last credit for the film expresses the whole crew's "gratitude and respect."

The Betsy episodes in *Taxi Driver* manifest Scorsese's obsession with angelic women rising above the crowd and his fears of sexuality as somehow compromising feminine virtue. When Travis first sees Betsy standing at the door of the Palantine Committee headquarters at Fifty-Eighth and Broadway, he rhapsodizes that she "appeared like an angel out of the open sewer. Out of this filthy mass. She is alone: they cannot touch her." Then Betsy and he have their disastrous date as Travis attempts to take her to see *The Swedish Marriage Manual*. Spurned, Travis doesn't examine his actions, but he instead flares out at Betsy. He tells his diary: "I realize how much she is like the others, so cold and distant. Many people are like that. Women for sure. They're like an onion." Then, putting his paranoid thoughts into action, Travis goes back to committee headquarters, terrorizes the employees, and yells his condemnation at her: "You're living in hell. You're gonna die in hell." The key elements in this sequence are the polarities: heaven and hell, angelic and demonic, women against men, insiders against outsiders. Travis's schizophrenic vision of life mirrors Scorsese's adolescent difficulties with the black-and-white sexual morality his Irish Catholic teachers hammered home to their Italian charges. As nuns warned about the dangers of "shaking your leg" in seventh grade, Scorsese's focus was elsewhere, he admits: "I was more into looking at the little girls' uniforms and wondering what was underneath the uniforms. Those uniforms became very striking to me, so that later in *Who's That Knocking?* and *Taxi Driver* I had them wear what looks like parochial school uniforms, a blazer and a pleated, Scotch plaid type skirt—Cybil Shepherd wears that in *Taxi Driver* as a kind of joke" ("Streets," 98). The uniform may well be a jest; the larger issues of men incapable of coping with women as equals in sexual relations are hardly comic. Travis cannot understand Betsy, cannot enter her world. So like Frankenstein's monster, he tries to destroy what he cannot embrace.

Schrader's original script allowed little room for an "angelic" Betsy. Schrader presented this career woman as one more manipulative female in a society based on status and success. In his vision "beneath that Cover Girl facial there is a keen, though highly specialized sensibility: her eyes scan every man who passes her desk as her mind computes his desirability: political, intellectual, sexual, emotion, material. . . . She is, in other words, a star-fucker of the highest order."[12] This concept remains in *Taxi Driver*'s final sequence. Travis is chatting with his buddies outside the St. Regis, Scorsese's home-away-from-home during his California years, when Betsy slithers into his cab.

After some talk about his heroism and celebrity, she purrs, "Maybe I'll see you sometime, huh?" But it's no fare for Travis as he slams down the meter, smiles, answers an emphatically negative though understated "Sure," and drives away. He recognizes the clay feet of his goddess and resigns himself to loneliness and the dark music of the night.

Travis's enlightenment about Betsy comes as a result of his encounters with Iris Steensma (Jodie Foster), a pubescent hooker working out of a tenement on East Thirteenth Street for a pimp named Sport (Harvey Keitel). As British critic Colin Westerbeck remarks, Betsy and Iris are traditional dramatic foils, with Betsy as "a goddess from the *haut monde*" and Iris as "a lost soul from the *demi-monde,* a demonic reincarnation of the untouchable Betsy, even looking vaguely like her."[13] The older Betsy, an affluent career woman living alone uptown flees porno theaters and fights off Travis's clumsy advances. The childlike Iris, a homeless runaway virtually imprisoned in the Lower East Side drug den, claws at Travis's zipper when he insists she keep her blouse on. Iris and Betsy are whore and madonna, young lover and older women, frivolous devil and beatific angel to a confused and frustrated Travis. Neither is a real person for him; they represent vague abstractions, dangerous alternatives, and bewildering challenges for this dim-witted paladin.

Casting the role of Iris led to one of Scorsese's daring choices. He wanted a young girl with a special look and settled on Jodie Foster, the original bare-bottomed Coppertone girl, a mainstay of family television series and several juvenile Disney classics, and the underutilized Audrey, Tommy's androgynous, thoroughly weird girlfriend in *Alice Doesn't Live Here Anymore,* whose most memorable line had been "You wanna get high on Ripple?" When Foster first saw the script, her reaction was surprise, since she felt "this was a great part for a 21 year old," yet she was only 12 at the time.[14] Her mother, Brandy, thought everything was fine, however, so Jodie was off for sessions with a UCLA psychiatrist mandated by the state regulators monitoring children's welfare on film sets. Foster passed her psychiatric examination with flying colors, convincing everyone she could impersonate a whore without losing her mind or her innocence. Unbeknownst to Foster, Scorsese and Schrader had chosen her because of what syndicated columnist Kathy Huffhines labeled her "unusual boygirl quality" suitable for roles "as a tomboy or a tramp or a little of both."[15] Travis, after all, wants Iris to be his child, his friend, his confidante; she's paid, however, to seduce him.

Jodie Foster as Iris in *Taxi Driver* (1976). Columbia Pictures. The Museum of Modern Art/Film Stills Archive.

Schrader and Scorsese were also cognizant of a recent study of rape and subliminal incitements to rape. Researchers had been surprised that, in group therapy, rapists often mentioned Foster's Coppertone ad with the puppy tugging at her swimsuit and baring her buttocks. As Schrader summarized the analysis by psychologists, the ad indeed had a prurient dimension: "It had just the right mixture for these rapists of adolescent sexuality, female nudity, rear entry, animals, and violence."[16] Unwittingly, Foster brought many sexual associations of violence and frustration to *Taxi Driver*; she had become a fantasy love object for a large number of disturbed individuals.

Travis fantasizes about saving Iris from her life on the streets, envisioning himself as Saint George conquering dragons and freeing virgins. Yet Travis proves a bloodthirsty Saint George in *Taxi Driver*; Scorsese has often labeled his psychotic protagonist as "somewhere between Charles Manson and Saint Paul. . . . He's going to help people so much he's going to kill them" (S. Braudy, 27). Violence becomes Travis's new religion; in the place of liturgy and sacraments, he embraces guns and blood. In a clearly Freudian substitution, Eros is displaced for him by blood lust. If he cannot be loved, he will be feared. Tender Travis, the would-be lover, becomes terrible Travis, the coldhearted destroyer.

The most famous sequence in *Taxi Driver* records this transformation as De Niro stares at the camera, as though he were rehearsing his role in a mirror, and menacingly demands a response to his insistent questions: "You talkin to me? Who you lookin at? You lookin' at me?" This sequence was an improvisation. In his youth Scorsese had fantasized about acting by standing before a mirror and imitating Alan Ladd in *Shane,* Victor Mature, and eventually even Marlon Brando and James Dean. Mirrors thus are linked in his consciousness with both artistic expression and the definition of the American male hero. As a result, he admits, "that's how a lot of mirror scenes in my movies came about" (Scorsese 1989, 42). Scorsese often uses his actors to reenact his own youthful rehearsals and discoveries. In *Taxi Driver* Scorsese and De Niro were improvising in an empty building in a noisy neighborhood. As De Niro worked on the scene, Scorsese, lying on the floor in front of him, kept instructing him to repeat his lines. The resulting footage, shot late in the production, provided an anchor for Travis's mental deterioration. Schrader the screenwriter freely admits that "it's the best thing in the movie. And I didn't write it!" (Thompson 1976, 11).

Martin Scorsese as a demented passenger with Robert De Niro as cabbie Travis Bickle in *Taxi Driver* (1976). Columbia Pictures. The Museum of Modern Art/Film Stills Archive.

Once violence becomes Travis's language, *Taxi Driver* begins to depend increasingly on visceral thrills. The bloodiest scenes emerge as the memorable ones. There is, for example, the shootout at the bodega when the clerk in a grocery store, wearing a Tulane University Green Wave T-shirt with the lettering emblazoned in superpatriotic red, white, and blue letters, consummates the murder by clubbing the corpse in rage. In another scene, one that film magazines reprinted under the caption "The Pussy and the .44," one of Travis's passengers, played by Scorsese, has him park outside 417 Central Park West while he watches the silhouette of his wife in a second-story apartment window and explains to Travis, "A nigger lives there. She left me two weeks ago. It took me this long to find out where she went. I'm gonna kill her." The passenger continues his murderous fantasy, prodding Travis to respond to his aggressive questions: "Did you ever see what a .44 can do to a woman's pussy, cabbie?" Scorsese's longtime friend

George Memmoli was to have played this role, but a serious accident the day before the scene was shot forced Scorsese to find a replacement. In most of his earlier films, Scorsese had done Hitchcock-like cameos or uncredited voiceovers; with this scene in *Taxi Driver,* he began in earnest his parallel career as a film actor. He also provided a harrowing counterpoint to Travis's mental collapse. Travis, spurned by a woman, seeks meaning through violence; this cab passenger seeks meaning and pleasure in violence.

Travis's quest for identity through armature, action, and violence can be seen in his monologues about a new "total organization," in which every muscle must be tight, junk food and other poisons renounced, and everything dedicated to "True force" so great that "all the king's men cannot put it back together again" (an allusion to the dangers of populism made clear by Robert Penn Warren's fictional account of Willie Long, *All the King's Men*). Travis first targets Charles Palantine, a latterday demagogue whose entourage includes the star-struck Betsy. Travis is too far gone at this juncture, however, to make his threat real. His Mohawk haircut, inappropriate battlegear, bulging pockets, and demented and solitary clapping (reminiscent of Charles Foster Kane's applause in *Citizen Kane*) mark him as every Secret Service agent's walking nightmare—the lone, crazed gunman.

Killing Sport and his henchmen proves much easier; no police seem to be patrolling the Lower East Side. This climactic sequence, with its prolonged shootout that pays clear homage to the Western and its bloody special effects, so gory that they prompted Pauline Kael to label *Taxi Driver* "one of the few truly modern horror films" (Kael 1979, 134), has been the focus of most criticism of *Taxi Driver*. To evaluate it fairly, one should consider the filmmakers' intentions. Schrader in his original script clearly wanted the mood of the sequence to differ vastly from the rest of the film. He provided the following extraordinary "screenwriter's note": "The screenplay has been moving at a reasonably realistic level until this prolonged slaughter. The slaughter itself is a gory extension of violence, more surreal than real. The slaughter is the moment Travis has been heading for all his life, and where this screenplay has been heading for over 85 pages. It is the release of all that cumulative pressure; it is a reality unto itself. It is the psychopath's Second Coming" (Schrader 1975, 100). The audience must be in tune with De Niro's performance to appreciate Travis's parousia. Madman Travis is an inspired zealot for whom violence has become an apocalyptic new religion. Julia Cameron—whom Guy

Flatley of the *New York Times* described as Scorsese's "new live-in Nightingale on the scene, . . . a seductive journalist who came to interview Marty and stayed for dinner and breakfast" (Flatley 1976, 39), and who eventually married Scorsese—emphasized the poetic aspects of De Niro and his performance, opining that he was "like a character in *The Dubliners,* walking alone on the beach full of feelings. In his silences, I see storm clouds threatening on the horizons."[17] Scorsese himself emphasized the religious, mythical, and historical dimensions: "Travis is a commando for God, in a sense. And look at the saints. He's full of their same energy, his just goes off in a different direction. He sees something ugly or dirty and he has to clean it up. . . . [I]n his eyes, he is doing good work" (B. Taylor, 15).

Rating boards demanded that the blood-and-gore in *Taxi Driver* be toned down, that scenes and dialogue be trimmed, and even that colors be altered; Scorsese has argued that the result is even more unabashedly dark than his original cut. Some of the terror is gone, however, and the film suffers for that absence, since the paradox remains that for Scorsese and Schrader, the greater the explicit gore, the clearer the moral theme. A reductio ad absurdum of machismo, fascism, and vigilantism, of martyrdom and blood sacrifice, depends on a disorienting excess of blood, gore, and suffering. *Taxi Driver* confronts the very dilemma Catholic writer Flannery O'Connor faced in parodying modern life: things must be disturbingly grotesque if anyone is to get the point. Just as the anxious O'Connor wrote in justification of her exaggerated fictions, so too does her ironic rationale hold true for assertively religious filmmakers like Schrader and Scorsese: "[T]o the hard of hearing you have to shout, and for the almost blind you draw large and startling figures."[18]

Many people coming to *Taxi Driver* expected just another Charles Bronson *Death Wish* or Clint Eastwood, *Dirty Harry* melodrama of a man who's had all he can take and sets out to right the world. Scorsese and Schrader struggled to transcend this genre by taking the action-hungry audience nauseatingly deep in the trough of gore, by exploding the righteous dimension of Travis's motivation, and by providing a nightmarish epilogue in which a demented society idolizes the assassin-terrorist-psychopath. No sane person can see Travis as a hero, the filmmakers' dialogue and visuals reveal, yet Betsy is seduced by him, and New York lionizes him. Catch-22 has come true here; everyone has flown over the cuckoo's nest, and the inmates are running the asylum.

Taxi Driver pinpoints the "sickness" of a culture addicted to guns, weaned on misogyny and pornography, addicted to celebrity and notoriety, and consecrated to consumption and imperial wars. Travis is, as Scorsese notes, "like a cross between a Gothic horror and the New York *Daily News*" (Thompson 1976, 54); he is Frankenstein, Dracula, and the Wolfman come true as current events. Travis is also, as cultural historian Robert Kolker admonishes, a refuge from "*The Searchers* and *Psycho*" (Kolker, 167). The Duke has let his mask slip, and everyone can see the Norman Bates lurking beneath. *Taxi Driver* shows that guns kill, that violence escalates, and that the blood-red tide is unleashed on the world when fanatics can take God's mission as their license to search and destroy.

Caught up in the excitement of the film's release, Scorsese gave a seemingly breathless interview to Richard Goldstein and Mark Jacobson of the *Village Voice,* a piece that they entitled "Martin Scorsese Tells All: 'Blood and Guts Turn Me On!'" but one that powerfully reveals his deeper themes. The style of the interview, with its incomplete sentences, unclear transitions, rhetorical questions, and restless energy, captures the chaotic rhythms of Scorsese's speech as he gushes forth ideas and impatiently demands feedback and approbation. But Scorsese's view of the relationship between Travis's violent murders and Christ's crucifixion emerges with luminous clarity in his jumbled statements. In his remarks the path from *Mean Streets,* in which one makes up for one's sins in the streets, to *Taxi Driver,* in which one sacrifices to redeem one's world, to *The Last Temptation of Christ,* in which the expiation of humanity's sins is miraculously accomplished, runs straight and true. Asked to explain the shootout in *Taxi Driver,* Scorsese begins by casually observing that "the whole thing has to do with, you know, the whole process that the character goes through to the point at which he wants to sacrifice himself—and it's going to be a blood sacrifice, right?"[19]

Thus, the final shots of the sequence, recorded from the viewpoint of a camera floating high in the sky and drifting back over Travis's path of destruction, is, in Scorsese's terms, "really kind of like a reexamination of the elements of the sacrifice . . . a ritualistic, religious experience. Like the Mass. Christ came down and said you don't have to kill any more lambs, right? He said, I'm gonna go up on the cross and it's gonna be a human sacrifice. . . . Do you understand my point? The idea of Christ coming to fulfill . . . not to, not to destroy, but to fulfill, you know, the prophecy and the idea was, you know, no more ritualistic blood sacrifices of lambs" (Goldstein and Jacobson, 29). When his interviewers then inquired if Travis actually thought that by his killings and his failed suicide attempt New York City would be cleansed, Scorsese said yes, that was the whole idea of Travis's insane mission, and he simultaneously admitted his own attraction to such fantasies: "I like the idea of spurting blood. It's really like a purification, you know, the fountains of blood. It's a personal thing" (Goldstein and Jacobson, 29).

Curiously, Paul Schrader used the symbol of fountains of blood when he conducted his seminar on "Redemption through Self-Destruction" at the American Film Institute. Schrader emphasized its roots in religion: "The idea of purgation through destruction, you know, is one that I was inculcated with as a child of the Church and all that bleeding-Christ consciousness—you know, there's a fountain that flows through Immanuel's vein and we will all be washed in that blood".[20] The confluence of Schrader's Calvinism and Scorsese's Catholicism bathes Travis's slaughter in the holy waters of ritual without absolving him. Travis has confused sacrifice with slaughter, *Taxi Driver* shows, so he cannot achieve martyrdom and salvation. Instead, his rewards will come from Caesar and mammon; he will be celebrated in an evil land as the new hero. Little wonder, then, that when they were making *Taxi Driver,* Scorsese told Schrader, "You know what's going to happen, we're both going to wind up in a monastery somewhere, you and I" ("Streets," 99).

Contemporary critics weren't intent on a monastery for Scorsese and Schrader when *Taxi Driver* was released; they had Shakespeare's "nunnery" or worse in mind. Typical of the response was Robert F. Moss's influential article for the *Saturday Review,* "The Brutalists: Making Movies Mean and Ugly," which pilloried Scorsese for "diving elatedly into the blood and mire".[21] At the Cannes Film Festival, when *Taxi Driver* was announced as the winner of the Golden Palm, there were persistent boos, and the jury president, Tennessee Williams, complained about the escalating violence in films that year.

Scorsese's real heartbreak with *Taxi Driver* came five years later, on 30 March 1981, when John Warnock Hinckley, Jr., opened fire on President Ronald Reagan outside the Washington Hilton. Hinckley later announced that his six errant shots were desperate attempts to win the affection of Jodie Foster (Iris). Hinckley had literally brought Travis to life and in doing so had rekindled the fiery debate about *Taxi Driver* and its effects on viewers. During his trial Hinckley claimed that 15 viewings of *Taxi Driver,* just like the devil, had made him do it; he was then acquitted on grounds of insanity.

Yet America at large in 1981 had little sympathy for would-be assassins and lone gunmen; the shadows of John Kennedy, Robert Kennedy, and Martin Luther King were long on the land. Even normally liberal antiadministration, anti-Reagan journalists like Lawrence Wright were staggered by the shooting. As Wright reports in his autobiography, he heard early accounts of the shooting on his car radio, and "by the time I crossed the river I was sobbing and pounding the steering wheel. . . . I had had enough of tragedy now. I could not bear another martyr."[22] For several months Scorsese was equally overwhelmed, and he refused to comment publicly on *Taxi Driver* or its aftermath. To his intimates, however, he confided that "For a while I didn't feel like making any more films" (Hoberman, 92). The more he thought about it, however, the more Scorsese realized that as a serious artist he must be true to his vision. At a press conference when he was again pestered by numerous questions on *Taxi Driver,* he finally turned on his attackers and offered his artistic credo, a statement that applies not only to *Taxi Driver* but to all his films, including the many even more controversial ones to come: "What am I supposed to do about [the Hinckley shooting]? Quit? Maybe my films do strike a nerve. That's what they're supposed to do. Isn't it? I can't and won't be responsible for every person that walks into a theater where one of my films is playing. I have a hard enough time being responsible for myself."[23]

Most of Scorsese's contemporaries had no such disclaimers to make; *Star Wars, E.T.,* and other such crowd pleasers rarely excited censors or politicians, theologians or lawyers. Scorsese, however, had chosen another path. His Travis Bickle, his Rupert Pupkin, his Jake La Motta, and his Jesus Christ raise hackles as they confront the issues of violence, sacrifice, expiation, sexuality, celebrity, and redemption. They leave audiences asking, "You talkin' to me?"

5

New York, New York (1977) and
The Last Waltz (1978)

Success proved Janus-faced for Martin Scorsese. As his dreams came true at Cannes, with *Taxi Driver* proclaimed a prizewinner, nightmares were forming back in Hollywood and New York. Scorsese was blindsided by demons, but Paul Schrader predicted the director's fall in spring 1976. Commenting on Scorsese's meteoric rise, Schrader foresaw a precipitous fall: "It will finally reach the point where Scorsese can get enough power that he won't have to deal with other people; then he'll be so cut off he'll make a big flop. It's a familiar pattern" (Schrader 1976, 13). Scorsese would consolidate his power on the elaborate set of *New York, New York,* yet this flawed musical drama would prove a calamitous flop.

New York, New York began propitiously. Scorsese, an avid reader of trade papers, came across a column in the *Hollywood Reporter* noting that producer Irwin Winkler had commissioned a script by Earl Mac Rauch about two fledgling talents and their romance in the big-band era and thereafter. Scorsese's agent, Harry Ufland, then proposed a package to Winkler and his partner, Robert Chartoff, with Scorsese as director and Liza Minnelli and Robert De Niro as stars.

Winkler jumped at the prospect of underwriting major young talents. Winkler told interviewers that the project was "a love story," suited to a "passionate man" like Scorsese who "grew up on the musicals at MGM"; in addition, Winkler said, he and Robert Chartoff were "looking for someone who could tell a story that on the surface was very simplistic and yet had an undertone of reality."[1] They hoped for a hit with sparkling music, big songs, an engaging romance, and a meaningful theme. *New York, New York,* the producers reasoned, could continue the tradition of *Cabaret,* another John Kander and Frank Ebb musical, by providing an Academy Award role for Liza Minnelli, a big part for Robert De Niro, glitzy production numbers, and serious insights about America's changing taste in music.

Scorsese, for his part, relished the prospect of making a big-budget, mainstream Hollywood entertainment film, imitating the old studio style as it encompassed his new ideas on what a serious musical could be. Scorsese joked with his associates that he wanted to work in every movie genre. By the mid-1970s he had toyed with gangster films and crime adventures in *Mean Streets* and *Boxcar Bertha* and had explored soap opera and romance in *Alice.* Critics hailed *Taxi Driver* as a modern horror classic, so *New York, New York* was to be his foray into film noir and the musical. After that, he reasoned, maybe he could do his biblical spectacle, *The Last Temptation of Christ.*

Scorsese began preproduction work on *New York, New York* long before shooting on *Taxi Driver* ever started. Liza Minnelli signed on at the inception and spent three years receiving video letters from Scorsese reminding her how interested he was in the project and in her preparation for this demanding role. Minnelli was shocked at the months of "research" she, Scorsese, and De Niro engaged in. As she recalls their groundwork, "We went to every jazz club in the world. And I must have watched 500 films with bands and singers from the period. It was hard to learn to sing in all those different styles."[2]

The background films came from Scorsese's collection. With the advent of home video recording, Scorsese became one of the world's premier archivists. His video library rivals his collection of movie memorabilia and takes its place beside the Martin Scorsese Archives, a comprehensive assembly of drawings, scripts, newspaper clippings, and photographs mirroring his career. Scorsese's intimates marvel at his collections and his memory for movie trivia. Scorsese needs but a few clues, and he can recall, shot by shot, arcane films. His imagination is suffused with vivid recollections of an infinite number of Hollywood features.

Musicals hold a special place in Scorsese's heart, for as he told *Newsweek's* Jack Kroll, "My first memories of the '40's are of my uncles in uniforms and those big musicals with the splashy Technicolor and the fake sets. When I think of my family, I think of those movies, and when I think of the movies, I think of my family. Maybe I was so ingrained with the movies that I had to go back and recreate that

Liza Minnelli conjures up memories of Judy Garland in *New York, New York* (1977). United Artists. The Museum of Modern Art/Film Stills Archive.

world which is half fake and half real. In my mind, that's my picture of the period."[3] Scorsese's father took him to the Paramount and Strand theaters to see Benny Goodman and Paul Whiteman, but the boy's keenest impressions were shaped at movie houses and in front of the television screen. *New York, New York* offered Scorsese the chance to recapture his childhood visions, to explore his roots in the Italian family, and to rediscover the marvels of studio productions. For him, the re-creation of an old, revered style of filmmaking was not just an idle homage but an examination of his roots. The movies were central to his psychic life and provided the emotional link to his extended family. As Scorsese explained to columnist Robert Lindsay, the nostalgic material in *New York, New York* was personal for him "in the sense that it evokes my aunts and uncles, and my mother and father, the whole period they lived in."[4]

Part of the magic in *New York, New York* for Scorsese lay in the opportunity to explore his cinematic heritage, the world of the soundstage. *New York, New York* was to be all fog machines, wind machines, klieg lights, painted sets, cranes, booms, extras, chorus lines, costumes, special effects, and ballyhoo. Before the shooting Scorsese kept proclaiming what joys lay ahead. Within a few days of beginning, he found himself seasick from rides on the crane and eager to get his feet back on the earth. The whole project, unfortunately, suffered from the same vertigo, a dizzying confusion of fantasy and documentary, romance and realism. *New York, New York* tried to give an account of New York as the glamorous painted skyline and New York as the city of broken dreams. The two towns came together, however, only in the title; in the body of the film, dreams and realities never quite intermeshed.

The troubles with *New York, New York* stemmed from Earl MacRauch's script. MacRauch, an intellectual and prose stylist, felt more comfortable with *New York, New York* as a literate novel than with *New York, New York* as a traditional script using dialogue and performances to carry its themes. The reluctant screenwriter admitted he didn't "like movies all that much" and saw them as "just something I do for a living."[5] MacRauch found himself imprisoned in the narrative confines of Hollywood's most hackneyed genre, the musical romance. Every professional writer knows the formula all too well: first the two attractive but gauche youngsters meet under trying and awkward circumstances and they sing a little, somewhat halfheartedly; then they discover their burning hatred for each other and dance a little, somewhat clumsily. In a little while the two become erotically fixated on each other and sing a lot, often beautifully; soon thereafter they fall madly in love and dance a lot, most majestically. Then they undergo a dramatic reversal of fortunes as they sing and dance quite buoyantly; finally they enact a blissful marriage or mournful separation, all with unforgettable musical accompaniment. The earliest description of *New York, New York* by Scorsese in 1975 indicates that Earl MacRauch's first working scripts fit the classic pattern perfectly; Scorsese announced a traditional tale as his next project: "It's about the decline of the big bands and a couple, a saxophonist and a girl singer in a band, who try to make a go of it but they have no money and they break up and then they get back together after they make it" (*Dialogue,* 84).

The success of *Taxi Driver* altered Scorsese's plans, however, and he confesses he got such a big head that he felt "no script was good enough" (Scorsese 1989, 69). Scorsese demanded elaborations, new scenes, new twists, and new insights, and MacRauch obliged. Soon Scorsese discovered the material was too voluminous.

The elaborations MacRauch provided form the bulk of his novel *New York, New York,* a satiric panorama of postwar America that uses Francine and Jimmy as barometers of larger realities. His romantic duo straddle several decades as the music of America changes, as the urban gives way to the suburban, and as jingoism yields to somber pragmatism. The characters' romance is linked at every stage to changes in society. Thus, in the novel when Francine meets her Jimmy, the narrator notes that Francine "liked the look of him in the Air Corps uniform, the bombardier's patch, and bombing of Dresden in his eyes."[6]

In Scorsese's film the first thing Jimmy does is ditch his army uniform and don a gaudy Hawaiian-style shirt emblazoned with pictures of the Statue of Liberty. Scorsese retains the suggestion that Jimmy and later Francine are an all-American couple, but he eschews Dresden and weighty allusions. MacRauch, on the other hand, frequently stops his narrative for commentary Scorsese avoids. MacRauch labors, for example, to analyze the gap between Jimmy's music and the WASP audience he plays for: "In playing jazz, he had overestimated the intelligence of the American public. The American public had no sophistication, had no heart, or manners either. It lived in an alcoholic vapor, watching propaganda films like a spasm of jelly on a movie seat, needing a blast of music every now and then only to light its light bulbs" (MacRauch, 238–39). Scorsese lacerates no "spasm of jelly on a movie seat"; he remains content to show young bands playing for aging audiences and one style of music uptown in Harlem and an other downtown at Radio City Music Hall.

Similarly, MacRauch parodies movie conventions and hackneyed screenplays throughout his novel and concludes the book in an over-heated summary of the film *New York, New York* might have been without the hand of Scorsese: "Long shot, love theme comes up, reverse angle shot, wide angle shot, camera tracks r——l and pans l——r, dolly shot, overhead crane shot, blimp shot—HOLD ON young lovers in a world of their own. SLOW FADE AND BRING MUSIC UP, and that should do it nicely. Keep it simple and poignant. Lights" (MacRauch, 248). Scorsese never contents himself with the nice, simple, and poignant; instead he labors to bring realistic characters and complex emotions to the fore, keeping the fake sets and painted backdrops clearly in the rear. The resultant dislocation throws *New York, New York* off kilter and fatally mars the film, but Scorsese struggles mightily to involve his audiences with authentic people moving through a never-never land straight from Tinseltown. The disequilibrium between his realistic story and the dreamy setting constitutes the largest flaw in his project, an error absent in MacRauch's novel. Scorsese succeeds so well in making De Niro's Jimmy and Minnelli's Francine true, modern, and relevant that the bogus settings loom as anachronistic conceits. The leading characters in *New York, New York* don't belong in the mythical world of Warner musicals; they're bittersweet modern lovers lost in a saccharine, old-fashioned world.

As Scorsese's vision and MacRauch's fiction drifted further apart, Scorsese asked his wife Julia Cameron to help rewrite the script. Eventually MacRauch withdrew from the collaboration; after more than two years of strenuous rewriting, he had had enough of filmmakers and their spouses. Scorsese then begged his old friend Mardik Martin to rework the Cameron-MacRauch material. Scorsese used Martin's transformed text as an outline that he constantly recast.

In long, largely unstructured rehearsals with De Niro and Minnelli, Scorsese used Martin's script as a springboard for inspiration. Scorsese then had the new material typed up and worked with the performers to create newer variants and more contemporary dialogue. Scorsese overlooked in large measure the effect the elaborate sets and stylized production numbers would have on the impromptu lines. As he, Minnelli, and De Niro rewrote the dialogue and refined the narrative, the sets and choreography were already being put in place. Sometimes the glittering surroundings or bustling extras overwhelmed the new intimate dialogue or situations. At other times the lines needed a more personal space. Yet the huge production had an energy all its own. It was if the show would go on, whether or not the players caught up.

In Scorsese's encounter-group-like rehearsals, the project began to move in unexpected directions. Scorsese began interjecting his turmoil over the collapse of his first marriage and the problems in his current marriage, as Liza Minnelli began recounting her fears that her career was wrecking her personal life. These career-versus-domestic-life dilemmas eventually found their focus in the question of children. Julia Cameron was expecting her first child even as her marriage to Scorsese was crumbling; De Niro's new wife, Diahnne Abbott, whose earlier child he had just adopted, was also pregnant, though the fact was disguised for her electrifying rendition of "Honeysuckle Rose" in *New York, New York*. Childless Liza Minnelli, who made no secret of her longing to be a mother, was portraying Francine, a singer intent on having her baby and then pursuing her career. Add to this mix a romantic liaison between Minnelli and Scorsese, and the result is a troubled production drifting out of control as the budget escalates from $6 million to $12 million, as the shooting schedule balloons from 14 weeks to 22 weeks, and as everyone senses that the project lacks a clear beginning, middle, and end.

The finest riffs in *New York, New York* flow from autobiographical improvisations. The most effective sequence, for example, occurs when Francine and Jimmy explode in a knock-down, drag-out brawl in the confines of a car as they vent their fury about her pregnancy and its effect on their career together. As Minnelli observes, "As it was written, it was just a normal scene that could happen anywhere to any couple," but a hyperactive Scorsese relentlessly goaded her and De Niro to "give it everything we've got" (Cagin, 40). Scorsese remained in the car with his principal, and he fiendishly egged them on. Some of his crew found the scene too frightening to watch and left the set in disgust. Finally, however, De Niro had an inspiration, which he described in a *Playboy* interview: "I thought it would be funny to show, out of complete rage, an insane absurdity, where you get so nutty that you become funny, hopping mad. I saw that the roof of the car was low and I hit it with my head, then I hit it with my hand" (Grobel, 80). Playing off De Niro, Minnelli began attacking him, bang-ing her arm against the seat and roof of the old car. By the end of the shooting, all three principals—De Niro, Minnelli, and Scorsese—ended up in the emergency room, but Scorsese had inspired footage. As he later remarked, a metamorphosis was taking place, and "my light, frothy musical turned out to be my most personal film" (Kroll, 84).

The tension between drama and music mirrors the split in *New York, New York* between Jimmy and Francine, De Niro and Minnelli, reality and fantasy, documentary realism and Hollywood glitter. To recognize the dichotomy in *New York, New York,* a title with an apt and revealing repetition, is to understand simultaneously its strengths and its weaknesses. The film attempts too many disparate things at once, with the result that it frequently teeters at the edge, threatening to fall apart.

Scorsese recognized the multitudinous splits in *New York, New York* but undertook the project, he declared, because he hoped to make a Hollywood film "with two central characters"; in his opinion "*Taxi Driver* has one, and *Alice* really only has one" (Pye and Miles, 215). In *New York, New York* he was seeking complexity and wanted, he told Guy Flatley, "to be fair to both characters, because I love them both. They just never can get together; they're star-crossed and that makes me sad."[7] The power of the film, Scorsese notes, derives from the irony that these two irreconcilable forces find themselves thrust together by fate. Scorsese structured shots throughout *New York, New York* to ensure that "Jimmy Doyle and Francine Evans are always in the same frame, whether they like it or not. They're stuck together" (Pye and Miles, 216). Scorsese exploits the chasm between Francine the entertainer concerned about popularity and Jimmy the narcissistic jazz artist dedicated to pure sound, between Francine the loving mother and Jimmy the self-destructive loner, between Francine the nurturing lover and Jimmy the insecure chauvinist.

When *New York, New York* began filming, Minnelli felt that she and De Niro might embody irreconcilable forces. In her perception of the earliest days of the production, there were two distinct forces on the set: "[T]here was the Scorsese unit—Marty, Julia, and Bobby, and my side with Fred Ebb, John Kander, and [the choreographer] Ron Field."[8] Minnelli's forces came out of the tradition of *Cabaret* and *Chicago*; things could be dark and grim in their art, but finally the music, the dancing, and the stellar performances provide the memorable elements. Minnelli does, after all, receive first billing in *New York, New York,* and her panache, show business connections, and celebrated parents linked this project to the 1940s tradition. During the production she occupied a dressing room once used by her mother. Every critic noticed the "Garland look" Scorsese chose for his star. As Hilary Ostlere declared, "We are given displays that are calculated copies of Judy Garland in her more hysterical days. The moviemakers have plotted towards it in a cold-blooded manner: Minnelli is dressed in black skintight pants and loose shirts and given lingering close-ups of her dark brown eyes—one of the few characteristics she's inherited from her famous mom. Pretty soon you get the feeling they're also making *The Judy Garland Story*."[9] One emotion-packed day on the set, director Vincente Minnelli visited and with tears in his eyes, told his daughter that she looked just like her mother. Some wags on the set teased Scorsese, who by this point was totally smitten with Liza, that he was getting a double dose of film lore with his new love and quizzed him whether he preferred the link to a pantheon director or the association with a superstar. Curiously, this teasing illuminates a bizarre pattern in Scorsese's romances: he woos either women in the movie business or women whose parents are movie folks. Like Jimmy Boyle, Scorsese desires women who share his obsessions and live in the universe of his art.

The prime shot for *New York, New York,* Scorsese's key image in his realization of the musical, reflects his preoccupation with Liza Minnelli, Judy Garland, Vincente Minnelli, and the old musicals, as well as his obsession with the New York of his ancestors. Scorsese has acknowledged that his vision of the film centers on an extended, self-consciously artistic close-up of Francine (Minnelli) as she studies her face in a mirror; in the background the Hot Club of France plays "Billet Doux," a piece of music beloved by Scorsese's uncles. This mirror shot, a favorite Scorsese icon, virtually stops *New York, New York* for a minute; it's a set piece of immense power, but it contributes little to the narrative flow. This visual stands as one of the few moments in Scorsese's canon that could be labeled precious. Arthur Bell of the *Village Voice* suggests that the only explanation for such indulgent filmmaking is Scorsese's infatuation with Minnelli: "I could only think of how much Martin Scorsese was in love with Liza Minnelli during the filming of *New York, New York.*"[10]

Scorsese balances this critical shot of Francine with an equally emotional image of Jimmy, one echoing his prime shot in *Taxi Driver.* At the jazz club in Harlem, Diahnne Abbott is singing "Honeysuckle Rose" when the camera drifts to a close-up of Francine getting drunk at her table and finally lingers on a shot of the desperately isolated Jimmy at a telephone—alone, just as Travis Bickle was when his women let him down. In this close-up Scorsese was revealing his own sympathy for and identification with Jimmy's plight. As the director explained to Guy Flatley, "The film is a *little* about the machismo thing, I'm a guy, and I understand the things beneath the chauvinism of Bobby De Niro's character. I see the vulnerability. He's trapped and frightened, like a child, and he doesn't know how to reach out. . . . A person has to express himself, whether he's a musician or a writer or a moviemaker" (Flatley 1977, 8). Scorsese's empathy with the Jimmy Doyle character helps him impose some continuity on *New York, New York*. The film begins and ends with Jimmy and his stylish dancing shoes, and the rewritten dialogue creates controlling symbol for the film: Jimmy's dream of a "major chord." This concept is introduced when, early in the film, Jimmy and Francine fight over the destination of a cab, just as they'll always argue over the destination of their lives, and she concedes to him and his rush to an audition. On the way to the small club in Brooklyn, Jimmy tells her what interests him most: music, money, and kissing. When Francine objects, "Always in that order?" he turns on the jive patter he's so proud of and answers, "Yes, always in that order, unless you happen to come across someone who grooves you and you want to groove with. Say you." Developing his idea, he eulogizes a "major chord": "The woman you want, the music you want, and enough money to live comfortably." Juggling priorities among romance, fame, and fortune becomes, then, the key to the film. Jimmy's order and Francine's never quite harmonize; they never find their major chord. Jimmy pursues Francine to Roanoke, telling her, "Didn't you understand that when I said major chord—I meant it about you?" Jimmy's real major chord, however, is the nightclub he opens when he is finally successful, a club named the Major Chord. When Francine sings her finale, "And the World Goes Round," at the Starlight Terrace at the climax of *New York, New York,* she dedicates it to "a friend of mine who is a great believer in major chords." If *New York, New York* has a thematic center, "major chord" defines the issue: how can an artist find "the music," "the woman," and "the money"? Scorsese clearly wanted to know, as did Minnelli and De Niro. Their work on this project allowed them to probe their lives.

De Niro's labor on *New York, New York* went far beyond the confines of a soundstage. As always, he made superhuman efforts to get into the skin of his character. For months he studied saxophone with Georgic Auld, the legendary Canadian saxophonist who plays Frankie Harte, the bandleader, in *New York, New York*. De Niro got so good that for a few sessions he toured with the Buddy Rich band.

De Niro's relentless gum chewing, his nervous but airy hand gestures, and his light-beard shave counterpoint his frenzied presence on stage. Jimmy cannot sit still when the music is playing; he wants to jump up and play what the script describes as a "magic solo, full of short riffs, staccato, crazy Coltranish sounds, in and out bursts against the rhythm,"[11] for, as he tells Francine, "If I can't do this, I'm not good for you, I'm not good for anybody." In De Niro's conception and Scorsese's plan, Jimmy's identification with jazz defines the musical split with the flexible Francine, who does demo records for pocket money, adapts her show to the audience, and takes her act to Hollywood. Francine is all show business, while Jimmy wants to be an artist.

New York, New York embodies the dichotomy between Jimmy and Francine, jazz and popular music, art and show business. As the principals were working on their personal script, they were also shooting the most elaborate production numbers done in Hollywood for decades. Scorsese was collaborating with production designer Boris Leven, the acknowledged master of studio productions. Also aboard was "special visual consultant" David Nichols, a Scorsese regular whose lack of a union card didn't hinder his input. Given a liberal budget, this troika spent weeks on the V-J Day sequence in which Francine and Jimmy meet at the Moonlight Terrace of the Biltmore Hotel, a dazzling confection, following Jimmy across Times Square, through the tickertape and honky-tonk of a celebrating New York, across a crowded ballroom to the forlorn table of Francine Evans. The crew worked weeks on this razzmatazz, shuffling extras, preparing montages, and blocking out ballroom promenades. In the end Scorsese had a rough cut that ran more than an hour, all just to introduce the characters.

Scorsese, mesmerized by lavish sets, painted backdrops, flip-screen transitions, extended montages, over-the-shoulder shots, backlighting, long rides in fake taxi cabs, artificial forests, studio snowstorms, papier-mâché train stations, and dancing extras, relished his time at Culver City so much that he lost track of *New York, New York* as one film. Thus, he spent more than 10 days filming a "Happy Endings" sequence, all without any idea of how it would fit into his new script.

Liza Minnelli (Francine Evans) and Robert De Niro (Jimmy Doyle) in *New York, New York* (1977). United Artists. The Museum of Modern Art/Film Stills Archive.

This intensively reflexive showpiece provides Minnelli with numerous opportunities to dance and sing, and it mirrors the overall plot of *New York, New York* well, but it eventually takes on its own life and seems distinct from the rest of the production—so distant, in fact, that Scorsese was forced to cut it from the film.

New York, New York came in way over budget and way behind schedule at an unreleasable length of four and a half hours. Scorsese showed his gargantuan opus to intimates and strenuously argued that it worked well. His producers weren't to be moved, however, and the cutting began. In its initial release the film ran approximately two and a quarter hours and included neither "Happy Endings" nor the mirror shot of Francine.

New York, New York had its world premiere at the chic annual Spring Gala at Lincoln Center on 21 June 1977, and as Scorsese ruefully admits, though *New York, New York* was "quite ambitious," it was "never marked for amazing success. It didn't *play.*"[12] Reviews were reverential but negative, and while Manhattan sites generated some box office, *New York, New York,* like many Woody Allen films, just couldn't survive outside Manhattan. Tom Allen in the *Soho Weekly News* observed that "no film ever had its spine snapped as quickly as *New York, New York.*"[13] Scorsese found himself lumped with Peter Bogdonavich, whose *At Long Last Love,* another musical flop, had destroyed his budding career.

In the face of adversity, Scorsese retreated to a tried-and-true strategy: he hustled and hustled and hustled some more. The two years following *New York, New York* proved the most frenzied and self-destructive period of his life. As his marriage crumbled, he became an inveterate womanizer; as projects floundered, he turned increasingly to cocaine; and as the adulation receded, he drifted deeper into the celebrity game of Mulholland Drive. His good friend Chris Holdenfield is charitable in observing that when Scorsese balanced editing on *New York, New York* with work on two documentaries, *The Last Waltz* and *American Boy,* as well as a commitment to direct Liza Minnelli's Broadway-bound show *The Act,* the young director had really "jumped on Mr. Toad's wild ride of rock'n'roll whoop-de-doo that took a couple of years to wind down."[14]

Scorsese's work on *The Act* stemmed from his affair with Minnelli. The theatrical project resembled a continuation of Francine Evans' chronicle. Discussing the project early in 1977, Scorsese told interviewers that *In Person* (the earliest working title) would be "an extension of *New York, New York,*" with the "same Francine Evans character" only in a different period of her life, "after she has made it, and now she has to find a new image."[15] In June 1977 Scorsese told Guy Flatley of the *New York Times* that "it picks up the singer ten years later, when's she's alienated from the people around her. She ends up alone, but she's still working" (Flatley 1977, 8). By late June the show was ready for a *Variety* review under the title *Shine It On.* Thematically, the review observed, *Shine It On* drew heavily on *New York, New York,* as it allowed Minnelli to confront the problems in her life through her character: "It has the basic plot theme of the film—a performer who is at once driven to professional success while failing in a series of masochistic personal encounters. . . . In both style and story, the show offers the idea that myth and reality in show business are often interchangeable and different faces of the same coin. That it does so without either invading or exploiting Minnelli's private life is a measure of the offbeat approach used by Scorsese and author George Furth."[16]

By the time *Shine It On* opened in Los Angeles in August 1977, Minnelli's private life and Scorsese's romance with his star would be viciously exploited by the press. Every day, a new story appeared, full of innuendo and condescension. The show was having trouble, Scorsese was being roasted for the failure of *New York, New York* and for the problems in *Shine It On,* and everyone was clucking about Minnelli's betrayal of Jack Haley and Scorsese's insensitivity to Julia Cameron. By September the gossip emerged from the back pages of trade papers to the entertainment columns of national newsmagazines. *Newsweek,* for example, offered a feature with the double-edged title "The Liza and Marty Show," in which Scorsese explained that he rehearsed music and drama separately because he felt that the music in *The Act* (the eventual Broadway title) should have no relationship to the book. He was repeating the errors of *New York, New York*'s rehearsals without sets and was honest enough to admit that things weren't going well on stage: "On stage, you've got serious transition problems. . . . I'm treating this like a work in progress. We keep patching it up but we haven't fixed it properly. Right now I feel we've done only two scenes properly from the whole work."[17]

Scorsese felt uncomfortable that the rehearsals and tryouts weren't going well enough to satisfy anxious backers. After releasing him so he could attend the Telluride movie festival and host a tribute to Michael Powell, the producers asked Gower Champion to save the show.

To spare Scorsese embarrassment, a story was released to the press lamenting his recent severe asthmatic attack. Insiders knew, however, that the real problem was Scorsese's inexperience as a theatrical director.

Though Scorsese left the production before *The Act* opened, the New York opening-night *Playbill,* 29 October 1977, lists him as the director. When the unenthusiastic notices came in, he got the blame. After the opening, author George Furth told *New York Post* interviewers that they shouldn't "blame us for the shape the show's in; it's all Scorsese's fault. Gower [Champion] has had only three weeks to repair the damage Scorsese did."[18] While Scorsese's official press release emphasized his illness and noted that he was recuperating in Europe, the daily press hammered away at his marital problems. When Julia Cameron sued for divorce and pursued claims for financial support, the daily press featured headlines of her charges that Scorsese was squandering his money and his health in flirtations with both cocaine and Liza Minnelli.

That drugs were on Scorsese's mind can be seen in his documentary short *American Boy,* a 50-minute examination of the life of his friend Steven Prince, a 25-year-old roustabout who had worked as a music promoter, starred in *Taxi Driver* as a fast-talking gun dealer, and now was addicted to heroin. Scorsese envisioned this garrulous con man as an emblem of America in the 1960s, a generation torn by the collapse of traditional values, shaken by the onslaught of random and senseless violence, galvanized by new forces in music, and seduced by visions of benevolent drugs. *American Boy* was intended as a companion piece to *Italianamerican* and part of a six-part series on American immigrants. Scorsese even announced that part 3 would explore the life of his writer-colleague Mardik Martin, though this project, like many of Scorsese's schemes during this period, never came to fruition.

Where *Italianamerican* treated life in Little Italy, *American Boy* chronicled the Jewish experience in America, as the short film intercut home movies of Prince's childhood with grim accounts of his entanglement in the drug scene. Prince, a natural storyteller, weaves tall tales about his clumsy encounters with narcotics agents and about his murderous acts of self-defense. The interview with Prince, partly scripted by Julia Cameron and Mardik Martin, was filmed in two weekends in George Memmoli's living room, and the audience for Prince's recollections includes Scorsese as interlocutor, George Memmoli, Martin, Cameron, and Kathy McGinnis. In the film's conclusion Prince is pressed to talk about the impending death of his father, and Scorsese's intent becomes clear. As Scorsese later told interviewers, *Italianamerican* explored "the America the fathers built," while *American Boy* dissected "the America the sons were destroying." In his involvement with rock-and-roll, violence, and drugs, Prince obviously served as an alter ego for Scorsese, an articulate doppelgänger for a troubled artist.

Scorsese's other documentary from this period, *The Last Waltz*—the finest concert film ever made—began as a celebration of the music of the Band, but the mammoth project eventually led Scorsese down a dark tunnel of drug dependency and despair.

Band member Robbie Robertson approached Scorsese about a concert film documenting the Band's farewell concert in October 1976, after concluding that the original plans to videotape or make a 16 mm film of their scheduled Thanksgiving concert didn't suit the occasion. Too many big stars were scheduled to appear, and Robertson saw the commercial prospects inherent in the stellar lineup of 1960s talent. Jonathan Taplin, who had managed the Band for four years and produced *Mean Streets,* made the connection between Robertson and Scorsese, an alliance fated to develop into a deep friendship. Recalling their relationship, Robertson observed in a documentary about Scorsese, "Martin Scorsese Directs," done for PBS in 1990, that their wives, Dominique Robertson and Julia Cameron, got "so fed up with us" that the rock star and film director moved in together as an "odd couple" in Scorsese's Mulholland Drive house, discovered their similar backgrounds as asthmatic kids racked by religious guilt, and partied together for a couple of years, until "Marty almost died" and they both decided "to do something else with our lives."[19] In the same documentary Scorsese proves more circumspect but does note that his emergence in the fast-track world of rock-and-roll music and of Mulholland Drive movie glamour led him to a "very crazy life style" for a couple of years, so crazy that it exhausted his physical reserves almost entirely and landed him in the hospital.

In fall 1976, however, the prospect of a follow-up to *Woodstock* documenting the end of the Band's 16 years on the road, a concert film celebrating their eight major albums and their influence on the whole world of rock, and a sociological statement marking another milestone in the history of the Age of Aquarius, proved irresistible to Scorsese. He ignored the facts that he was desperately behind in the work on *New York, New York,* caught up in the production of *American Boy,* and working hard to bring a new project, *Prizefighter,* with

Robert De Niro, to Broadway and the soundstage simultaneously, as he continued to woo Liza Minnelli, supervise *The Act,* and cope with the birth of his daughter and the collapse of his marriage to Julia Cameron. In their first meeting Robbie Robertson and Scorsese sketched out the details of the film, and Scorsese found himself making the same commitment he would make so often in the future in very much the same terms: "I can't do it, but I have to do it" (Cagin, 40).

When he agreed to film *The Last Waltz,* Scorsese did something unprecedented in concert films: he prepared a shooting script and scheduled rehearsals for all the talent. Though Scorsese admits that the shooting script was ignored in the actual film because logistics limited communications, the existence of his proposal for a concert indicates Scorsese's desire that his film complement the music. Eventually Scorsese had the 300 pages of instructions bound in a red leather volume and gave it to Robertson as a Christmas present. The volume, he told journalist Stephen Silverman, had "all the camera set-ups, every Band lyric and chord choreographed" to his specifications and represented about three weeks of "visualizations."[20]

The Last Waltz was the first concert film to be shot entirely in 35 mm and the first to use a 24-track recording system. Seven of the world's finest cinematographers handled the cameras during the seven-hour-long concert, detailing 37 songs, of which Scorsese eventually used 26. Their collective efforts surrounded him finally with more than 400 reels of highly professional color film, to which he eventually added numerous reels shot on location at the Band's Malibu recording studio and home base, Shangra-La, as well as still more footage shot in the MGM studios for coverage of Scorsese's favorite Band pieces, "The Weight," "Evangeline," and "The Last Waltz Suite." Scorsese remained undaunted by all this accumulated celluloid because he was awed by the Band's music. He told interviewers that "This music is my life. *New York, New York* was the music of my father; *The Last Waltz*—it is mine."[21]

During the shooting the cameras had to abide by rock producer Bill Graham's edict for concerts in his auditoriums—no one can interfere with audience sight lines. To his associates Scorsese exclaimed, "What I wouldn't have done sometimes to move my camera just six inches closer!"[22] The limitation may, however, have helped to shape a successful project. For one thing, it encourages Scorsese not to include images of the audience; *The Last Waltz* keeps its focus on the stage and musicians, capturing the mechanics of rock-and-roll perfor-

Bob Dylan joins The Band for its farewell concert in *The Last Waltz* (1978). United
Artists. The Museum of Modern Art/Film Stills Archive.

mances. As Scorsese explained to David Sterritt of the *Christian Science Monitor,* he was spellbound by the troubadours: "Musicians are
outlaws. They're a subculture, just like the guys in *Mean Streets*. It
doesn't matter if they're jazz musicians of the 40's, or rock musicians
of today. They have their own language and life-style. I feel at home
with that."[23]

Graham's restrictions also forced Scorsese to relinquish his plans of
an orchestrated filming. Instead, Scorsese told critics from *Rolling
Stone,* he had to adopt standard concert film survival strategies: "We're
just scanning and zooming. Nothing elaborate."[24] This simple approach became, as author Roger Greenspun notes, the virtue of *The
Last Waltz*. Distilling the essence of the performances and capturing
every detail of the musicmaking, Greenspun notes, "looks like simplicity itself," but "the apparent simplicity is really a kind of lucidity
and assurance about what to do and when and how to do it."[25]

If the film has a central theme, the concept is developed in the interview footage Scorsese shot later at Shangra-La and intercut with
the concert footage, using the band members' remarks as an analytical

commentary on their performances and as a digest of the influences on their music and their sense of their place in the American musical tradition. In one intense interview, Robbie Robertson justifies this final concert. The road, he asserts, "was our school. It taught us our sense of survival. . . . But you can press your luck. It's taken some great ones, Hank Williams, Otis Redding, Janis, Jimi, Elvis. It's a goddamn impossible way of life—no doubt about it."

Unfortunately, Scorsese would soon discover how impossible it was to live the life of a rock-and-roll musician, a film director, a Hollywood actor, and a media celebrity. Writing about *The Last Waltz*, Stephen Harvey from the Museum of Modern Art described "the cock-of-the-walk" attitudes and the "offstage sniggers about nonstop, nubile groupies," arguing that all this adolescent behavior seems "a little cloying for anyone who was never a member of the club or who's long since outgrown it."[26] Working with the Band and living with Robertson on Mulholland Drive, Scorsese quickly joined the club.

Then there was the question of the snowstorm in Hollywood that eventually wired John Belushi. Catherine Evelyn Smith, Belushi's last companion on the night of his death and his admitted drug supplier, had dated Levon Helm of the Band, and through Helm she met Belushi (Woodward, 354). Robert De Niro, a Belushi intimate, frequently did drugs with the comedian and once required medical care for an accident that occurred when the two friends were taking cocaine (Woodward, 354). Scorsese moved in this circuit and told several journalists that he had abused cocaine for a year or so, though he saw his drug involvement as only a small part of his troubles in Los Angeles.

As usual, a welter of projects were vying for his attention. Mulholland Drive neighbor Marlon Brando sought Scorsese's talents for a major film and whisked both De Niro and Scorsese away for a short vacation in the South Seas, one that turned into a long visit, but no film resulted. Jay Cocks, a friend of Robbie Robertson and Scorsese, pitched a film to them called *Nightlife,* about fraternal rivalry, but it never materialized. Julia Cameron urged Scorsese to fulfill his plans to film *To Forget Palermo,* about an Italian politician's romance with an American magazine writer, as Robert De Niro focused on the *Prizefighter* project. Also in the hopper were scripts for *Haunted Summer,* about Mary Shelley; a Mother Cabrini biography; *The Last Temptation of Christ*; some Edith Wharton stories; and a historical drama titled *The Gangs of New York*. In addition, Scorsese's appearances in his films and his success in demanding scenes encouraged agents to propose a career in acting. Paul Bartel convinced Scorsese to play a gangster in *Cannonball* (1976), and Sam Fuller approached him to play an Italian recruit in *The Big Red One*. The television producers of "Helter Skelter" also made him an attractive offer to star as Charles Manson in their miniseries.

But Scorsese was overwhelmed by it all and befuddled. As he later lamented to Mark Jacobsen of *Rolling Stone,* the move to Hollywood had disoriented him and the hustle had corrupted his values. In this "filmmaker heaven" he found himself a "zombie": "I mean my head was shook up. I did things differently than I had before, I seemed to have values I hadn't had before. I started living in a negative way. . . . I began to be very unhappy and I'd wake up at night. Awake at night! Awake so I never fell asleep, drove me crazy. I wanted to walk around, but it was L.A., so you don't, so I walked around my house. It was a nightmare!" (Jacobsen, 108). Making *New York, New York,* Scorsese danced the Los Angeles, California, shuffle, and like his screen protagonists, Francine Evans and Jimmy Doyle, he found fortune and fame, but like them also, he went home alone at night haunted by the emptiness of deserted streets.

6

Raging Bull (1980)

Labor Day 1978 found Martin Scorsese in the hospital; hustling and partying were playing havoc with his frail constitution. Among his visitors that afternoon was Robert De Niro, concerned about Scorsese's deteriorating health and stalled career. De Niro, a bankable star, goaded his friend about their "prizefighter" project, intended for Broadway and the screen, baiting Scorsese with his reiterated mock-heroic lament "You know, we can make this picture" (Scorsese, 1989, 76).

De Niro had been an apologist for this fight movie since the early 1970s, when Pete Savage, coauthor of Jake La Motta's popular autobiography *Raging Bull*, approached him with material about the controversial middleweight champion from the Bronx. Pete Savage, whose real name was Pete Petrello, had been La Motta's friend for years, and the boxer's best-selling autobiography recounts their misadventures as juvenile delinquents in a tough Italian neighborhood and their subsequent, often-bloody rivalries in the ring, around the gym, about women, and with each other. Savage, who pursued a career in entertainment, convinced De Niro that this chronicle of a street fighter from the Bronx who wins the championship belt despite a public furor over his alleged ties to organized crime, only to find himself trapped in the nightclub business, convicted on a dubious morals charge in Florida, and brutally imprisoned, could prove the acting role of his life. Savage so believed in the project that he stuck with De Niro for a decade, developing the deal despite obstacles and eventually receiving credit as associate producer with Hollywood veterans Irwin Winkler and Robert Chartoff, who decided to give Scorsese a chance to redeem himself from the *New York, New York* debacle.

De Niro was wild about the prospect of playing Jake La Motta and he engaged the ex-champ as his personal trainer. When Scorsese contemplated a show and movie, De Niro threw himself into physical conditioning. Between April 1978 and April 1979, De Niro and La Motta sparred more than 1,000 rounds. At first La Motta declined to wear protective gear, but soon the tyro De Niro managed to knock out Jake's upper teeth, crush his ribs, and break his nose. La Motta found himself boasting to journalists that "[De Niro] was a natural. He coulda been a pro."[1]

Handsome praise from a ruthless slugger more likely to maul his opponents than to flatter them, a man whose career was notable for his willingness to schedule tough matchups and for his ability to go toe to toe with the hardest hitters. Like a bull, La Motta moved forward relentlessly, driven by rage, blind to his own injuries.

La Motta's autobiography, *Raging Bull,* purportedly "the true story of a champ," provided justifications for his excesses. Coauthors Joseph Carter and Peter Savage structured the memoir thematically, beginning with Jake's odyssey toward a reformatory and ending with his release from prison in Florida. In their first-person narrative, they have La Motta emphasize his nagging guilt over a bookie he believed he murdered; they frequently show La Motta their narrator hypothesizing that he sought physical punishment in the boxing ring for his moral lapses.

La Motta's life, as recast by Savage and Carter, is replete with characters who symbolize larger institutions. For example, there's the kindly but unworldly priest who challenges the boxer to take up Christ's cross and the slimy racketeer luring the frustrated challenger into a pact with the mob. There's Vickie, the beauty La Motta courts, marries, abuses, and divorces. And there's Joey, his chauvinistic brother, who, like La Motta represents all Italian males, torn between home and the streetcorner, between the church and the mob.

Scorsese was mesmerized by the material in *Raging Bull*: the impoverished Italian American ghetto, the preening mobsters, the icy blond, the overwhelming Catholic guilt, and the omnipresent violence. Although he abhorred sports and knew nothing about boxing, he loved the milieu so much that he entreated Mardik Martin to prepare a script. Martin labored on the text for two years and fell in love with the material Scorsese loathed—La Motta's legendary bouts before, during, and after his championship reign from 16 June 1949 to 14 February 1951. Martin's work emphasized the drama in La Motta's landmark fights: the brutality and controversy in the Reeves fight, the growing obsession with Sugar Ray Robinson in their many confrontations, the ignominy of the Billy Fox loss, the glory in the victory over Marcel Cerdan, the ecstasy of the come-from-behind victory over Dauthille, and the agony of Jake's decline. Scorsese couldn't live with Martin's script, but this early work did guarantee that boxing would take its rightful place in the drama. Martin's fanatic involvement with boxing lore made heavy punches central to La Motta's story.

Scorsese then asked Paul Schrader to rework *Raging Bull*. Schrader had completed a flurry of writing the year before, but his pen had been still for a while. For about a year the only script he finished was his *Raging Bull* rewrite. Discussing his contribution with John Gregory Dunne, Schrader claimed that he provided Scorsese with "a spine" for the picture, reshaping the project until it was "purely about Jake." Schrader also noted that when he completed his contribution, *Raging Bull* "was no longer about the whole boxing world, no longer about Italians, but simply about one man—and primarily seen through his brother. The theme was about redemption by punishment and the falseness of that premise" (Dunne and Schrader, 87).

Predictably, Schrader, who was working on a feature about the porno industry, *Hardcore* (1979), also focused on the sexual themes in *Raging Bull*. In his autobiography La Motta offered some startling confessions about the "strange thing about me and broads": "There were times, sometimes months on end, when I'd be impotent. Sometimes I felt I'd go out of my mind about it because it would happen all of a sudden, without warning, and it seemed like for no reason at all. I couldn't figure any reason for it, physical or psychological, and then after I was about ready to commit suicide, I'd be all right again."[2] The ever-analytical Schrader made those hidden reasons the center of his script, climaxing in a masturbatory sequence when La Motta is thrown into "the hole" of the Florida prison. This confrontation with himself and his despair forms a key moment of illumination in Scorsese's eventual film, but in Schrader's rendering the scene is more a catalog of La Motta's sexual fantasies and suppressed fears. Schrader envisioned a montage in which, in part, "the image of Jake hitting Vickie might be accompanied by the sounds from a love scene between them" and intercut with "1940's black and white pornography," "a body building ad," "Li'l Abner comics: Daisy Mae's tits seem about to fall free," "Vickie's pretty young face double exposes with Sugar

Ray Robinson's," "On a bed, a Girl is going down on Joey," and "Vickie is in her underwear in a bedroom. A pair of black arms come in and embrace her body."[3] After this montage, La Motta wails out his confused sexual anguish in a veritable breakdown: "Why, why, why? I'm a man, I'm a man. I'm no faggot. I'm not a faggot. Ma, why? What do they want? My cock's not enough. What do they want from me? Why? Ma? Why?" (Schrader and Martin, 95). Where Martin emphasized the punches scored on others, Schrader saw the cruel blows to the self.

Scorsese appreciated the strengths of both visions and eventually gave full screenwriting credit to Martin and Schrader, but he and his star, Robert De Niro, wanted more. To quiet their reservations about the screenplay, they took off for a sojourn in the Caribbean, where the world-weary director and hyperactive star revised the script in a few soul-searching weeks.

Their greatest contribution to the script of *Raging Bull* was an unprecedented colloquial language, choking with profanities and blasphemies but true to their memories of life in an Italian ghetto. In the place of literary dialogue, the two friends substituted non sequiturs, half-formed ideas, angry blasphemies, poetic insults, and sustained cursing. Critic Joe Baltake correctly identifies this strength in *Raging Bull* when he lauds the "incredible off-the-cuff dialog" that makes it possible for the principals to "recite it and interact as if they really do live together and hate it."[4] Filmmaker Steven Spielberg admitted that this realistic dialogue made him embarrassed because he felt like a voyeur, an unnoticed eavesdropper, "on real situations with real people whose dignity and privacy I should respect" ("Martin Scorsese Directs"). In *Raging Bull* Scorsese and De Niro peep into the tenement windows of the Bronx, uncovering ugly realities and recording harrowing dialogue.

An interesting example of the shift from literary conceptions to naturalistic dialogue can be found in the famous "steak" scene in *Raging Bull* when La Motta fights with his wife over the time she is taking to prepare his dinner. In the original script the impatient boxer explodes in a diatribe about his career: "Wait! I'll wait. But let me tell you, if this steak was the middleweight championship, I'd show you how I'd wait. I'd eat it raw. I'd drink the blood. I'd eat it before it came out of the cow—that's how I'd wait" (Schrader and Martin, 6). De Niro, however, saw that this extended analogy was too complex a conceit for a bruiser like La Motta. So the star substituted the most famous eruption in the film, as La Motta expostulates a disjointed syllogism: "Don't overcook it! You overcook it, it's no good—defeats its own purpose." Discussing his creation, De Niro admitted to interviewers that "I knew it didn't make sense, but in a way it did—it was like a double negative of some sort, but it seemed perfect for that!"[5]

The perfection of *Raging Bull* depends on exactly this "double negative of some sort"; the more the characters try to express their love, the more they fall into ritualistic exclamations of hatred; the more passionate they feel, the more they wallow in the banal phrases of profanity; the more they struggle to communicate, the more they face their own inarticulateness. The script as revised by Scorsese and De Niro works best in its visceral explosions and reveals most in its loud confusions and bombastic rhetoric, as it forces tortured characters to expose hidden facets of themselves in superheated litanies and profane cursing. As the players tear at one another's wives and families, at sexual inadequacies and marital infidelities, at short penises and open vaginas, at homosexuality and impotence, at anal intercourse and oral sex, they stand condemned by their charges, exhausted by their psychic blows, and enervated by personal demons. Their bodies and souls are laid bare for all to see, often so powerfully that one is torn between the desire to continue peeping and the urge to avert one's eyes.

To heighten the intimacy, Scorsese accentuated Schrader's focus on the two brothers, merging the friend and brother of La Motta's autobiography into one character. Scorsese had been working for months with his good friend Jay Cocks on a "Night Life" project about an older brother, an animator, and a younger brother, an agent for William Morris. This violent screenplay emphasized their sibling rivalry, insane jealousies, struggles for success, and love affair with the same girl. "Night Life," while never realized, provided the inspiration for the focus on Joey La Motta (Joe Pesci) and his battles with Jake in *Raging Bull*. Where the original autobiography looked at the whole neighborhood to explain Jake's rage, Scorsese's project took a more Freudian tack, emphasizing the marriage bed, progeny, brothers, and the ties of blood. The split between Jake and Joey in Scorsese's *Raging Bull* focuses on one issue: the insane Jake bellows in mad rage that his wife, Vickie, and his brother, Joey, have cuckolded him and ruined his life.

Because of the changes his script made in La Motta's autobiography, Scorsese and company insisted that "it would be a mistake to confuse the real Jake La Motta with the character in the film played by Robert De Niro."[6] The best approach to the film, Scorsese maintained, would be to reject the idea of an adaptation of the autobiography and instead to see *Raging Bull* as "Bobby's and my view" of Jake La Motta.[7] Critic Andrew Sarris refines this idea when he opines that *Raging Bull* "tells us less about La Motta's dismal life than the deep feelings the subject has stirred up in Scorsese, De Niro, and the scenarists, Paul Schrader and Mardik Martin."[8] As usual, Scorsese emphasizes personal filmmaking over the boxing record, artistic involvement over documented fact, and moral complexity over simplistic lessons.

When shooting began on 16 August 1979, Catherine Scorsese's birthday, Scorsese was convinced that *Raging Bull* would be his "swan song for Hollywood" and that he would spend the next decade "living in New York and Rome" making "documentaries and educational films on the saints . . . films for television, that sort of thing" (Holdenfield 1989, 49). Scorsese knew his $14 million budget revealed more about De Niro's status as a star than his stature as a director. Scorsese approached *Raging Bull* as a suicidal attempt to bring everything inside himself out onto the screen; the enterprise, he recalls in his autobiography, was "a kamikaze way of making movies" in which you "pour everything in, then forget about it and go find another way of life" (Scorsese, 1989, 77). In an equally violent metaphor, Scorsese also described making *Raging Bull* as preparing "a punch in the face," one that would shake audiences and "make them feel something" (Holdenfield 1989, 49).

Eschewing color for black-and-white photography, substituting montage for continuity, offering a loathsome protagonist instead of a hero, emphasizing the sordid instead of the respectable, highlighting defeats and self-doubts instead of victories and exultation, *Raging Bull* seemed an anti-*Rocky,* a tale of the fall down the museum steps and not the run up. In *Raging Bull* Scorsese masterfully reworks his favorite themes, retribution and personal salvation, again demonstrating that real men don't make up for sins in church but instead find atonement in the streets. Balancing physical suffering and spiritual growth, *Raging Bull* often seems ready to embrace what sociologists call "the penitent syndrome," a delusion that novelist Robert Stone describes as a "bizarre coupling of the machismo sense with the religious impulse and with the desire for physical humiliation. . . . It's as if they're inclined to compete with Christ to see who can take it more" ("Streets," 47).

In Scorsese's film audiences must seek a rationale for Jake's pride in being able to absorb all the punishment the world can dish out. At a superficial level, Jake's masochism reflects his feelings of guilt and inadequacy. The film hints at this theme when a dejected La Motta muses in his locker room over his many undeserved defeats, "I dunno. Maybe I don't deserve to win. I've done a lot of bad things. I dunno." Scorsese, however, explores subtler religious themes in *Raging Bull*. Scorsese cautioned British journalist Philip French that *Raging Bull* is about "redemption, a man reduced to nothing, fighting his way back."[9] An appreciation of *Raging Bull* demands, Scorsese told Mary Pat Kelly, a recognition that his Jake La Motta operates on a unique spiritual plane, that his fights bring him closer to God and the eternal: "[H]e's on a higher spiritual level, in a way, as a fighter. He works on an almost primitive level, almost an animal level. And therefore he must think in a different way, he must be aware of certain things spiritually that we aren't because our minds are too cluttered with intellectual ideas, and too much emotionalism. And because he's on that animalistic level, he may be closer to pure spirit. . . . [T]hat's the idea around the film and that's what I like about it—that, and the idea of being born again" (Kelly, 1980, 32).

Most critical reactions to *Raging Bull* reflect the reviewer's willingness to appreciate Scorsese's religious vision and to value the mystical approach to salvation he promulgates. Those who could suspend disbelief and see Jake as a contemporary martyr lavished praise on *Raging Bull*, while others, more skeptical about Jake's rebirth and beatific visions, attacked the picture's endless violence and bloody excesses.

Boston Phoenix critic Stephen Schiff, attuned to the manifest religiosity of the movie, argued that Scorsese transformed La Motta into "a holy vessel, a martyr who suffers for our sins, is tempted by the Devil (in the form of the Mob) and sacrificed on the altar of our bloodlust; and who finally, when's he's imprisoned in Florida, undergoes a conversion, giving up his violence and turning into what Scorsese deems a good end, entertainment. This is a peculiarly Catholic conception—the redemption of blood by spirit and spirit by blood—and the movie abounds in Catholic religious imagery."[10] Schiff recognizes all the mystical touches but bridles at the idea of Scorsese "transforming an icon of violence into a religious icon" (Schiff, 3). Reviewer Veronica Geng of the New York *Soho News* felt no such reservations, proclaiming *Raging Bull* "a tremendously powerful biography of a soul—a story of violent spiritual desire told in terms of physical violence."[11] Geng is especially cogent discussing the Catholic concept of a prelapsarian universe, the Fall in the Garden of Eden, and the need for atonement and rebirth in *Raging Bull*: "The whole human race took a dive with Original Sin, and La Motta's fall is just a version of the Fall. He's obsessed with not actually going down—he gives away the [Fox] fight on points, by standing there and taking a beating in the face—and much later, in the last fight we see, when he loses his championship to Sugar Ray Robinson, he shouts, 'You never got me down, Ray.' But in the harsh theology of the movie, everybody goes down one way or the other, and La Motta goes down the other way" (Geng, 59).

Predictably, the *Variety* reviewer proved less sympathetic to Scorsese's religious trappings, complaining that "what seems to be on the minds of Scorsese and his screenwriters is an exploration of an extreme form of Catholic sadomasochism" and warning potential exhibitors that mainstream audiences might not be enchanted with the idiosyncratic theological framework imposed on the boxing genre, a framework creating "a pervasive feeling of guilt and frustration."[12] Boston critic David Rosenbaum echoed the *Variety* reservations and went on to denounce *Raging Bull* as "a masochist's delight," a laborious opus in which Scorsese confuses pain "with Christian martyrdom." For Rosenbaum, "Martin Scorsese's Christmas present to his audience is an empty cross and an invitation to climb on. It's not Christianity; it's the Ramrod room."[13]

The chasm between opposing critical camps evaluating *Raging Bull* mirrors the debate that surrounds Scorsese's career: Is he a religious mystic or an apostle of violence? Do his films lead to Calvary and redemption or to the Ramrod room and perdition? Is this ex-seminarian uniquely pious or outrageously blasphemous? For Scorsese's acolytes, his excesses lead audiences back to the eternal light, allowing them to see though they once were blind. For his detractors, Scorsese extinguishes all the bright with his guilt-ridden, dark vision.

Some of the most searing moments in *Raging Bull* come in the boxing matches, and critics are divided in their assessment of these harshly brutal, relentlessly bloody, almost-surrealistic images of human bodies being pounded into living gargoyles as gore and sweat splash across frenzied spectators. In this animal fury Scorsese intuits a mystical power; others witness only mindless slaughter. Scorsese filmed the ring footage in *Raging Bull* during the first months of production, around the Christmas holidays. Partly because of British director Michael Powell's casual observation that red gloves and brightly colored boxing trunks didn't suit the atmosphere of La Motta's personal history, and partly because he was beginning his well-publicized campaign to convince Kodak that its color film was deteriorating far too rapidly, Scorsese used black-and-white film stock for *Raging Bull,* except in the "home movies" montage, an echo of the similar dichotomy in *Mean Streets* between the "fiction" film and the "unstaged" candid footage.

In filming La Motta's fights, Scorsese decided, he told reporter Howard Kissel, to ignore Hollywood's traditional approach: "I wanted them to look like fight scenes in no other movie, so they were shot from intricate angles and sometimes we only got one setup a day."[14] Whereas other directors employed multiple cameras to capture the same action from different angles, Scorsese decided to work with only one camera, putting it in the ring with the fighters. As a result, recalls Michael Chapman, his cinematographer, the shooting sessions required intensive preparations and fancy footwork: "We treated the fights like a dance. . . . [W]e had everything extensively choreographed ahead of time" (Wiener, 34). For one sequence, Scorsese studied Hitchcock's shower scene in *Psycho* frame by frame, then recast the action in the boxing ring.

Scorsese was so proud of this boxing footage, which occupies only about 10 minutes of screen time in a film more than two hours long, that he carried all his storyboards to New York University to lecture future filmmakers on the desirability of elaborate preproduction planning and on the necessity to abandon preconceived approaches when the shooting leads in another direction. Summarizing his lecture in an article for a popular audience, Scorsese recalled, "I showed the storyboards I drew for the fight scenes in *Raging Bull* on a screen and compared them to how the actual movie came out. In some cases it was absolutely identical. I put the storyboards up on a screen and I showed the scene in video, and said, 'That shot corresponds to this one, shot number one, and that cuts to this,' and it was exactly as storyboarded by me'."[15] Yet for some sequences, Scorsese admitted in his lecture, the plan didn't foresee all that the shooting would accomplish. A key example of a change in concept came, Scorsese confessed, in his treatment of round 13 of Jake's final bout with Sugar Ray, a round that the ring announcer describes as "the hard luck round" and that the film presents as Jake's Golgotha. This episode, Scorsese told the students,

Martin Scorsese surveys the ring in *Raging Bull* (1980). United Artists. The Museum of Modern Art/Film Stills Archive.

took 10 days to shoot, though it constituted only 20 seconds of film; in the editing Scorsese was forced to rethink his vision: "During the editing, we put it together the normal way, shots one, two, three, four, and so on—it was a total of 36 setups. We realized after we put it together that we had our structure, but we then discovered other values of movement, lighting, special effects, and started juggling the shots" ("Second Screen," 25). Editor Thelma Schoonmaker received an Oscar for *Raging Bull*. In her statements about the award, she has reiterated her belief that "Marty deserves it," since his planning makes her cutting possible and his assistance in the editing room assures the quality of the final cut ("Martin Scorsese Directs").

In his fight sequences Scorsese eschews Hollywood's traditional boxing soundtrack—which orchestrates catcalls, thunderous applause, Bronx cheers, doleful groans, and pregnant silences—in favor of what critic Stephen Schiff describes as "eerie, booming noises" and mixes where "lions roar and hyenas cackle" as "press photographers' flash-bulbs hiss" (Schiff, 1). *Boston Globe* reviewer Michael Blowen astutely noted that this peculiar, hyperreal soundtrack contains the same "raging sounds" that are made by the crowds lining the path to Calvary in Scorsese's later film, *The Last Temptation of Christ,* hammering home Scorsese's theological bent by identifying the boxing arena as "a metaphorical recreation of the crucifixion."[16] The vehicle of the metaphor—desperate, lonely men fighting for survival as predatory animals assail them with their hunting cries—isolates the athletes and establishes the confines of the ring as the combatants' last avenue for salvation. Scorsese felt he so expanded the import of the battles between Jake and his opponents that, as he confided to *Rolling Stone* columnist Mark Jacobson, audiences would discover that *Raging Bull* "wasn't about boxing" (Jacobson, 108). Forcing viewers into the ring and bloodying the audience's noses, Scorsese hoped, would make them confront La Motta, the raging bull, and sympathize with his need for purification, expiation, and vindication.

Raging Bull marks the giddy moment in Scorsese's career when his genius brushes closest to insanity, when his insight smacks of the absurd, and when violence fuses with spiritual rebirth. During the shooting his friend and protégé Jonathan Demme sent Scorsese a picture of Jake La Motta with the inscription "Jake fought like he didn't deserve to live." Analogously, Scorsese filmed *Raging Bull* as though he would never touch a camera again. By their passion both Scorsese and La Motta overcame seemingly impossible odds.

Scorsese's daring is evident in his portrait of Italian male chauvinism. Scorsese exposes the phallocracy of La Motta's environs with dialogue that redefines the rating board's tolerance for explicit sexual banter. In La Motta's world what counts is "balls" and "cock"; men are measured by the way they strut their masculinity, and women are derided as "cunts" and "pussies." The double standard is writ large in this Bronx ghetto where married men flock to the summer dances at St. Clare's Church on Tremont Avenue and the Holy Name Society and Mother Seton Guild blissfully ignore the absence of spouses but where married women are expected to avoid contact with men, look after the children, and keep their mouths shut and their legs crossed.

La Motta's principal witticism in *Raging Bull,* an offhand barb about Tony Janiro—"I've got a problem. I don't know whether to fight him or fuck him"—defines the dilemma of his life. La Motta is always confusing love and hate, fighting and fucking, most notably with his wife, Vickie (Cathy Moriarty). La Motta's passion for Vickie is beautifully captured in a love scene before an early Robinson fight as he orders her to disrobe slowly and embraces her fervently. Convinced that depleting his sperm in the act of love will limit his fighting prowess, La Motta runs to the bathroom to pour cold water on his penis. Originally Scorsese had planned to have La Motta put his erection in a glass of cold water and had hired a body double for De Niro. He rethought the scene, however, remembering what a challenge the obscenity-larded screenplay already posed to the R rating he and the producers wanted. The scene as shot nevertheless establishes quite potently the antithesis between Vickie's soft curves and the hard muscles of professional fighters. Concurrently, it suggests that Jake sees his beloved as an obstacle in the way of the championship belt.

In training camp, Jake and Joey muse on the weakness of women and in a classic example of projection agree that "any woman—given the right time, the right circumstance"—would fornicate, despite marriage vows or moral compunction. As Jake moves closer to the boxing crown, he becomes convinced that he is being betrayed by Vickie. She, in turn, discovers the best way to hurt him. In their most heated encounter, she drives him mad with her mock-confession: "I fucked them all; I sucked your brother's cock and his cock is bigger than yours." As a victim of male chauvinism, Vickie exploits her spouse's weaknesses fully.

On set, newcomer Cathy Moriarty, felt victimized herself because the director and his good friend, Robert De Niro, often avoided her and kept her ignorant of script changes. To film the fight sequences, Scorsese had Moriarty watch with no knowledge of what was coming next; that way, he reasoned, her responses would be natural. She, of course, was terrified of working cold. In one sequence, where Jake and Vickie argue, De Niro slapped Moriarty unexpectedly hard so Scorsese would get a natural reaction from the stunned actress. Moriarty confessed to journalists that "sometimes I did feel intimidated, but I think that's the way they wanted me to feel" and that there were "times that I wanted to cry but I decided that I didn't want to, that it was important not to show I had been hurt" (Weiner, 33).

Unorthodox as his methods may have been, Scorsese did obtain a performance from Moriarty that stunned audiences. Vickie La Motta, as played by Moriarty, was the demure blond who is all fire within, the virginal-looking angel who is pals with all the wiseguys, the looker who is sweet around children and sultry around Mafia dons. *Raging Bull* linked Cathy Moriarty and the role of Vickie La Motta forever, and the actress, despite great reviews, didn't work much in the subsequent decade.

As always, Scorsese infused his personal concerns into his film about Jake La Motta. Scorsese heightened attention to marriage and fidelity, a theme that receives scant attention in the original autobiography but reflects Scorsese's concern for both his parents and his recent nuptials. Charles Scorsese retired around the time Scorsese began production of *Raging Bull*. Catherine Scorsese complained that her husband was bored, so she induced her son to use his father as a consultant on costumes. Soon Charles found himself cast as a feature player in *Raging Bull,* in a largely silent role as the Mafia chief's henchman. Scorsese featured his father in a homage to his parents' wedding, as he filmed "home movies" of the La Motta's wedding reception on a tenement roof—an allusion to the Scorseses' wedding party, held on a roof because they couldn't afford a hall.

Scorsese's mind centered on family and marriage because on 30 September 1979, just before shooting on *Raging Bull* began, he married Isabella Rossellini in the city hall of Bracciano, a town near Rome. The couple had met when Rossellini interviewed Scorsese for Italian television during the filming of *New York, New York*. Present for the wedding ceremony were both of Scorsese's parents, actress Ingrid Bergman, and director Roberto Rossellini. This third marriage for Scorsese proved his shortest, though it did afford him an opportunity to appear with his wife in Roberto Benigni's comedy *In the Eye of the*

Pope. As often is the case in Scorsese's romances, his intimacy with Rossellini strengthened his ties to the film industry and to film history. Isabella Rossellini was, after all, the child involved in the 1949 love affair between Ingrid Bergman and Roberto Rossellini that scandalized Hollywood. Later Isabella Rossellini would shock Hollywood again with her performance as an abused woman in David Lynch's *Blue Velvet*.

Marriage in *Raging Bull* threatens to derail Jake La Motta's career; this tension between a man's career and his home life is Scorsese's most frequently explored theme. Scorsese often shows his protagonist's mission endangered by the snares of matrimony, whether that mission lies on mean streets, in the ring, or across time in Jerusalem. The other danger in *Raging Bull* is posed by the Mob. Like other Scorsese heroes, from J.R. to Henry Hill, Jake La Motta has to deal with the good fellas, the wise guys, the silk-suited gangsters. If Vickie represents his unattainable angel, Tommy and his cronies, modeled after the infamous Blinkie Palermo and Frankie Carbo, serve as Jake's inescapable demons. Jake may beat and subdue Vickie, but he can never escape the regulars at the Debonair Social Club. They see that he takes the dive against Fox and that his monies are invested in a glitzy nightclub; they're even there when he's reduced to introducing Emma and her fabulous 48s at a run-down strip joint.

In its focus on mobsters and on "the fix" in boxing, *Raging Bull* draws on the emotions central to *On the Waterfront* and Marlon Brando's landmark performance as Terry Malloy. In fact, to conclude *Raging Bull* Scorsese pictures La Motta backstage at the Barbizon Plaza Hotel preparing for "an Evening with Jake La Motta," a series of dramatic readings from Paddy Chayefsky, Budd Schulberg, Rod Serling, William Shakespeare, and Tennessee Williams, among others. Robert De Niro, who won the Academy Award for Best Actor for his portrayal of Jake La Motta, after gaining more than 60 pounds to embody Jake's physical decline and spending more than $8,000 to have makeup expert Michael Westmore redo his cauliflowered nose 14 times, suggested to Scorsese that the most poignant monologue for the ex-champ was not a lofty soliloquy from a dusty classic but the central boxing speech in their experience, Brando's "I coulda been a contender" lament to his brother Charlie in *On the Waterfront*. Scorsese agreed, and the two perfectionist filmmakers shot this sequence of De Niro playing Jake La Motta playing Marlon Brando playing Terry Malloy to his dressing-room mirror 19 times. Scorsese, who plays a

Robert De Niro as the overweight former middleweight boxing champion Jake La Motta in *Raging Bull* (1980). United Artists. The Museum of Modern Art/Film Stills Archive.

Barbizon stagehand in *Raging Bull,* cued De Niro during the takes, as they reinterpreted the celebrated cinematic variant on the theme of the American dream:

> It wasn't him, Charlie. It was you. You 'member that night in the Garden you came down my dressing room and said, "Kid, this ain't your night. We're going for the price on Wilson." You 'member that? "This ain't your night!" My night—I coulda taken Wilson apart! So what happens? He gets the title shot outdoors on the ballpark, and what do I get? A one-way ticket to Palookaville. *You* was my brother, Charlie. You shoulda looked out for me a little bit. You shoulda taken care of me just a little bit so I wouldn't have to take them dives for the short end money. . . . [Y]ou don't understand! I coulda had class. I coulda been a contender. I coulda been somebody—instead of a bum which is what I am. Let's face it. It was you, Charlie. (Schrader and Martin, 100)

De Niro and Scorsese, avid film buffs and Brando devotees, mine these lines admirably. Critic Andrew Sarris admitted that their reworking of this scene left him speechless: "I can only gasp at the deeply affecting aptness and audacity and virtuosity of the conceit. Between them, De Niro and Scorsese and their associates end up with a breathtakingly new dimension of memory and regret" (Sarris, 55). Scorsese refers to this sequence as the "redemption scene" in *Raging Bull,* arguing that watching the new La Motta, a man at peace with himself, audiences should recognize that "we should all have such peace" (Rafferty, 1983, 192). De Niro's recitation of Brando's lines achieve, Scorsese asserts, his central goal in *Raging Bull*: "I wanted to show there was hope for the resolution of the soul, to show it simply with an unsympathetic character; that is, to take all the unsympathetic things from myself and throw them up on the screen" (C. Taylor, 48).

Many reviewers of *Raging Bull* deny that this dressing-room sequence provides enough evidence of Jake La Motta's spiritual rebirth. Rex Reed, for example, blasted *Raging Bull* as a "relentlessly despairing look at a punchy, inarticulate, ignorant, sub-mental punching bag from an Italian neighborhood in the Bronx who lives a thoroughly loathsome life from first frame to last" and complained that when the film ends De Niro, "Bloated, beer-bellied, porcine, and disgustingly vulgar, doing Brando's 'I coulda been a contender' speech . . . you don't know if you're supposed to laugh or cry."[17] John Simon, writing for the *National Review,* concurred, arguing that Scorsese had little of interest to say: "*Raging Bull* does not even communicate what the rage of this bull is about, why he is so preternaturally jealous (even for a street-bred Italian) of his faithful wife, why he will turn even on his loyal and helpful brother, [or] how he works out his eventual salvation if that is what it is."[18] Even the normally supportive Steven Harvey warned readers of *Inquiry* that De Niro's last speech is subject to various interpretations, that the message is ambiguous: "If this speech could be applied to any one figure, it's La Motta, but what's terrifying is that his reflected face betrays nothing—he's learned it all by rote."[19]

The title cards with which Scorsese chooses to end *Raging Bull* suggest that he did not feel equivocal about La Motta's salvation. The original script ended with images of Jake shadowboxing, a description of Jake as "still alive, still a contender, a forty-two year old man fighting for his shot," and a citation from St. John's Gospel, chapter 3, beginning with verse 3: "Verily, verily I say unto thee except a man be born again, he cannot enter into the kingdom of heaven." By the time *Raging Bull* was completed, Scorsese decided to change the citation to later lines in St. John's Gospel, chapter 9, beginning with verse 24: "So, for the second time, the Pharisees summoned the man who had been blind and said: 'Speak the truth before God, We know this fellow is a sinner.' 'Whether or not he is a sinner, I do not know,' the man replied. 'All I know is this: once I was blind and now I can see'."

Scorsese was totally responsible for the new text. His collaborator Paul Schrader maintains that it does not fit the film: "I had no idea it was going to be there, and when I saw it I was absolutely baffled. I don't think it's true of La Motta either in real life or in the movie; I think he's the same dumb lug at the end as he is at the beginning, and I think Marty is just imposing salvation on his subject by fiat. I've never really got from him a terribly credible reason for why he did it; he just seemed to feel that it was right" (Schrader 1990, 133).

In this new "now I can see" citation, Scorsese was commemorating Jake's new understanding and peace, but as his title card went on to note, he was also "Remembering Haig P. Manoogian, teacher, May 23, 1916–May 26, 1980, with love and resolution, Marty." Those who knew Manoogian would recall that he challenged all his New York University students to *see* and linked the idea of seeing with the essence of art and religion. As a headnote, for example, to his text *The Filmmaker's Art*, Scorsese's mentor had cited the Victorian critic John Ruskin: "The greatest thing a human soul ever does in this world is to see something, and tell what it saw in a plain way. Hundreds of people can talk for one who can think but thousands can think for one who can see. To see clearly is poetry, prophecy, and religion, all in one" (Manoogian, vii). Scorsese found poetry, prophecy, and religion in La Motta's life and struggled in *Raging Bull* to make audiences share his vision. By filming *Raging Bull,* Scorsese also fulfilled the trust Haig Manoogian had placed in him and fittingly thanked his teacher for aiding him in the movement from blindness to sight. By the time *Raging Bull* began to receive its just critical accolades, Scorsese also knew that like Jake, he had to be born again. *Raging Bull,* he confided to Philip French, marked both the end of his first decade of professional filmmaking and a major milestone in his artistic development: "It ends everything. I've got to start all over again" (French, 14).

7

The King of Comedy (1982)

Martin Scorsese launched his campaign to revitalize his career by abandoning his fancy digs on the West Coast and settling into a spartan apartment in New York City. The move from Mulholland Drive to Manhattan symbolized Scorsese's apostasy from the new Hollywood catechism of megahits aimed at a youthful, T-shirt-buying, designer-jean-clad audience, so smitten by special effects that they would gladly spill tons of popcorn over their Reebok and Nike athletic shoes if the thrill were great enough. As Scorsese explained to *Rolling Stone* interviewer Anthony DeCurtis, the 1980s in Hollywood were inhospitable to his personal, small films aimed at sophisticated audiences: "The whole mood of the country was different. Big money was being made with pictures like *Rocky* and eventually the Spielberg-Lucas films. At that time they were the myth-makers and to a certain extent, they continue to be. I mean, *New York, New York* was a total flop and it opened the same week as *Star Wars*. So at that time I knew which way the wind was blowing, and it certainly wasn't in my direction."[1] At the large Hollywood studios, which were being relentlessly acquired by conglomerates, eager MBAs were more attentive to ledger books than to cinematic worth and confirmed Scorsese's sad analysis of his commercial prospects.

Statisticians for the Motion Picture Association of America (MPAA) counseled would-be filmmakers that more than 85 percent of the American filmgoing audience were under 40; in fact, a substantial majority were under 25.[2] The same surveys revealed that a small cadre of filmgoers, roughly a quarter of the American public, were frequent ticket buyers, coming more than once a month and accounting for more than 84 percent of all admissions (Litwak, 113). Studios dedicated themselves to pleasing this young adventure-seeking audience by providing romantic thrills and by reiterating successful fantasy ploys in well-publicized sequels. No wonder Scorsese exclaimed in despair that reviewers critical of his works for their lack of women's roles should see the larger issue, Hollywood's lack of roles for recognizable human beings of any gender: "Looks what's around! Aliens! Talking to Blue Screens? Ducks Coming from Space! You're talking about parts for women? Parts for men! Humans! Parts for humans we're talking about; where are they?"[3]

As a player in the Hollywood "star wars," Scorsese had intuited a dramatic shift in the dream factory, one that film historian Todd McCarthy later astutely characterized as a renunciation of the so-called A-feature, a big-budget, serious picture aimed at a mature, urban, literate audience, and a deification of B-movies, sensational, exotic formula films appealing to the basest instincts of the mass audience. This move from complex, challenging narratives with subtle themes, round characters, and ambiguous conclusions to mindless chases and duels, cardboard villains, clear victories, and happy endings, McCarthy argued, shaped the corporate mind-set in Tinseltown: "This process of transmogrification says a lot about Hollywood today: its ability to recycle its past; the shift towards a younger target audience; the ever-increasing dominance of form and style over content; the obsession of younger directors with the films of their youth; and the triumph of pop culture as the honorable object of attention of even the most prestigious filmmakers."[4]

The shift in studio orientation and audience expectations proved especially burdensome to Scorsese as he tried to market his first film to be released in the 1980s, *Raging Bull*. For all the attention critics lavished on this black-and-white epic of guilt and salvation, and despite all the praise Scorsese received from his colleagues in the industry for the film's dazzling camerawork, challenging script, and masterful performances, he and the financiers in Hollywood knew *Raging Bull* would be a hard sell. Scorsese warned British journalist Karen Moline that "it was a tough picture. I don't know if you'd go to see it as entertainment—it's painful to watch and the emotional impact is pretty strong."[5] American audiences needed no warnings. The toughness, pain, and strong emotional impact of *Raging Bull* provided no appeal for the mass audience. They were content with frothier entertainments, so *Raging Bull* did modest business, even as reviewers proclaimed it Scorsese's masterpiece and critics lauded it as the decade's best movie.

As Scorsese attempted to recover from his disappointment, another bombshell exploded. On 30 March 1981 John Hinckley shot President Reagan and declared that his fixation on Jodie Foster and *Taxi Driver* made him do it. In the following months, Scorsese would suffer the full scrutiny of journalists, television interviewers, and media theorists. All of America wanted to know more about the effects of celebrity on assassins, about the peculiar impulse that drove Mark David Chapman to kill John Lennon in December 1980, about the erotic projection that inspired John Hinckley to shoot a popular president, and about the messianic fervor that eventually caused Arthur Richard Jackson, on 15 March 1982, to slash Theresa Saldana, who played Lenore La Motta, Jake's sister-in-law, in *Raging Bull*. Undoubtedly, all these incidents led Scorsese to his next project, *The King of Comedy*. *The King of Comedy* would embody Scorsese's views on celebrity and ambition, hero worship and eroticism, notoriety and violence, entertainment and news, media sterotypes and eternal verities, horror and black comedy, popular culture and high art, popularity and salvation.

As is often the case with Scorsese's features, *The King of Comedy* had been in development for a long time—in this case more than a decade. Scriptwriter Paul Zimmerman, a film critic for *Newsweek,* had been inspired by a 1970 "David Susskind Show" on autogrpah collectors and by an *Esquire* feature on a man obsessed with talk shows. In a moment of insight, Zimmerman recalls, he came to his central thesis: "My God, they're just like assassins."[6] Zimmerman's script interested Paramount's leading director, Milos Forman, who began developing the material with the screenwriter Buck Henry under the title *Harry, the King of Comedy*. After three years of delays, the Paramount project aborted, and Zimmerman sent his original script to Scorsese, who wasn't interested but who did pass it on to Robert De Niro.

De Niro was notorious for carting around bags of paperback novels and scripts, all with feature roles he could play. From his earliest days in acting he had always been a dynamo, a one-man studio, with visions of producing and starring in an infinite number of projects. De Niro told Zimmerman he "really loved" *The King of Comedy* but had "five pictures to do first" (Brown, 73). Meanwhile De Niro attempted to convince Scorsese, who had just finished *Alice Doesn't Live Here Anymore,* that this dark comedy about television should be his next project.

Coincidentally, when Scorsese evaluated the script in 1974, he was fascinated by the prospect of doing a comedy and was working with

Zimmerman's rival film reviewer at *Time,* Jay Cocks, on a feature about Borscht Belt comedians, emphasizing the pain and fear that go into standup routines. Scorsese didn't like Zimmerman's script, however; he considered it too superficial and simple, a one-joke gag ("Martin Scorsese Directs"). Scorsese told De Niro he "didn't go for it . . . didn't understand it," and begged off the project.[7]

Zimmerman continued refining the script, however, and De Niro promoted it all over Hollywood. Finally in 1978, when De Niro was negotiating with novice Israeli producer Arnon Milchan about doing a film on Moshe Dayan, the actor showed the would-be investor Zimmerman's script and got a commitment for a shooting budget of between $10 million and $15 million. De Niro lined up Michael Cimino to direct, but the boondoggle of *Heaven's Gate* intervened.

Meanwhile Scorsese and De Niro completed *Raging Bull*; at the time of its release, Scorsese began an exhausting lecture tour through Europe, continuing his crusade against fading color film stock. Kodak responded with an improved film and Scorsese switched his emphasis to the need to preserve film properly, to make copies of studio originals, to restore mutilated classics like *Lawrence of Arabia,* and to ensure that colorized prints didn't entirely replace black-and-white originals. The controversy and travel exhausted Scorsese, and he was in physical collapse when De Niro appeared at his bedside to cajole him into a major project, *The King of Comedy.* As Scorsese recalls their encounter, De Niro "made it seem like a lark . . . and I was exhausted so I was susceptible to an *easy* film" (Blowen, 1).

Scorsese reread Zimmerman's script and discovered new angles in its treatment of comedy, facets that critic Dave Kehr accurately labels "comedy as violence, comedy as salvation, and comedy as psychosis."[8] Scorsese also found the autobiographical element central to all his projects. As he explained in press releases, "I went back and reread Paul Zimmerman's script and realized it addressed a lot of issues of our times and it also helps clarify what has happened to Robert De Niro—who plays the young comic, Rupert Pupkin—and myself over the past decade. Even though I didn't write it, I could identify with Pupkin's struggles."[9] Scorsese committed himself to the film in the belief that *King of Comedy* could examine American society as it explored the psyche of one dispossessed individual, that the outsider's anguish would make audiences understand the passions inside all individuals, and that Rupert Pupkin would serve as a vehicle for De Niro and him to work out their misgivings about the past 10 years:

their shattered private lives, their unbounded ambition, and the complications attendant on their celebrity.

The King of Comedy was conceived with Dick Cavett in mind as Jerry Langford, the talk-show host. But Scorsese saw more affinities to the "Tonight Show" and Johnny Carson, so he approached the graying eminence of late-night television about playing Jerry Langford. Carson demurred, evincing no interest in doing the constant retakes filming required; he preferred the spontaneity of television but did offer to advise Scorsese and De Niro during the production. Meanwhile Scorsese made overtures to Jerry Lewis to play Langford, and De Niro began watching inexperienced performers work in comedy clubs. He also attended celebrity galas with autograph hounds; De Niro eventually recruited his contacts to play autograph seekers in The King of Comedy.

Then Scorsese and De Niro took the script out to Long Island to hammer out a new version. Zimmerman had been worried about this "collaboration" but was delighted to discover that "the script Marty and Bobby returned to me was all mine—with maybe one new scene"; their real contributions came, he felt, in "the creative overlay," in an interpretation that gave the film a tone "tougher" and "darker" than the original script called for (Brown, 72).

As these preparations were being made, the still-ailing Scorsese turned his attention to preproduction on other projects, including a television miniseries of 10 to 20 hours' duration on the "history of early Christianity and its links to paganism" (Pirie, 139). Then the Directors Guild of America issued strike threats that would shut down any project not already rolling. Panicked, Arnon Milchan ordered Scorsese and De Niro to start shooting in July 1981, a full month before their target production date. As a result of the hasty beginning, Scorsese was exhausted, De Niro harried, and the production crew disorganized.

Bringing a big-budget film to New York before all the details were ironed out made the work on King of Comedy most exasperating. In his autobiography Scorsese compares making this film with living with an out-of-control dinosaur: "[T]he tail was so big it was wagging and slamming into everything, perhaps not intentionally, but destroying things as in a Godzilla movie" (Scorsese 1989, 87–88). Union troubles, botched permits, difficult accommodations, stalled clearances, unruly spectators, power problems, uncertain weather, and the complications of street scenes in midtown Manhattan kept nerves on edge.

Martin Scorsese checks the look of *The King of Comedy* (1982). The Museum of Modern Art/Film Stills Archive.

King of Comedy's first stage of production took 20 weeks, and Scorsese began to harbor doubts about his future as a mainstream American director. The scale of Hollywood feature film production was beginning, he told colleagues, to seem excessive: "I had a bad experience with *The King of Comedy* in terms of rising costs. The actual machine began to beat me down, and I worked very slowly. I had forgotten what it was like to do a film under pressure. I thought maybe I had just gotten old, and I wondered how I ever did film at a different pace."[10] All the troubles were compounded, Scorsese felt, by his own perfectionism. His involvement with a project so consumes him, he admits, that he cannot allow any aspect of the production to be flawed.

The King of Comedy exceeded its $14 million projected budget by almost $5 million, yet its American box office take was less than one-sixth that amount. Scorsese, increasingly convinced that his dream "to make experimental pictures within the mainstream" was an impossibility in the era of Lucas and Spielberg, was confounded by the fact that *The King of Comedy* was, he knew, "a good movie," yet as he

Robert De Niro as Rupert Pupkin in *The King of Comedy* (1982). Twentieth Century-Fox. The Museum of Modern Art/Film Stills Archive.

observed, "I didn't like making the picture. I didn't like cutting it. And I don't like to see it" (Siskel, 5).

Robert De Niro proved equally unhappy with *The King of Comedy,* viewing his portrayal of Rupert Pupkin as the largest gamble of his acting career, a risk that just didn't pay off. In several interviews De Niro analyzed his approach to the role to define just what went wrong; paradoxically, his director, Scorsese, has gone out of his way to laud De Niro's performance as his finest work ever. De Niro, as usual, began with an animal image to structure his portrayal of Pupkin, whose very name is a portmanteau word with canine overtones. For De Niro, Rupert (another portmanteau word, blending *rude* and *pert,* his conflicting qualities) was "Gawky. A bird whose neck goes out as he walks . . . a chicken"; De Niro hones in on Pupkin as a "spindly" man "with white shoes, like a cartoon" (Grobel, 86). In De Niro's interpretation Rupert's unflagging attempts to emulate Jerry Langford, like demons' attempts to emulate human beings, always come up one detail short: his barbershop haircut has the shape of Jerry's but lacks the finish expensive stylists provide; Rupert wears white bucks with his polyester sportcoats, whereas Jerry wears designer silk jackets and understated soft leather shoes; Rupert's tie is a garish red ready-made, whereas Jerry wears a restrained, off-white, hand-tied cravat. Rupert is the unbalanced schmuck who aspires to the charmed life of the beautiful people but always treads in dog droppings, sits on bubble gum, or cuts his hand in a fray. As critic Stephen Schiff notes, De Niro carefully limns one Rupert who glides carelessly through fantasy sequences hobnobbing with the elite and another Rupert who awkwardly stumbles over reality, "so we can compare the way Rupert sees himself with the way we see him; in the fantasies the gestures are not quite so crude, and the laughter isn't quite so bellicose."[11] The effect of these careful modulations and studied contrasts, author Paul Zimmerman suggests, was to "make Rupert sympathetic even when he is so ruthless and obnoxious. Bobby develops this wonderful vulnerability, this openness and innocence, that I now see as essential" (Brown, 72–73).

De Niro's humane approach to Rupert Pupkin and his masterful presentation of both Rupert's fantasies and Pupkin's realities reinforce Scorsese's focus in *The King of Comedy,* his desire to explore his and De Niro's lives and careers during the 1970s. *The King of Comedy,* Scorsese declared in the production notes distributed to the press, "is a very personal film for me and for Bobby. It's a way of reexamining our own early ambitions, seeing what we were like then and what we are now" ("Scorsese and De Niro," 3). Developing this idea in later interviews, Scorsese maintained that *The King of Comedy* so vividly chronicles everything that happened to the two friends since *Mean Streets* that he could watch only parts of it at any one sitting: "It's so grim. For me it's about how my fantasies and De Niro's fantasies have come about. We were like the guy in that movie. We wanted to get into show business. We were fascinated by celebrities. Now we're a part of it. It's very strange" (Siskel, 15).

Part of the strangeness, Scorsese acknowledges, arises from the film's ambiguous, almost-dualistic point of view. While the dialogue and camera angles sometimes encourage identification with the struggling Rupert, substantial segments of *The King of Comedy* present Pupkin as a nerd and seem to take the aloof, cynical perspective of Jerry Langford. Flipping from one consciousness to the other, from possessed social climber to cold professional, the film seems torn between its fascination with Rupert's implacable energy and its horror at Pupkin's dementia. This mixture of pity and terror, normally associated with classical tragedy, seems out of place in a modern comedy. Much of what should be casual laughter is throttled by the serious themes. Audiences are left unable to decide whether to laugh at or about Rupert—indeed whether to laugh at all. *The King of Comedy* emerges less as a comedy than as a disorienting descent into a chaotic, off-balance, psychotic universe, haunted by material success and spiritual bankruptcy, extraordinary fame and debilitating emotional emptiness, stylish power and impotent despair.

The bleakness of this terrain reflects the angst Scorsese was experiencing. His marriage to Isabella Rosselini had just collapsed, and she had gone public with her side of the split, declaring that it was impossible "to be with a person who is completely dedicated to his work" (Hoberman, 40). For his part Scorsese would say only that "It's impossible for me to talk about it. You find all sorts of ways to punish yourself" (Hoberman, 40). *The King of Comedy* provided Scorsese with a venue to dissect the ambition and obsessions that played havoc with his personal life, with both male leads, the irascible Pupkin and the detached Langford, serving as his alter egos. As Scorsese explained to Janet Maslin of the *New York Times,* ambition is a deadly vice in *The King of Comedy*: "I wanted to look at what it's like to want something so badly you'd kill for it. By kill I don't mean kill physically but you can kill the spirit, you can kill relationships, you can kill everything else around you in your life."[12] In *The King of Comedy* Rupert may be the ugly loser, an abrasive, discomfiting quid-nunc, but Jerry Langford is just a beautiful loser, a polished, ingratiating nonentity torn from the pages of *Being There.*

Scorsese's casting of Jerry Lewis, a star whose career was on the wane, as Jerry Langford startled the Hollywood establishment. But Scorsese had long been a fan who shared the French enthusiasm for "Monsieur Lewis."[13] At NYU, Scorsese had challenged his students to analyze *The Nutty Professor,* arguing that this slight comedy was "the greatest multiple personality film every made" and positing a simple exegesis: "Buddy Love is Dean Martin. Professor Kelp is Jerry Lewis. The movie is the result of Jerry's years in psychoanalysis. He wants to be Dean Martin and Jerry Lewis at the same time."[14] *The King of Comedy,* another multiple-personality film, reiterates this comic theme in the persona of Rupert Pupkin, who desperately wants to be a Jerry Langford clone, an apotheosized new star in the late-night constellation. *The King of Comedy* goes on to reveal, however, that if Rupert could just penetrate the maze of offices protecting this hollow king or break through the doorman and concierge levels of

Jerry's apartment house instead of being stranded on the street, Rupert would discover that the emperor has no soul, only designer clothing on loan from a television network.

The King of Comedy plunges into the deep end of Langford's private life and demonstrates how uncomfortably icy and still the waters are. Langford's Xanadu, a beige penthouse in a downtown apartment house, reeks of wealth and boredom, of a privacy bordering on solitary confinement. The wall unit with three televisions emits no sound, and two sets are turned to test patterns. The answering machine's playback contains only stale business calls, and Jerry's pre-prepared dinner-for-one looks as cold and unappetizing as a frozen TV dinner. Jerry Langford shuffles through this affluent wasteland in what reviewer Stephen Schiff recognized as "the most economical, lived in portrait of power since Marlon Brando's Don Corleone"; in a radically unappreciated performance, Schiff notes, Scorsese has coaxed from his normally hyperactive, almost-spastic comedic star a physical tour de force of restraint: "Lewis makes his eyes dead and his body rigid until he's all sleep repression; every unseemly emotion, everything not ready for prime time, seems to have settled into the absorbent wattles around his neck, or into the muscles around his mouth that coil furtively as if straining to hold back venom" (Schiff, 4). For the characterization Lewis actually wore his own clothes and brought his dog to the set; critic Michael Bliss found in the Lewis–Langford pet an ironic metaphor for the whole scene, noting that this "ridiculous Pekinese" with its "sullen face and pampered accouterments" actually mocks "its owner's situation" (Bliss, 136–37). Whether it was the dog or the apartment or his body language, Langford in The King of Comedy evidences so little vitality and so little humanity that Lewis's wonderful improvised lament about life as a late-night television host—"I'm just a human being, with all the foibles and all of the traps, the show, the pressure, the groupies, the autograph hounds, the creeps, the incompetents"—rings as false as Nixon's "I'm not a crook" and Checkers speeches. If Langford were "a human being," he wouldn't have to work so hard to convince others of his foibles and his problems. When Langford is finally mummified in tape by his inept, demented kidnapper-worshippers, the irony of The King of Comedy becomes visually apparent: Rupert and Masha can immobilize Langford's body, but fame has already crippled his soul. Their mummy is a zombie underneath, and everything about late-night television is really a horror show.

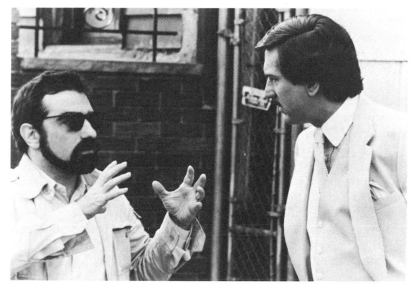

Martin Scorsese and Robert De Niro collaborate on the set of *The King of Comedy* (1982). Twentieth Century-Fox. The Museum of Modern Art/Film Stills Archive.

The King of Comedy offers some inspired satiric sequences, such as the on-screen marriage of Rupert Pupkin and his black girlfriend Rita (played by De Niro's recently estranged wife, Diahnne Abbott), a masterful spoof of the Tiny Tim–Miss Vicky cornball nuptials on the "Tonight Show"; the prolonged bungling use of bizarre cue cards to orchestrate ransom demands; and the laboriously reflexive shtick with Scorsese appearing as a harried television director disingenuously assuring his star, concerned producers, and casual passersby that breathtakingly dull material is convulsively "funny," a skit that quickly cuts to images of an overstimulated Masha clumsily disrobing before the captive and bored Langford as she exclaims, "Let's have some good American fun!" These sequences make Scorsese's feature, in Jack Kroll's words, "a scarifying anatomy of modern mania"[15] and convince David Denby that the project is "fired by a mercilessly exact loathing of show business."[16]

Scorsese injects more venom, when in an echo of *Taxi Driver*'s unsettling epilogue, Rupert Pupkin achieves his insane goal. His nationally broadcast monologue seemingly satisfies audience expectations, his demented kidnapping ploy is dismissed as a desperate publicity stunt, and his subsequent jail term of six years evaporates into two years and nine months at Allenwood, the infamous white-collar federal country club–prison where he pens his best-selling confession, *King for a Night*. Pupkin eventually obtains his own late-night show, and the golden-throated announcer reminds Rupert's fans that they've been "waiting and waiting and waiting" to welcome home "the legendary, the inspirational, the one and only King of Comedy!" Their adulation, of course, is unbounded.

As Stephen Harvey writes, Pupkin's apotheosis constitutes "Scorsese's sickest joke of all," the epitome of gross humor, yet this phantasmagoric conclusion also allows *The King of Comedy* to be experienced as "a feel-good farce, replete with what scans like an upbeat finish,"[17] a *Rocky* of the airwaves. Those who identify with Pupkin and his guests can cheer his victory; more critical audiences can contemplate his celebrity as evidence of the lunacy of hero worship in America and of the absurd randomness of celebrity. Professors Krin Gabbard and Glen Gabbard seize on this possible dual-edged appeal to argue, in their complex survey *Psychiatry and the Cinema,* that "we are not even sure if the renown that Pupkin enjoys at the end of the film is in his head or in reality."[18] Either way, however, the Gabbards maintain, Scorsese has achieved his goals: "He has apparently sought to make two movies: one for a naive or "right" audience, who may find De Niro's Pupkin to be as adept as any other standup comedian presented by Johnny Carson, and who may assume that the film is another in a long series of American entertainments about a little guy who beats the system. The other film . . . is addressed to the ironic or 'left' audience, who are more acquainted with cinematic codes. Scorsese has asked this audience to think more critically about America's television heroes" (Gabbard and Gabbard, 211).

Fascinating as the Gabbards' deconstruction of *The King of Comedy* may be on theoretical grounds, it is undercut somewhat by Scorsese's pronouncements on his intentions: "[*The King of Comedy*] is a movie about a guy who isn't very talented who becomes a celebrity only because he appears on a successful talk show. It's in the nature of our society that Andy Warhol's proclamation about everyone being a celebrity for 15 minutes is coming true. Television holds this tremendous lure for people. In some cases, it legitimizes our existence. Some people don't think an event is true unless it's been on television" (Blowen, 8). On other occasions, however, Scorsese has observed that he was attracted to the script of *The King of Comedy* by the unevenness of Pupkin's monologue, a weird pastiche of jokes about growing up in Clifton, New Jersey, with parents who "couldn't afford my childhood," a mother so tied to the bottle that "her alcohol was two percent blood," a sister Rose who grew up to be "a fine man," and classmates who beat him so frequently that "the school worked it into the regular curriculum." Scorsese admits that it's hard to reject Pupkin's final assertion that "It's better to be a king for a night than a schmuck for a lifetime," and this irresistible charm may make the whole monologue a success. Robert De Niro also acknowledged the power of this monologue, arguing that it is a "great" moment: "I thought there was no need to improvise or ad-lib. The whole routine that Pupkin had at the end was word for word—the whole timing and the way it builds. I loved the monologue. I don't know what other people thought, but I thought it was great" (Paris, 36). Those who agree with De Niro's assessment see the conclusion of *The King of Comedy* as a just recognition of Rupert's skills; those who find Pupkin Scorsese's "guy who isn't very talented" bemoan the absurdity of his success.

Professional reviewers were divided in their reactions. Howard Kissel from *Women's Wear Daily* thought that "When we finally see him deliver his standup routine at the end of the film, it turns out to be quite funny—one has the feeling he could have been successful as a comedian without the machinations we have spent the last 90 minutes watching."[19] Yet Michael Bliss was convinced that the monologue was a bleak failure and a perverse disappointment: "By *The King of Comedy*'s end there is nothing to laugh about except morbidity: ruling over the film's ironic black humor is the ultimate comic king, the figure who saves the nastiest joke for last, the ruler plenipotentiary of emptiness and waste" (Bliss, 141). Indeed, the split in audiences and reviewers, reinforces Scorsese's theme: our inability to judge Rupert, mass media, and celebrity objectively. John Simon, in a contentious passage meant to excoriate *The King of Comedy*, may have defined the film's greatest strength. Simon blasts the "muddle" of the film in a cogent catalog of possible interpretations: "The monologue strikes me as only slightly less funny than most such monologues. . . . Are the filmmakers saying that Pupkin's comedy is junk, but that on the *Langford Show*, introduced by Tony Randall, it enchants an audience of Pavlovian fools? Or are they saying that Pupkin does have that minimal talent needed to make anybody's success in this abysmal business? Is the film about weirdos cannibalizing their betters, or are there no betters, and are large numbers of—if not, indeed, all—Americans a breed of imbeciles? Is the satire specific or all-inclusive?[20] Scorsese's satire is simultaneously specific and all-inconclusive in *The King of Comedy*. He lets neither audience nor performer off the hook: the business is "abysmal" if it deifies either Jerry Langford or Rupert Pupkin. Yet the business does serve a breed of imbeciles clamoring for autographs and groping for souvenirs. Scorsese's vision balances media culpability with audience responsibility in its depiction of a kingdom of comedy where it is folly to be wise.

Scorsese's mise-en-scène reinforces the idea of a diminished landscape populated by stunted personalities, a wasteland patrolled by cyclops. Scorsese told interviewers that because "all the characters are fascinated by television," he tried to "shoot it like a TV film" (Kissel, 24). Analyst Robert Kolker celebrated Scorsese's success at capturing the "flat, neutral" television style, noting that "the lighting is even and low key; the camera almost always at eye level and largely steady; the editing, except for some fantasy sequences, remains close to the standard shot—reverse shot of television and ordinary filmmaking" (Kolker, 209). Interpreting this style, Dave Kehr remarks on the impact of Scorsese's regimen: "Every shot is lit (if not overlit) in an even, tepid, sourceless manner, and the color of the release prints has the thin, dull tone of DeLuxe processing at its worst. It's a TV image, with a cold, false cheer and a compulsive cleanliness; it's like watching the inside of a refrigerator."[21] Scorsese related the stark, static quality of his visuals—stolidly realized by cinematographer Fred Schuler, who usually worked on frothy, topical comedies like *Stir Crazy* and *Arthur*—to both the nature of the media and the personalities of his characters: "Everybody in this movie is *impassable*; they're like rocks. . . . Everybody's so rigid that just a medium shot of them talking to each other would do" (Rafferty 1983, 187).

Scorsese's visual genius does break through occasionally in *The King of Comedy*. The title sequence, for instance, echoes *Raging Bull's* fascination with flashbulbs and their stereoscopic effect on the actual. As Jerry Langford is assailed by fans, everything switches to slow motion, movement is distorted, and finally reality is reduced to a freeze frame with color washed out by overexposure of Masha's hands splayed against the windows of a limousine, as the soundtrack lyrics promise "I'm gonna love you." The sequence provides a stunning introduction to a love that threatens to destroy, an obsession kept safe behind a glass television screen, and a human hunger distorted by bright lights and ambition.

Similarly, a frantic sequence with Rupert barging through Langford's reception area recalls the Keystone Cops in its absurdist chase through the halls of a sterile, compartmentalized television conglomerate. And an improvised scene at Langford's country estate is filmed with such nervous energy and through so many shifting perspectives that it becomes, Richard Schickel comments, "As good as anything to be found in a modern comedy of ill manners."[22]

Researching for *The King of Comedy,* Scorsese found himself so caught up in the milieu of television comedy that he contemplated doing a short documentary on Ernie Kovacs; his 30-minute study would, he thought, fit smoothly into Michael Powell's proposed television series "13 Ways to Kill a Poet." Though the Kovacs short was never made, it reveals Scorsese's work pattern: after a feature film, Scorsese likes to collapse for two weeks, often taking a rest cure at a hospital, and then he undertakes a small project—a documentary, a commercial, or a music video—just to keep the creative juices flowing.

In January 1982 Marilyn Beck of the *New York Daily News* reported that Scorsese was "furiously editing" *The King of Comedy* and that the distributors, Twentieth Century-Fox, were so pleased by the roughly assembled footage that they had decided to strike it off their summer release schedule "and unveil it as a major year-end release."[23] How much of this gossip-column item was hype is uncertain, but the sad fact is that by November 1982 Scorsese was still shaping the film and the studio was insisting on more shooting. Again the *Daily News* put a press agent's release in its news columns, quoting Sherry Lansing of Twentieth Century-Fox declaring that "The studio agreed to extra shooting even though it cost extra money" and promising that "the end result would be a masterpiece, one of the five best films of all time."[24] Subsequently *The King of Comedy* was ballyhooed as the opening-night film at the Cannes Film Festival. Yet as John Simon noted, there were persistent rumors that studio interference was "obliging the filmmakers to make the humor less black" (Simon 1983, 576). Industry insiders, *Village Voice* critic J. Hoberman observed, "know Lewis fans will hate the movie and they're afraid all the people who hate Lewis won't go near it" (Hoberman, 4).

Ironically, Scorsese's attempt to make a mainstream feature was backfiring. Few major studio releases by established directors received so much bad word-of-mouth in the industry. Reviews of *The King of Comedy* in the popular press were mixed but tended to the positive, and a few were ecstatic. But the trade press was uniformly grim and downbeat. The influential trade weekly *Variety* was typical. Its reviewer chastised *The King of Comedy* as "a royal disappointment," a film that was so "totally unsatisfying and bleakly cynical" that to say "hardly worth waiting for is too much praise."[25] Saluting the performances, *Variety* noted that this "off center teaming of director Martin Scorsese and star Robert De Niro" would enjoy some enthusiasm "in certain limited quarters," but that enthusiasm was unlikely to be shared by "the majority" (*Variety,* 1983, 18). The review castigated Scorsese for misunderstanding the comic genre and for ignoring the average moviegoer, constantly hammering at the idea that Scorsese the intellectual New York maverick could never connect with a middle American audience. *New York Daily News* columnist Marilyn Beck then viciously attacked *The King of Comedy* before the film even opened as "the most irresponsible film to hit the screen since Scorsese's *Taxi Driver* . . . perhaps potentially more dangerous than the 1976 film that reportedly served as an inspiration for John Hinckley, Jr.'s attempt on the life of President Reagan."[26]

These impassioned critiques fueled pessimism among exhibitors and set the stage for a slim box office return. Scorsese's New York black comedy quietly suffered the fate of Woody Allen's bittersweet Manhattan romantic comedies; in the words of one reviewer, "Outside of the Manhattan first-run ghetto where Scorsese is Favorite Son, audiences have been shunning his current *The King of Comedy* in droves" (Harvey, 44). Marilyn Beck, undoubtedly smarting from the bitter attack Scorsese and his associates mounted on her review in February because it predated the official release of *The King of Comedy,* was happy to pinpoint the commercial failure of the film and of Scorsese films in general; in her influential "The Big Screen Scene," she gleefully reported that "the weak business being recorded by Martin Scorsese's *The King of Comedy* is causing anything but joy. *Comedy* has done okay in a few large cities, but has absolutely bombed elsewhere—following the pattern of his earlier pictures. *Raging Bull,* for all its urban success and all the acclaim it received, was no big money maker, and even the much praised, much discussed *Taxi Driver,* despite its popularity in some major markets, turned in only a modest profit. As for *New York, New York,* it was an outright failure—everywhere."[27] Hollywood numbers-crunchers acted with precipitous speed. *The King of Comedy* was whisked off the silver screen almost as unceremoniously as Rupert Pupkin was carted from the Langford show to prison.

Howard Kissel, columnist for *Women's Wear Daily*, informed his readers that despite the "reasonably good reviews" for *The King of Comedy*, the lack of public response had Twentieth Century Fox "thinking of withdrawing it after only two weeks" (Kissel 1985, 24). Kissel then described a meeting between Scorsese and the distributors, during which the accountants explained to the filmmakers why the scant monies generated by the film and the lavish profit-participation deals involved in the project made further exhibition financially undesirable. When Scorsese asked that it be shown for a longer time at just one theater in Manhattan, Fox quickly retorted, "That might work if the picture had cost $5 million . . . but it wouldn't help at all for a film that, like *King,* had cost $15 million" (Kissel 1985, 24).

Scorsese was finding himself increasingly out of step with Hollywood. His return to New York City symbolized the distance between Tinseltown and his Manhattan base. All his personal projects with limited budgets were, industry pundits agreed, too small and specialized to attract large audiences. And now it seemed that his "big budget" feature *The King of Comedy* appealed to too small a segment of the population. Scorsese, it seemed, could never reign as king of cinema, because his act was too classy. Unlike Rupert, he couldn't be mediocre enough to succeed, and unlike Langford, he couldn't drain the life and humanity from his art in the name of professionalism and popularity. In February 1983 Hollywood was telling Scorsese he would always be a schmuck from the Lower East Side, no Rocky, no Luke Skywalker, and surely no Indiana Jones.

8

After Hours (1985) and *The Color of Money* (1986)

In February 1983, Martin Scorsese gave a soul-searching interview to
Janet Maslin of the *New York Times* in which he detailed his fears that
Hollywood was changing and his worries that dedication to his craft
was destroying his personal life. Impending middle age was, he confessed, changing his attitudes: "At 40, you do start to think about
things differently. I must say I can understand why people eventually
stop making pictures—because to make films in such an impassioned
way, you really have to believe in it, you've really got to want to tell
that story and after a while, you may find that life itself is more important than the filmmaking process. Maybe part of the answer for
what the hell we're doing here has to be in the process of living itself,
rather than in the work" (Maslin 1983, 23). Scorsese had, he acknowledged, one more tale he had to tell, so he ended the interview with a
reference to his departure the following Sunday "to look for new locations for the next picture" (Maslin 1983, 23).

That next picture was the *dream* project of his life, his adaptation of
Nikos Kazantzakis's 1954 novel *The Last Temptation of Christ*. Kazantzakis, a nonbeliever, had created controversy in Greece by limning
an untraditional story of the Messiah in demotic Greek. Scorsese
wanted to bring this populist existential Christ to the American people
in his modern guise, not as a comforting Hallmark-card Jesus, sure of
his powers, but as an unsettling, tortured Jesus, unsure whether his
inner voices are divine or demonic, and torn between his love of the
flesh and his need for the divine.

Kazantzakis, his translator Peter Bien admits, did not believe in any
traditional God; nor did he believe in a spiritual afterlife. Kazantzakis,

140

Bien observes, felt that this world would "somehow, through its own dematerialization, produce its own materialistic renewal in another cycle"; in his story of the Messiah, Bien argues, Kazantzakis attempted to assist our inevitable evolutionary transformation.[1] Kazantzakis, like the Catholic philosopher Teilhard de Chardin, envisions a God-who-is-to-be, born of humanity's ascent to the divine, and in his prologue to *The Last Temptation of Christ* identifies his Messiah's struggles with the mystic destiny of civilization: "Struggle between the flesh and the spirit, rebellion and resistance, reconciliation and submission, and finally—the supreme purpose of the struggle—union with God: this was the ascent taken by Christ, the ascent which he invites us to take as well, following in his bloody tracks."[2]

Kazantzakis's themes, the need for salvation and transformation, the struggle between flesh and spirit, and the choice between rebellion and reconciliation, parallel Scorsese's interests from *Mean Streets* through *Taxi Driver* to *Raging Bull*. No wonder, then, that Scorsese's classmates at NYU recommended the novel to him in 1960. But at that time the young cineast wasn't ready to tackle Kazantzakis. A decade later in 1972, on the set of *Boxcar Bertha*, Barbara Hershey, then the quintessential flower child, gave her copy of *The Last Temptation of Christ* to Scorsese, proclaiming him the director for an adaptation and herself the woman for the role of Mary Magdalene. Scorsese recalls that Hershey's gift haunted him for the rest of the 1970s: "It took me six years to finish it! I'd pick it up, put it down, reread it, be enveloped by the beautiful language of it" (Corliss 38). *The Last Temptation of Christ* was, Scorsese would tell interviewers, "the story I want to make more than any other. It's what I'm always trying to get at . . . at least, indirectly" (Blowen 1988, 31).

To realize his dream project, Scorsese turned to his trusted colleagues, actor Robert De Niro, scriptwriter Paul Schrader, production designer Boris Leven, and agent-counselor Harry Ufland. These principals agreed with Scorsese that his Kazantzakis adaptation would be "a small, personal, please-let-me-do-this type of film, one that nobody—or at least very few people would have seen," because religious movies "have a very limited audience" and are normally not "commercially viable."[3]

De Niro and Scorsese had been seeking another collaboration, and they traveled to Russia with their friend Michael Powell to develop an art film with the British director, only to see the project produced by Powell's colleague Frixos Constantine but directed by Emil Lotianou. In this curiosity piece, *Pavlova—A Woman for All Time* (1982),

Scorsese was drafted to impersonate Gatti-Cassaza, director of the Metropolitan Opera House, in a minor role. All the while Scorsese kept mulling over *The Last Temptation* project, doing research and preparing storyboards. Eventually Scorsese worked for more than 18 months on this first attempt to film *The Last Temptation of Christ.* As early as 14 April 1982, Ed Naha, in his "Screen Scoops," could announce that Schrader was working on a script and De Niro was committed to playing Christ.[4] Harry Ufland was flashing his trump card, the triumvirate of Schrader, Scorsese, and De Niro, the progenitors of *Taxi Driver* and *Raging Bull,* all over town, trying to flush out willing gamblers.

The more De Niro explored characterizations of the savior, the less he liked the prospect of incarnating Christ Almighty and the more tepid his enthusiasm became. De Niro finally withdrew from *Last Temptation,* though he did not abandon his friend. As De Niro recalls his discussions with the director, he told Scorsese that "I just couldn't relate to it. People have so many preconceived ideas about Jesus, myself included, that I didn't want to bother"; aware, however, that this religious epic was "Marty's trip" and might need some aggressive promoting, De Niro did make a concession: "I told Marty, if he had trouble getting it off the ground and if he really wanted me to do it, I would've done it. It was something I was telling him as a friend; if he needed me, I was there—but if I had my choice, I wouldn't do it" (Paris, 32). Scorsese never took his friend up on the offer, though many observers agree with Richard Gehr that De Niro's "passion and anger" could have "realized the project's inherent power" and created a movie that religious extremists "might *really* have crucified Martin Scorsese for directing."[5]

Paul Schrader, unlike De Niro, found himself more committed to *Last Temptation* with each revision of the script. Schrader and Scorsese saw this version of Christ's life as the culmination of their trilogy of works together; false saints like Travis Bickle and mystic heroes like Jake La Motta, they were sure, pointed the treacherous path to Golgotha. As always on a Scorsese project, endless reshapings reflected frequent shifts in emphasis. Nevertheless, Scorsese consistently told co-workers how much he admired Schrader's ability to condense a long, lyric, philosophical novel into a crisp, poetic scenario of fewer than 100 pages, while maintaining all its concepts and sustaining its emotions. Scorsese praised Schrader's script as one of the best ever written and made no secret of his desire to bring it to the screen as faithfully as possible.

Schrader's earliest drafts indicate his espousal of American vernacular as a parallel to Kazantzakis's demotic Greek. His Christ would have none of the rhetorical grandeur of the King James Bible. Indeed, in some scenes it's hard to tell Schrader's Jerusalem from the mean streets of Little Italy or the avenues of Bay Ridge, Brooklyn. Consider, for example, Schrader's vision of the apostles John and Judas discussing the prophets:

> John: "Isaiah knew right from wrong. How long ago did he live?"
> Judas: "I don't know. Before Jeremiah."
> John: "No, Jeremiah was before Ezekiel."
> Judas: "Get off it."
>   (*to Peter*)
> Peter (shrugs): "Beats me."
> Jesus (thinks): "I'm not sure."[6]

This realistic slice of life emphasizes Christ's humanity and fallibility as it defines the social status of his disciples. Like Pasolini in his *The Gospel According to Matthew,* Schrader and Scorsese focus on the impoverished classes that support Christ and the agrarian–peasant–revolutionary bias of his crusade. Their savior comes from crowded backstreets. His mantle is dusty, his gait often weary, and his message frequently hard to hear and contradictory. His ministry terrifies and confounds.

Like Pasolini, Schrader focuses on the literal level of Christ's miracles. His drafts for *Last Temptation* contain one overpowering scene of Christ and his sacred heart, a motif much adored by pious and evangelical Catholics. As envisioned by Schrader, his Christ "reaches into his chest and pulls out his own bloody heart. He offers it at arm's length to the disciples. Blood drips from the ventricles" (Schrader 1982, 45). This blood symbolism prepares audiences for Schrader's literal presentation of the transubstantiation of Christ's body and blood at the Last Supper. In Schrader's conception the Eucharistic Offering was physically real. Christ offers his apostles actual flesh and blood in Schrader's version of the first Communion: "As they do [eat the bread], the bread and wine transubstantiate into flesh and blood in their mouths. Peter is the first to cough up the bloody flesh. The others, sickened, follow. They wipe their bloody mouths" (Schrader 1982, 73). Agape here is as real as it is symbolic; charity and the body of Christ are commingled.

Similarly, Schrader feels compelled to make Christ's earthly temptations real seductions of the flesh. Schrader's early drafts for *Last Temptation*—some of which were pilfered and copied by religious zealots opposed to any revisionist treatment of Christ's life—emphasize sexuality as the demonic alternative to sanctity. Schrader's savior is mesmerized by the lustful snake of concupiscence and struggles to divine its meaning. In a key voiceover the troubled Messiah muses on a vision of two snakes copulating: "So this is sex. Men and women coupling. This is why they were thrown out of Paradise (watches the snakes). But everything is of God. And everything has two meanings, one obvious, one hidden. What are they telling me?" (Schrader 1982, 82). The dance of the snakes fuses in Christ's consciousness with the allures of Mary Magdalene. In Schrader's most controversial sequence, Christ identifies erotic fulfillment with the ineffably sacred:

> Jesus: I never knew the world was so beautiful. I was blind. (Kisses Mary's breasts again) I didn't know that the body was so holy. But now I understand.
> Magdalene: Understand what?
> Jesus: That this is the road.
> Magdalene: What road?
> Jesus: The road on which the mortal becomes immortal; God becomes human. I was so stupid: I tried to find a way outside my own flesh. I wanted clouds, great ideas, death. But now I know: A woman is God's greatest work. And I worship you. God sleeps between your legs. (Schrader 1982, 81–82)

These words come during the dream or fantasy of the last temptation, an alternate reality eventually rejected and repented by Christ, yet they do crystallize the main elements Scorsese and Schrader emphasize in their conception of the film—the warring worlds of the flesh and the spirit in which humanity strives to achieve salvation. Their Christ struggling to link humanity and divinity mirrors the modern quest to reconcile knowledge with faith, science with tradition, sexuality with transcendence, responsibility with freedom.

Somber themes like these philosophical tangles, scenes the unsympathetic might view as blasphemous, and the prospect of an oversize budget for a spectacle appealing to select audiences made *The Last Temptation of Christ* a hard sell. So Harry Ufland, who had been Scorsese's agent since he first saw the director's short films at NYU, spent months searching for backers. Support finally came from the unlikeliest of quarters, the three most powerful men at Paramount Pictures: Barry Diller, Michael Eisner, and Jeff Katzenberg. Ufland found himself faced with the ungodly task of placating this unholy trinity so that Scorsese could promulgate his iconoclastic gospel. Unfortunately, the deal turned out to be less than heavenly; there was a good bit of hellfire for everyone involved, right around the corner.

Initially, however, everything seemed propitious, and Scorsese cast Aidan Quinn as Jesus and Harvey Keitel as Judas. As they developed their characterizations, Scorsese delegated Boris Leven, his production designer on *New York, New York*, *The Last Waltz*, and *The King of Comedy*, to scout locations for the film in Morocco and Israel. Leven's sketches inspired Scorsese, and Scorsese developed drawings covering more than two-thirds of Schrader's script. Costumes were purchased, arrangements for accommodating cast and crew were set, and actual shooting was less than one month away when Paramount pulled the plug. With more than $4 million already spent, the Paramount production was shuttered and the costumes sold to the crew making *King David*.

To understand the demise of this Scorsese project is to discover the realities of 1980s Hollywood. Paramount Pictures formed but a small part of the Gulf and Western conglomerate. So long as Paramount Pictures showed a profit and contributed to the public profile of Gulf and Western Industries, everything was grand. But *The Last Temptation of Christ* proved suspect on both counts. Accountants questioned whether a $14 million religious spectacle based on a cerebral novel by a Greek atheist could produce an adequate return on investment. Meanwhile public relations experts queried whether a film that might offend potential customers for other Gulf and Western products promoted the "synergy" Gulf and Western desired among its operations. The filmmakers and the producers were buffeted by the larger concerns of the conglomerate; decisions were reversed, reaffirmed, modified, reapproved, and then revised.

Scorsese finds his metaphor for these months of heartbreaking tension and negotiation in the novels of Kafka, especially *The Trial*. His situation, he explained to Paul Attanasio, was much the same as Joseph K's predicament in Orson Welles's film version of Kafka's *The Trial*. Every day Welles's Joseph K is told of the judge's interest in his case, and every day he is then disappointed to hear the same words, "You'll have to wait." Scorsese remembers a similar fate: "That's the way it was trying to make this film. Katzenberg would tell me, 'Listen, Marty, I just want you to know, Michael Eisner really wants this film made.' And then a week later, Eisner would say, 'Katzenberg is the one who's really behind this picture.' And then I'd hear, 'Barry Diller is really behind you on this point. He wants this picture finished, he wants it done' and then I'd hear, 'The *only friend you have here* is Michael Eisner.' Every day, every half hour, it would change" (Attanasio, 1). Scorsese kept open reservations on every plane to Israel, as he played the waiting, dealmaking, more waiting, more dealmaking games of the conglomerate.

There were budgeting problems on Paramount's *Last Temptation,* and delays exacerbated them. Big film budgets, Scorsese discovered, were like avalanches; although they're slow to start, once they're moving they gather momentum at a dazzling speed. Sporting the Paramount logo on equipment meant, Scorsese quipped, that with every setup on location, "it costs $500 just to turn your head" (Farber, 35). Gradually the projected cost for *Last Temptation* rose from $12 million to $16 million, and producer Irwin Winkler requested provision for an additional 10 days of shooting. That request, which Scorsese subsequently admitted was unnecessary, sealed the film's fate. Studio executives, alarmed at a project based on the other side of the world, out of their ken and control, stampeded to shut the project down, even as a dieting Aidan Quinn was flying to the Holy Land ready to begin work. Scorsese's later offer to cut the budget to $7 million and to cut shooting time to 60 days couldn't resurrect the project; Paramount would perform no Lazarus-like miracles.

Budgeting quagmires were accompanied by pressure from fundamentalist religious groups. The America Family Association, based in Tupelo, Mississippi, initiated a letter-writing campaign against *The Last Temptation,* thereby igniting much of the Moral Majority to take further action. Martin Davis, chairman of Gulf and Western Industries, was disturbed by the turmoil and saw little reason to jeopardize the company's good name for such a small project.

The fundamentalists rallied their forces with the patently false assertion that Scorsese intended to portray Jesus as a homosexual. Ill-informed or not, the campaign was potent, as Scorsese informed Gene Siskel: "I can't overestimate the effect of the fundamentalist protest, because when we began scrambling to find other funding, the same sort of letters from the Moral Majority began showing up on the desks of whomever we talked to. I think we dealt with 26 people between Thanksgiving and Christmas, and a number of them said, 'We like the script, but we can't touch this picture.' It was almost like we were being blacklisted" (Siskel, 7). Harry Ufland later reported that the death knell in America came when a major theater circuit owner, who also owned several cable systems, encouraged exhibitors to refuse to show any such film and informed Home Box Office he would refuse to televise this film if they bought it (Litwak, 106). Ufland continued championing the project around the world and interested Jack Lang, minister of culture for France, in the possibility of government funding for Scorsese. French clerics intervened, and the prospect disappeared.

Scorsese, emotionally and physically devastated by the abortion of his cinematic child, told journalists, "It was as if someone had died."[7] And while he tried to find some consolation, speculating that God had been with him on the project and "was trying to tell me I just wasn't ready" (Grogan, 42), the director spent his free time in parleys with old friends, searching for a new career. At lunch with director Brian De Palma, Scorsese morosely weighed his limited employment prospects. After rejecting college teaching because of the abysmally low pay and complete lack of status, Scorsese realized that "there doesn't seem to be anything else I can do. I can't write novels. I could write scripts, but I'd only want to direct them" (Holdenfield 1989, 49). Reinvigorated by his discovery of the inevitability of his vocation, the middle-aged director went out seeking projects. The indefatigable Scorsese was on the comeback trail.

Scorsese had clear criteria for his next undertaking. First and foremost, the budget had to be limited. Stung by his experiences with behemoth productions on *The King of Comedy* and the canceled *Last Temptation,* he told his friends that "if you want to do something unique today, you have to do it cheaply" (Orth, 110). Scorsese's declaration ran counter to Hollywood's axiom that small films were for small talents and that every production must be a blockbuster.

Scorsese also wanted to find a script where the focus was on people and not on special effects. His domain was the soul and not the solar system, the torment of Jake La Motta and not the ecstasy of Rocky, the claustrophobic streets of New York and not Indiana Jones's temples. Scorsese was pained by the omnipresence of blue-screen special effects. Summarizing the opinions of the so-called New York school of independent filmmakers, Scorsese told David Pirie that "We all seem to be agreed that making something like *Star Wars* is a murderous experience: with the use of blue screen as an effects background you can't even have people move an inch while they're talking, so even shooting a simple dialogue scene becomes impossibly tedious. This is one reason why all of us are so involved in finding ways of simplifying, ways of making films faster and cheaper" ("Confessions," 139). Scorsese wanted to get his cameras back on location, use the crane and dolly, create chases in real space and time, improvise, capture the human dynamic, and convey his emotions, his dilemmas, his life through his characters. Working with a limited budget challenged him, Scorsese told James Truman, to find out "what I have to express" and was "almost like playing at being one of the studio directors of the Thirties and Forties and Fifties, who were given a certain kind of film to make, and they had to do it" (Truman, 80). Scorsese was challenging himself to be auteur, an artist who shapes productions to reflect his concerns, his core of themes, as he imposes his signature on the film in its mise-en-scène.

Scorsese found the vehicle for his aspirations in a project being promoted under the title "A Night in Soho" but eventually released as *After Hours*. Scorsese's lawyer Jay Julien brought him the proposal from the Double Play Company, an independent production group headed by actor Griffin Dunne and actress Amy Robinson, who played Teresa in *Mean Streets*. Double Play specialized in contemporary romances like *Chilly Scenes of Winter* (1979) and *Baby, It's You* (1983)—both small, literate productions aimed at sophisticated urban audiences. "A Night in Soho" had been written by Joseph Minion as a class assignment at Columbia University, and this dark comedy— parodying both Orson Welles's film noir detective stories, *Touch of Evil* (1958) and *The Lady from Shanghai* (1948), and Alfred Hitchcock's misogynistic romances, *Marnie* (1964), *Rear Window* (1954), and *The Birds* (1963)—was championed by the instructor, Dusan Makavejev. Makavejev, smitten by Minion's perverse humor and clever plotting, carried the student script to Robert Redford's Sundance Institute, where he happened on Amy Robinson and consummated a production deal. Originally the plans called for a budget of $3.5 million, but when Scorsese entered the package, David Geffen signed on as coproducer with the proviso that an additional $1 million be available to facilitate speedy completion.

Like many independent productions, *After Hours* was financed by a bank loan on the promise of an eventual studio distribution pact. This arrangement made it possible, Stephen Farber notes, for Scorsese to use a New York based NABET crew "rather than a more expensive

Martin Scorsese and Griffin Dunne work on the interpretation of the script for *After Hours* (1985). The Geffen Film Company. The Museum of Modern Art/Film Stills Archive.

IA crew" (Farber, 35). The cast took diminished salaries in exchange for increased participation in the profits.

Scorsese committed himself to an eight-week shooting schedule, with more than a dozen setups every day; on *The King of Comedy* he had managed only four or five setups a day. To speed things up, Scorsese worked closely with cinematographer Michael Ballhaus, who in 10 collaborations with Rainer Werner Fassbinder in Germany had established himself as a master of improvisation, a magician with high-speed film stocks, and a virtuoso in elliptic narrative modes. Ballhaus's ability to create the new European images rivaled Scorsese's memory for classic American shots; together they fused the finest of the old traditions with the best of the new. Ballhaus revivified Scorsese's career, giving him a new lens on reality and assisting him in rethinking his visual strategies. Scorsese helped Ballhaus understand the American scene, but Ballhaus brought Scorsese up-to-date on all the camera tricks of Europe's Second Wave, the gifted progeny of France's New Wave.

Like these European auteurs, Scorsese expanded the text of *After Hours* into a complex cinematic creation, a skillful combination of an autobiographical essay, philosophical tract, and social commentary disguised as a manic, slapstick sitcom. *After Hours* draws heavily on the heritage of the Keystone Cops and Charlie Chaplin, with its marauding vigilantes, bumbling burglars, and inept but lovable hero. Yet the film also echoes the bleak defiance of Beckett in its frustrated performance artists, the absurd terror of Ionesco in its victimized women and their tortured psyches, and the claustrophobic humor of Pinter in its sly semantic confusions and misunderstandings. The uptown, computerized, antiseptic locales of *After Hours* owe much to David Hockney, while the downtown, visceral, tribal environs of the film are linked by careful allusion to the universe of Edvard Munch's *The Scream. After Hours* is also suffused with the specifically Catholic angst and ennui of James Joyce. Scorsese's comedic homage to Joyce's *Ulysses* propels its Bloom, Paul Hackett (Griffin Dunne), to a Night Town cursed by a sad chorus of "no . . . no . . . no," not Molly's orgasmic "yes . . . yes . . . yes."

Yuppie Hackett, a frustrated skirt-chaser, pursues his Marcy (Rosanna Arquette) through Soho, only to discover her grief and witness her suicide; the rest of his journey leads to further confrontations with other unbalanced women, such as Kiki (Linda Fiorentino), Julie (Teri Garr), and June (Verna Bloom). Nothing Hackett does can effect an escape. Only when he is completely encased in bandages, immobilized and virtually entombed, objectified and kidnapped, does chance intervene and propel him back to another imprisonment, a job he abhors. The film concludes, ironically, at dawn, with Hackett confronting a "Good Morning" on his computer monitor but the greeting merely reemphasizes the horrors that await him uptown and downtown.

In his remarks on *After Hours,* Scorsese highlighted the affinities he felt for the beleaguered Paul Hackett. Right before shooting began Scorsese himself had moved from an apartment on Fifty-seventh Street (the beginning of Hackett's cab ride) to a loft in Tribeca (similar to Marcy's pad), and the transplanted director shared Hackett's disorientation and alienation from the new bohemia downtown. Scorsese's identification with Hackett also had to do with personal relationships and loneliness. Hackett, a seemingly rational, sensitive, "nice" man, cannot connect with others; his efforts to relate to women especially end in catastrophe. This facet of the script fascinated the thrice-divorced Scorsese, who was once again working on a serious relationship, this one with Barbara De Fina, an experienced hand at independent filmmaking. Eventually the two would wed, and she would serve as the producer on his future films. When he made *After Hours,* Scorsese was preparing to share his life with De Fina and saw the project, he told Maureen Orth, as "really a self-examination I'm trying to do, and the only way I know how to do it is on film. I seem to be trying to analyze the negative. It's dangerous. The people around you may not survive, relationships may break up, but maybe you remain alive. In a sense it gets down to a very religious idea, which is salvation. How do we redeem ourselves?" (Orth, 102).

No one who knew Scorsese could miss the self-examination in *After Hours,* having heard Paul Hackett's touching reminiscence about having his tonsils out: "When I was a kid, I had my tonsils out. Didn't have enough room in the hospital, so they put me in the burn ward. The nurse warned me not to take the blindfold off or the operation would have to be done over. I took the blindfold off and I saw—." Paul's story is interrupted, and he cannot use his fable to explore Marcy's fixation with burn imagery. Scorsese's childhood tonsillectomy became the source of the symbolic wound in his films, and Scorsese's reaction to his surgery was complicated by the lies his mother told him beforehand. Catherine Scorsese prepared the timid Martin by promising him he was going to a wonderful circus. Even after decades of therapy, Scorsese cannot forgive her; her deceit marked his first encounter with human duplicity and feminine wiles, and provided him a terrifying glimpse into the heart of darkness.

In *After Hours* Scorsese weaves his imagery of hurt and betrayal into a tapestry with Joseph Minion's own well-developed images of pain and evil, the scars from serious burns. Minion grounds Marcy's character in her burns, real and imagined, and her predilection for matches and candles. In Minion's script Marcy shies away from anything hot and brings burn ointment home from the drugstore, leaving it where Paul will see it. She later seduces him with her seminude body, flashing her inner thigh in such a way that to Paul "it appears to be covered with scars."[8] As they become intimate, she recounts a brutal, six-hour-long rape ordeal, only to change the mood inexplicably by asserting half-jokingly that the rapist was her boyfriend and that she "slept through most of it" (Minion, 27). Later when Paul explores her bookshelves, he finds a medical textbook on burns with "graphic, hideous photographs of human third degree burn victims" (Minion, 34).

Paul is so mesmerized by the aura of suffering and scarring Marcy projects that when he finds her corpse after her suicide, he compulsively strips it, looking for the nonexistent scars. Audiences attuned

Paul Hackett (Griffin Dunne) massages sculptress Kiki (Linda Florentino) in *After Hours* (1985). The Geffen Film Company. The Museum of Modern Art/Film Stills Archive.

to Scorsese's methods will recall the nurse's injunction not to take the blindfold off and will recognize that Paul Hackett has just been privy to a secret he is far too naive to comprehend. This pattern of discoveries and unveilings too personal and complex for Paul to fully appreciate is repeated in his encounters with women in Soho. It is, after all, *after hours,* and new rules apply. Paul wants to grapple with naked bodies; instead, he must wrestle with exposed souls.

Scorsese viewed the courtship calamities in *After Hours* as both comic and tragic. If Paul Hackett's ordeal smacks of the buffoonery of a Punch and Judy show, it also mirrors some of the most unsettling phenomena in America, the dislocations that result from a redefinition of sex roles. Raised as an Italian Catholic male, Scorsese never denies his puzzlement about women; in the words of the old streetcorner canard, his alter ego protagonists "can't live with them and can't live without them." Paul Hackett's bewilderment, Scorsese told journalists, mirrors his own confusion: "I identify with the character in many ways. It's the everyday anxieties that a man goes through, especially in dealing with women and dealing with the proximity of sexual encounter. If, let's say, you've been married and you get a divorce, and you're gonna start seeing women again. You go on a date—it's hard! It's not easy! You have dinner with them, you talk, you look, and the flirting goes on, and then, oh, my God, what about performance? What about sexual performance? Whaddaya gonna do? It's terrifying, it's absolutely terrifying" (Attanasio, 2). Hackett's encounters mine the terror in comically grotesque ways. The women he meets challenge his definitions of masculinity and undercut his confidence. Kiki, for example, wants the discipline of bondage and role-playing, not his intimacy and honesty. Julie the barmaid seems immured in a world of the Monkees and mousetraps; her dementia threatens the order of his universe. Gail, an inveterate practical joker, looses armies of gay vigilantes against him, while the more mature June subtly ensnares him and transforms him into a living sculpture.

Scorsese's war of the sexes inflicts losses on both men and women; its internecine struggles hold but Pyrrhic victories. Linda Fiorentino, who plays Kiki, shared an illuminating anecdote about working with Scorsese on *After Hours* with London *Times* regular Karin Moline: "But this day we were shooting a scene where I'm tied up on the floor, and I was really nervous because Marty's parents were on the set and I was wearing a see-through shirt and was a little embarrassed. So we're lining up the shot and I'm lying on my side and Marty says he wants me to meet someone. I look up and it's Brian De Palma. Brian bends down and shakes my little finger and says, 'I love the way Marty dresses his women'" (Moline, 3). The elements here define Scorsese's sexual universe. His parents, symbolic of the restraint of Little Italy and the sanctions of the Roman Catholic church, have always been uneasy about the nudity in Scorsese's films; this day they were the guests of the mature producer Amy Robinson, who had upset them grievously years before with her full frontal nudity in the lovemaking sequences in *Mean Streets*. Brian De Palma, on the other hand, represents the New York University heritage of grainy, gritty, confessional, priapic cinema. Between the elderly, courtly, Old World Scorseses and the cosmopolitan De Palma lies an iconic feminine form, brazenly exhibitionist, assertively sensuous, yet cruelly pinioned in a quest for greater discipline. Across the set stands the fictional Paul Hackett, titillated by Kiki's carnality yet disturbed by her flagrant kinkiness. Looming above the scene, riding his infamous crane, director Scorsese labors to shape enduring art from all these chaotic, contradictory impulses, seeking a balance between tradition and change, guilt and liberation, responsibility and freedom, as he painstakingly explores the terrain of his loves and lusts.

Scorsese, fascinated by the veritable maze of Hackett's quest for female companionship, warned reviewers that there was no escape for his stranger in a strange land. The principal idea in *After Hours,* Scorsese laughingly told James Truman, concerned the answer to Hackett's final lament—Hackett moans that "All I wanted to do was go out with a girl and have a nice time. Do I have to die for it?" The answer the film provides, Scorsese asserted, is an emphatic *yes,* and this paradox drew him to the project: "That fascinated me, the idea of not giving this guy anywhere to go. And the concept of him being decent—the more decent he was the more trouble he got in. It was like a silly little morality play" (Truman, 80). Joseph Minion's script made the beleaguered Hackett sound like Jake La Motta confronting his devils in solitary confinement: "You know—I just came downtown to get laid and now all these people wanna kill me—Maybe I, maybe I deserve it. Maybe I deserve to die, I don't know—They could be right—I don't know" (Minion, 94).

Scorsese, riddled with a similar guilt, embraces *After Hours* as the only one of his films he can watch: "It's because Griffith acts out all my reactions. He tries to be decent about all the things that happen to him. He's really an Everyman moving through this netherworld, being morally put through his paces. This poor guy acts it out for me—to watch him squirm in and out of all these situations is therapeutic" (Kissel 1985, 24). *After Hours* proved equally therapeutic to Scorsese's career. As he was making his feature, Scorsese realized that his chronicle of Griffith's nightmarish adventures was a surrealistic "reaction against my year and a half in Hollywood trying to get *The Last Temptation of Christ* made" (Fein, 1), right down to the lingering shot of Hackett studying graffito envisioning a man's penis being swallowed by the shark from *Jaws,* a not-too-subtle projection of Scorsese's fears of being castrated by the blockbuster mentality. Scorsese couldn't help but feel potent as an artist when *After Hours* garnered him the Cannes Film Festival's accolades as the year's best director, when reviewers like Andrew Sarris proclaimed that *After Hours* marked Scorsese as "the most talented of his generation's non-mainstream filmmakers,"[9] and when trade papers like *Variety* conceded that this low-budget comedy "will be a must for serious-minded filmgoers and stands as one of the quality entries of the fall season."[10] Scorsese had demonstrated his ability to work quickly, to get every dollar up there on the screen, and to garner attention for a small film.

As usual, the completion of a feature propelled Scorsese toward a respite in a shorter work, a casual entr'acte, so when Steven Spielberg approached him with an offer to do a television episode as part of his "Amazing Stories" series on NBC, Scorsese accepted. "Mirror, Mirror," Scorsese's half-hour project, based on a short story idea of Spielberg's and scripted by the author of *After Hours,* Joseph Minion, is similar to Scorsese's NYU short, *What's a Nice Girl like You Doing in a Place like This?* (1963). Sam Waterson plays Jordan, a popular horror-fiction author modeled on Steven King, who appears on the "Dick Cavett Show" proclaiming his freedom from fears and marveling at his audience's credulity. Soon thereafter Jordan begins to see a phantom (Tim Robbins) reflected in windows, glasses, and mirrors. Overwhelmed, Jordan eventually becomes the phantom and leaps from a window.

Scorsese has categorized this television enterprise as nothing but a vignette about paranoia, but it did capture the attention of reviewers. Ed Siegel of the *Boston Globe,* for example, lauded "Mirror, Mirror" as the "most creative outing" in Spielberg's series and saluted Scorsese as "the country's most creative director."[11] Siegel and other reviewers praised Scorsese for his willingness to create an open-ended story. As Siegel noted, there are many possible questions about Jordan's fate: "Is he a victim of his narcissism? His isolation? His imagination, more fetid than fervid? Are his visitations a reverse-Scrooge curse of God for exploiting the masses? Is the 'House of Wax' phantom a reminder of horror films that didn't rely on massive bloodletting for terror? Or is he succumbing to the urban paranoia that plagues the antiheroes of Scorsese's *After Hours* and *Taxi Driver?*" (Siegel, 16) The answers reside in the show itself, which contains these themes and more, including the death-dealing nature of mass media and celebrity, the difficulty in maintaining a marriage, and the snares of materialism.

Scorsese worked six days on "Mirror, Mirror," twice the usual time for an episode, contriving unusual camera movements to evoke Jordan's mental imbalance. Scorsese frames all his interior shots to emphasize the sterility of high-tech decor, making Jordan's success just as cold as Jerry Langford's in *The King of Comedy.* Scorsese eventually regretted all this labor because, he complained to Peter Biskind when NBC aired the show on 9 March 1986, "the network neglected to tell anyone it was on"[12] so "Mirror, Mirror" never got the audience it deserved.

Scorsese's appearance as an actor in Bertrand Tavernier's *Round Midnight* (1986) also suffered from audience neglect. Tavernier overestimated the American popular audience's interest in jazz, and despite stellar contributions from saxophone legend Dexter Gordon and musical direction by Herbie Hancock, this backstage tour of the postwar music scene, inspired by the lives of Bud Powell and Lester Young, failed at the box office. Scorsese had met fellow film buff Tavernier in Paris at lunch with producer Irwin Winkler, and the two directors discussed the possibility of jointly filming a documentary on the legendary Winkler's career as producer. The French Tavernier, impressed by Scorsese's New York accent and his staccato speech patterns, saw that the American director would be perfect to play Goodley, the fast-talking manager of New York's famed jazz emporium Birdland, in *Round Midnight*. Scorsese, who like Alfred Hitchcock, had a habit of playing small roles in his features, including a recent turn as a spotlight operator in *After Hours,* was daunted by Tavernier's offer of a larger role, yet he acceded to the request. His days as an actor, Scorsese later recalled, were mortifying: "Oh, it was terrifying. I felt like I was too heavy—a little bald—I talk so fast people laugh at me. So I find it embarrassing. I find it humiliating. I did it as a favor for Bertrand Tavernier. It was an honor to be in it, but I feel bad about it. I feel people are laughing at me" (Ansen 1987, 51).

Scorsese's next film centered on performances by two of Hollywood's leading male stars: the elder statesman of sincerity and suavity, the sixtyish Paul Newman, and the "top gun" among the young Turks, the prince of brashness and boyish twentysomething charm, Tom Cruise. Newman initiated the project when he telephoned Scorsese, in the fall of 1984 and asked him what he thought about Eddie Felson, a question part trivia quiz and part proposition. Twenty-five years earlier Newman had played Fast Eddie in Robert Rossen's classic *The Hustler.* Walter Trevis had since published a sequel, and Newman's lawyer, Irving Axelrod, who would eventually coproduce the film with Barbara De Fina, was urging his client to pick up the cue stick again.

Newman proved easy to convince. He told the *New York Time's* columnist Myra Forsberg that he wanted to do the project as soon as he read *The Color of Money* because Trevis's prose "reminded me that Eddie wasn't completed at the end of the first film like some other people I had played."[13] For his work in *The Hustler* Newman had been nominated for an Oscar for Best Actor, but as so often happened to him, he didn't win. His lack of an Oscar stirred a controversy in Hollywood, since the age of 60 wasn't normally the best time for actors to garner awards. Newman had been nominated for *Cool Hand Luke* (1967), *Hud* (1963), *Absence of Malice* (1981), and *The Verdict* (1982), but his fireplace mantel remained bare of statuettes. Academy members, concerned with both the oversight and Newman's advancing years, awarded him a special Oscar for "memorable and compelling screen performances, for personal integrity, and dedication to craft." When Newman called Scorsese, however, he had the Best Actor Oscar in mind; he had recently screened *Raging Bull* and marveled at De Niro's performance, and he also recalled the Oscar that fellow Actors' Studio veteran Ellen Burstyn had won for *Alice Doesn't Live Here Anymore*. Newman, the old pro, knew that Fast Eddie Felson was a Cadillac of a role and that Scorsese could drive him to an Oscar.

Scorsese had little interest in making sequels, but the relished the notion of working with one of Hollywood's legends; Scorsese, an avid Newman fan, even revered *The Silver Chalice,* a work Newman disavowed. Scorsese also admitted he wanted to know more about the fate of the hustler: "Most movie characters you don't care what happens to them after the movie ends, but I was always fascinated by that guy Eddie Felson in *The Hustler*. Fast Eddie, a great pool hustler. He's self-destructive. He says too much; he takes an extra drink. I thought there were more stories in that guy."[14]

Problems arose, however, when Newman and Scorsese sought an Eddie Felson story to pursue. Two scripts were already available, one by Walter Travis and the other by Darryl Ponicsan. Newman owned the options to these materials and to the novel *The Color of Money,* but Scorsese wanted to spin his own Fast Eddie yarn, an independent narrative inspired by the original, true to its characters and themes, but markedly modern. To pursue his ideas, Scorsese solicited the assistance of novelist Richard Price, who had made a reputation among insiders for his works *Bloodbrothers,* filmed by Robert Mulligan in 1978, and *The Wanderers,* directed by Philip Kaufman in 1979.

Price and Scorsese flew to California to convince Newman of the need for an original script, free of flashbacks to the earlier film and of awkward allusions. The pair's meeting with Newman in February

1985 proved disconcerting. Scorsese recalls that the pale-skinned New Yorkers felt like vampires at noon when the tanned Newman strode onto a porch overlooking the beach at Malibu. Newman's casual conversation about the giants he had worked with, including "Gadge" (Elia Kazan) and "Tennessee" (Williams), reminded Scorsese of how huge the gap in generations was. Newman's roots went deep into the old Hollywood; Scorsese, even after 20 years in the business, remained the fledgling outsider.

Novelist Price later reconstructed their initial parley about *The Color of Money* as a minimalist scene in a Jim Jarmusch film: "We were in Malibu—me and Marty Scorsese—the two New York guys on the beach. Marty's sitting there with his jacket and his nasal spray and I was smoking a cigarette, hunched over coughing. And then Newman comes out, all tanned up, Mr. Sea and Ski, eating a grapefruit. It was like something out of *Stranger than Paradise*" (Forsberg, 21). The grapefruit led Newman to rhapsodize about the Israeli melon he had had for breakfast, and this gourmet chatter disarmed the tough guys from the Bronx and Little Italy. Scorsese, sweating in his blue blazer and uncomfortable in dark sunglasses, felt, he told David Ansen, that he and Price were "two New York scuzzballs," "two New York Lower East Side–type guys," allowed to glimpse a world they could not enter and to relish "a sensuality [of which] we have no idea."[15] For the moment Newman's hustle had worked.

The rowdies from the East nevertheless convinced their svelte host that a new plot must be developed, and in one afternoon they extemporized a central concept and a rough treatment for Price to flesh out. Price had little idea what he was getting into. Over the next 10 months, he estimated for columnist Bruce Cook, he wrote more than 1,000 pages of draft script, met with Paul Newman three dozen times, and saw Scorsese even more frequently; the project became so burdensome that it filled Price's dreams: "I had a vision of myself spending the rest of my life rewriting *The Color of Money*. I'd get gray. My child would grow up and go off to college, and still I'd be doing revisions."[16] Then Newman insisted on a month's rehearsal before the shooting so they could refine their lines, and Scorsese agreed because he hoped to cut expenses by having every detail prepared before production began in Chicago in January 1986.

Despite the fact that Paul Newman lured Tom Cruise, an eminently bankable young star, into the deal, finding a studio to underwrite the project proved arduous. Scorsese first took the package to Twentieth Century-Fox and received an enthusiastic response from Sherry Lansing, then a vice-president. When Lansing left Fox—one small switch in Hollywood's nonstop game of musical chairs, titles, and executives—Fox rejected *The Color of Money.* So it was off to Columbia, where Guy McElwaine promoted the package. When McElwaine left Columbia, that studio ended further negotiations. Meanwhile Paul Newman carried the offer to Touchstone Pictures, a branch of Disney Productions, and Touchstone approved it, though with a parsimonious budget and onerous production controls. Scorsese and Newman both had to defer substantial portions of their salaries as guarantees the film would be completed within budget projections.

The backing from Touchstone was not without its ironies for Scorsese. Disgruntled Paramount executives who fled that studio formed the core of Disney's reorganized staff. Michael Eisner from Paramount emerged as head of the Walt Disney Company. His assistant at Paramount, Jeffrey Katzenberg, now headed Disney's television and movie operations. As a result of this shuffling, Scorsese bemusedly noted for Michael Blowen, he "ended up making [*The Color of Money*] for the same people who cancelled *The Last Temptation of Christ*" (Blowen 1988, 97). Hollywood in the 1980s for Scorsese was Kafka with a Hitchcock twist. While Scorsese jested with friends that the only picture he would ever make again with Disney was *Bambi Does Dallas,* the press agents at Disney assured the world that, like most of Touchstone's talent, Scorsese had signed a two-year, multipicture pact. The widely circulated press release quoted Scorsese as saying, "I'd like to run a gamut of small dramatic pictures and even family pictures—I don't know—maybe even animation."[17] For all this hype, a cartoon by Scorsese remains an unlikely prospect, as does a "family" picture.

Touchstone did have the good sense to allow Scorsese, Newman, Price, and Cruise to film *The Color of Money* much as they had planned. For a mainstream Hollywood production, it bears the unmistakable stamp of the individuals who worked on it, especially Scorsese. From his first, uncredited voiceover—a device he employed in *Who's That Knocking* and *Mean Streets*—Scorsese shades the meaning of the film, shifting the focus from the game of nine ball to the psychology of his characters and their moral dilemmas. *The Color of Money* in Scorsese's hands proves as autobiographical as *Mean Streets,* as focused on expiation and redemption as *Raging Bull,* as taut and explosive as *Taxi Driver,* and as philosophically bemusing as *After Hours.*

"Nine-ball is a rotation game," Scorsese solemnly intones in his title sequence, and "that is to say luck plays a part in nine-ball, but for some players, luck itself is an art." *The Color of Money,* a sizzling collaboration of the most talented players in the Hollywood hustle, proved Scorsese's luckiest project and, despite its obvious flaws, ranks among his finest accomplishments. *The Color of Money,* Scorsese's breakthrough film, a hit that crossed over from art house to neighborhood screen and brought Paul Newman his well-deserved Best Actor Oscar, guaranteed Scorsese renewed status as a "bankable" director and made possible the realization of his dream to film *The Last Temptation of Christ,* as it paved the way for the even more successful, more popular *GoodFellas* (1990) and *Cape Fear* (1991).

Developing the script for *The Color of Money,* Scorsese and Price hit on a concept that enabled them to relate their lives to Eddie Felson's tribulations. Autobiographical art, Scorsese has always insisted, ensures the proper involvement of actors, directors, and writers, and inspires the perfect dynamic for the whole crew. Artists must see their own souls, their secret dreams and nightmares, up there on the screen; this credo informs all Scorsese's films. For Price and Scorsese, the game of pool becomes the symbol connecting Fast Eddie to all the other participants in *The Color of Money.* In Price's and Scorsese's hands, Eddie's gifts as a pool player provide a metaphor for Newman's and Cruise's craft as actors, for Price's gifts as a writer, and for Scorsese's skills as a director. The film focuses, Price explained, on one question: "What would happen to us if we couldn't write or direct?" (Denby 1986, 36). All the principals knew what monsters they would become—monsters like the Eddie who shuns the game, eking out a fringe existence selling second-rate liquor with first-rate labels and staking other pool hustlers.

When an inspired pool player like the flaky Vincent (Tom Cruise) shatters Eddie's self-imposed exile from major league action, Eddie impulsively does everything he can to corrupt his protégé, but eventually Eddie must acknowledge his own blindness, adjust his moral vision, shape up, and be true to his gifts. Richard Price, well trained in analyzing scripts, recognized *The Color of Money* as a prototypical Scorsese narrative: "It became another movie about salvation through mortification—a typical Scorsese theme. The getting of wisdom by

Paul Newman as "Fast" Eddie Felson instructs Tom Cruise (Vincent Lauria) on the fine art of the hustle in *The Color of Money* (1986). Touchstone Pictures. The Museum of Modern Art/Film Stills Archive.

living out your evil impulses to the end" (Denby 1986, 36). In re-sponse to Price's exegesis, Scorsese added his perceptions about the deeper narrative structure: "Eddie has become everything he hates—a slick guy. He meets a young guy who reminds him of himself at that age and starts to corrupt him. But then, at a certain point, the two poles cross" (Denby 1986, 36). Eddie, another of Scorsese's misguided and reluctant saints, cannot live without pool and cannot betray the purity of the game, not for all the money in the world.

Scorsese's secondary theme in *The Color of Money,* the seductiveness of wealth and the allure of the hustle, in pool halls, Hollywood, and corporate America, reflected, he told David Ansen, his concern with America's yuppie mania. His "mini-morality play," the director pon-tificated, "really reflects our values: money and success and especially this yuppie thing. Who would have thought in the late '60's that some-day we'd see a generation that was interested in making money on the stock market? Not that that's necessarily bad, but if that becomes the golden idol in your life—it's putting false gods. That is the Second Commandment isn't it? Don't put false gods in my place" (Ansen 1987, 51). As usual, Scorsese's hold on dogma is weak—he never gets the numbering of commandments right or outlines theology cor-rectly; he deserved expulsion from the seminary on purely scholarly grounds. But he does masterfully explore morality and ethics. His heart is stronger than his head, his conscience more developed than his creed. Winners and losers in *The Color of Money* are never clear and Fast Eddie shares more wisdom than he knows when he cautions that "sometimes you have to lose in order to win."

Scorsese wisely assessed his losses and victories in directing *The Color of Money* for Touchstone. His evaluations mingle exaltation and regret. On the positive side, Scorsese realizes he shot "a real studio film" with "real stars" on time and well within budget as he reached out to a sizable mainstream audience that had not seen his earlier films ("Martin Scorsese Directs"). While the original plans called for 50 days of shooting at a cost exceeding $14 million, Scorsese econo-mized, completing the filming in 49 days for approximately $13 mil-lion, yet he maintained a glossy, high-voltage, big-budget "look." His producers and the other studios noticed these numbers and the glitzy result, so Scorsese was again viewed as a director with integrity and artistic talents, a hot commodity in a trendy town with an eye on the bottom line. Scorsese's credentials were reaffirmed, as was his bankability.

Yet Scorsese's regrets and misgivings loomed large. Historically, studio-produced films were similar to chess and pool, Scorsese explained to columnist Anthony DeCurtis, for individual artists had to see if they could "be expressive" within the well-established conventions of a genre and within the confines of a budget and production routine (DeCurtis, 64). For him, Scorsese continued, such restraints were becoming onerous: "You see if you can be expressive within it. I don't know if you can. I always have that problem. Loving the old films, I don't know if I can make them. I mean, *New York, New York* was obviously revisionist. But with *The Color of Money,* I went half and half, and it should have been one way, I think" (DeCurtis, 64).

Much of the "half and half" Scorsese laments occurs in the conclusion of *The Color of Money,* when Fast Eddie resurrects his billiards career in a major Atlantic City tournament only to be hustled by Vincent and forced to forfeit the title match. Eddie then turns on Vincent, challenging him to a showdown, an honest confrontation over a pool table. Eddie, clearly the morally superior force and the more complete human being, goads Vincent "Come on, let's clear it up," and the film ends with a close-up of Eddie admonishing Vincent and the world, "Hey. I'm back." The outcome of the private, one-on-one match is unclear, but the message is overwhelmingly upbeat and uplifting. Sooner or later Fast Eddie will beat Vincent's "ass" and save the young man he once corrupted, just as he has saved himself. Winning and losing fuse on the path to personal salvation, for Vincent must lose the game to be redeemed, an ironic echo of the confusion of winning and losing in the art of hustling.

The problem with this tangled but triumphant conclusion is, as David Denby notes, that "when the setting shifts to a big tournament in Atlantic City, Scorsese shoots the competition room as if it were a cathedral. The end of the movie is almost pious. Fast Eddie has become a pool room saint and we feel there's a degree of irony missing, as if Sylvester Stallone has somehow barged in to dictate the ending."[18] Though Scorsese's major films always have troubling conclusions, normally the problem involves overly rich ambiguities, ironies, and complexities: Will Alice reach Monterey? Is Travis saint or assassin? Is Jake sacred or profane? Is Pupkin king or clod? In *The Color of Money,* however, Scorsese conforms to Hollywood's oldest tradition, the happy ending. Eddie's "I'm back" recalls E.T.'s voyage home, Rocky's victorious call to Adrian, and Indiana Jones's inevitable conquests. As Vincent Canby temperately observed in the *New York Times,* the filmmakers "didn't adequately prepare for the twist that ends the film, which is more emotionally soothing than believable."[19] While he preferred not to pander to mass tastes, Scorsese acknowledged when he was making *The Color of Money* that fantasy and sentimentality meant bigger box office returns, as did a glorious victory culminating in a joyously happy ending. These conventions, he lamented, cheated audiences as they excited them. Happy endings, he told David Ansen, were still Hollywood's ultimate hustle, yet the audiences loved to be manipulated: "Look how corrupt [American moviegoers have] gotten, with films like *Top Gun* and *Rocky*. They have been corrupted; it's a pity. . . . They're being shortchanged, the audience. They're going for easy emotions, and it's a pity. I really feel that" (Ansen 1987, 51). But to survive in Hollywood, Scorsese had to meet audience expectations by sinking the nine ball in *The Color of Money*.

On his way to winning audience approval in an upbeat conclusion, Scorsese tried many fancy combinations in *The Color of Money*, learning more from colleague Michael Ballhaus about economical and stylish camera setups and from friend Robbie Robertson about using music to counterpoint and complement action. All Scorsese's films demonstrate his concern for the integration of visuals and music, but his mastery of the craft of camerawork and musical composition increases in each. As he told Chris Holdenfield, *The Color of Money* became his advanced seminar on using the camera and music within budgetary confines and studio restrictions: "*The Color of Money* was a good commercial exercise for me. I learned a great deal about structure and style. Learned what may not have worked" (Holdenfield 1989, 51). In this feature, Scorsese bragged, he finally got the "elegant" look of a moving camera he long aspired to ("Martin Scorsese Directs"), and he used a soundtrack to maximum effect.

The editing and final mix for *The Color of Money* were done in Scorsese's production offices at 1619 Broadway, the famous Brill Building, the legendary capital of Tin Pan Alley. Yet for all the musical heritage that surrounded him, Scorsese had to be surprised by the next offer of a project that crossed his desk. Just as he finished *The Color of Money* and began looking for a short film to undertake, Quincy Jones asked Scorsese if he would be willing to make a music video with America's popular and eccentric vocalist Michael Jackson.

Arrangements were made quickly, with Scorsese receiving a hefty fee and Jackson putting up more than $2 million to finance a 16-minute short, "Bad" scripted by Richard Price, who had written *The*

Color of Money and was in the process of drafting his next feature, *The Sea of Love*.

"Bad," which premiered on CBS on 31 August 1987, is loosely based on the life of Edmund Perry; its driving rock beat counterpoints an overly moralistic tale of a black boy who escapes the ghetto to attend prep school but then returns to Harlem, where his old friends challenge him to be "bad" and live the macho life. Unlike the real Perry, this protagonist, Darryl (Michael Jackson), dances his way emphatically through all moral quandaries in what the *Wall Street Journal* describes as "a 'Beat It' style heartwarmer" of which "Walt Disney would have been proud."[20] Jackson had chosen Scorsese because he loved *Raging Bull* and wanted to work in black-and-white. Scorsese, for his part, was lured by the generous budget, the media attention and guaranteed audience, the unusual array of talent involved, and the fortuitous timing. "Bad" gave him both commercial exposure and a respite from feature production.

The late 1980s would not, however, prove a quiet time for Scorsese. His success with *After Hours* and *The Color of Money* put his career in high gear. Marlon Brando was hounding him again; the king of American actors wanted Scorsese to direct him in a comedy written by Andrew Bergman in which Brando was cast as God and Michael Jackson was his costar. Paul Schrader was eager to develop a joint project on George Gershwin. And there were many other prospects: De Niro looked perfect for the gangster epic *Wise Guy*, scripted by Nick Pileggi; Touchstone had approached him about a big-budget production of *Dick Tracy*; and Scorsese was also renewing his interest in adapting Edith Wharton's *The Age of Innocence* for the screen.

If the decade had begun with Scorsese, like Fast Eddie, wondering how to sell his strong liquor under different labels, it ended with his triumphant demonstration that he was *back* and Hollywood would never be the same pool game again.

9

The Last Temptation of Christ (1988)

In November 1986 *American Film* published an interview with Martin Scorsese in which he vented his anger at the American film industry in general as he hectored Paramount Pictures for its precipitous cancellation of *The Last Temptation of Christ*. His tone was both unsparing and despairing as he fulminated about his aborted biblical epic: "Hopefully, I can still get *The Last Temptation of Christ* made someday, but it won't be in this country. At all. Forget it, that film has nothing to do with the American film industry" (Biskind, 70). Around the same time, Scorsese was conferring with Michael Ovitz, the superagent behind Creative Artists Agency (CAA) who had represented both Paul Newman and Tom Cruise in *The Color of Money* and was about to sign Robert De Niro. Scorsese recognized that Ovitz was fashioning a monopoly in Hollywood by prepackaging film deals based on talents his firm represented. Ovitz was replacing the studio system with an innovative, agency-based arrangement that presold stars and organized worldwide distribution and exhibition in advance of production, thus ensuring smoother financing. Scorsese intuited that Ovitz had been the power behind the scenes propelling *The Color of Money* through the hierarchy of Touchstone. Scorsese wanted Mike Ovitz, Tinseltown's best game player, hustling for him.

As it became clear that Ovitz craved the prestige of representing a respected artist like Scorsese, the New York wunderkind began to talk about his loyalty to his old agent Harry Ufland, about Ufland's unflagging devotion to *The Last Temptation,* and about the importance of *The Last Temptation* to his artistic fulfillment. Ovitz understood, better than Scorsese knew. When Scorsese announced his break with Ufland and his contract with CAA and Ovitz, beginning 1 January

1987, Ovitz was pressuring Universal and Cineplex Odeon theaters into producing, distributing, and exhibiting the film with Scorsese as director, Ufland as executive producer, and Scorsese's wife, Barbara De Fina, as coproducer.

Scorsese meanwhile had gone to England to present a series of lectures, had shot commercials for his friend Giorgio Armani in Milan, and had begun work with Robbie Robertson on some music videos. He also found time to fly to Tetiaroa to see Marlon Brando about possible joint film productions. All this time Ovitz was convincing Thomas Pollock of Universal to commit to *The Last Temptation* and courting Garth Drabinsky of Cineplex Odeon to guarantee North American exhibition in top-ranking theaters.

Scorsese had kept his options on Kazantzakis's material current, largely because Paul Schrader was competing for the material. Schrader's contract for scripting *The Last Temptation* included a clause guaranteeing him the right to direct the film if Scorsese lost interest or couldn't secure funding. In 1985, sensing that Scorsese was discouraged by the Paramount debacle, Schrader wrote Scorsese, informing him that he had potential backers in France and Egypt and warning Scorsese that "I will walk over your back to get this movie done"; the startled Scorsese replied, "You will have to pull the script from my dying hands."[1]

Universal wasn't that eager to grab *The Last Temptation*. Instead, like Ovitz, the studio was eager to secure the Scorsese connection. As Aljean Harmetz of the *New York Times* reported, Scorsese's religious epic was seen as a low-budget artistic exercise with little prospect for box office success, and there was speculation in Hollywood that "Universal had given Mr. Scorsese $6.5 million to make this personal film so that a grateful filmmaker would come to the studio with his next more commercial venture."[2] Universal hoped, of course, that Ovitz would remember the studio when he had a surefire winner. For under $7 million, Universal's accountants figured, they could put a lot of "goodwill" on the ledgers.

Universal recognized that *The Last Temptation* could generate controversy. To defuse the tensions, the studio insisted that the project have a new working title—"The Passion." And Universal hired two conservative religious opinionmakers, Tim Penland and the Reverend Larry Poland, as consultants on the marketing of the project. Penland and Poland would inadvertently play a larger role in the film's promotion than anyone could have foreseen. Asked to make suggestions about the script's acceptability to born-again audiences, the pair called for revising almost two-thirds of the text, and resigned when Universal did not respond to their pleas. Then they spearheaded the assault on *The Last Temptation,* condemning it as an "insult to Christians."[3]

At the outset of the project, however, Scorsese deflected worries about religious controversy by assuring Universal's executives that he wanted to make the film so he could "get to know Jesus better" (*Scorsese* 1989, 120), by accepting a budget less than half that of the average Hollywood film, by agreeing to "a long term multi-picture arrangement under which the filmmaker will produce, direct, and develop projects" exclusively for Universal,[4] and by reiterating his constant refrain that *The Last Temptation of Christ* was based not on the Bible but on a novel by Nikos Kazantzakis.

By April 1987 Scorsese was scouting locations in Morocco. His experience with Paramount convinced Scorsese to simplify. Thus, when he found an ancient village named Oumnast near Marrakech, he based his operation there and shot *The Last Temptation of Christ* in and around this primitive outpost.

In summer 1987 Scorsese rewrote Schrader's script with the help of Jay Cocks. Schrader was aware of the revisions but refused Scorsese and Cocks the right to on-screen credit. Although Scorsese took the case to arbitration, the Writers' Guild sustained Schrader's argument. In his presentation Schrader asserted that his first script, "with the exception of two scenes, is exactly scene for scene, the movie that's on the screen" (James, 19). The arbiter agreed.

Shooting on *The Last Temptation* began on 12 October 1987, and Scorsese worked with messianic fervor. Barbara Hershey summarized the production company's mood when she observed that "it meant so much to Marty, it was like a crusade."[5] Scorsese admitted that "this film for me is like a prayer. It is my way of worshipping" and rejoiced in the difficulty of the shooting, arguing that "It was important this film be made in a special way, under great hardship. I wanted to get more on a one to one level with God, without anything in the way" (Grogan, 40–43). Scorsese's loudest complaint about the shoot was the absence of his favorite device, a large crane; his wife Barbara De Fina would authorize only a small crane. He never let her forget this hardship, constantly chiding that she kept his Jesus earthbound.

Scorsese shot *The Last Temptation* in just over 10 weeks in Morocco at a cost of approximately $6.7 million. Before undertaking his Jesus

Director Martin Scorsese preparing a scene in *The Last Temptation of Christ* (1988). Universal Pictures. The Museum of Modern Art/Film Stills Archive.

project, Scorsese reviewed the image of the Savior on film and was most impressed by Roberto Rosselini's epics, *The Acts of the Apostles* (1968) and *The Messiah* (1975), which Scorsese subsequently attempted to distribute in the United States. From Rosselini, Scorsese confessed, he discovered the importance of the primitive setting to Christ's mission: "Rossellini's historical films opened up my mind to the point that, of course, if Jesus is in Nazareth, it's going to look very poor. Therefore, you don't need big art direction. When you film in places like North Africa, people are still living in the same conditions they have been for thousands of years."[6]

When he got to the desert, Scorsese made another discovery. The endless sands, oppressive heat, and preternatural silence warp one's perceptions and redefine one's place under the sheltering sky. Scorsese was quick to admit that many sequences in *The Last Temptation of Christ* "take on the tone and mood of the desert," because when he was in Morocco he "got a real sense of timelessness, of everything moving at 120 frames per second—extremely slow motion, almost like a trance. That's part of the effect that I wanted from the movie, and it's part of the reason the movie is two hours and 46 minutes long!" (Scorsese, "Second Screen," 25)

Another major contributor to the tone for the movie and the source of its hypnotic, trancelike rhythms is Peter Gabriel's musical score. Without its multicultural New Age sound, *The Last Temptation of Christ* would be leaden and mute. Gabriel's score accounts for much of the doleful sorrow, a good bit of the cacophonous shock, and a large part of the raw sensuality.

The inspiration for Scorsese's visuals came from a recondite source, the scholarly journal *Biblical Archaeology Review*. Scorsese wanted his images of the redeemer to be authentic. All his life Scorsese had clipped articles about Christ and saved them for future reference, but after the failure of the Paramount project, he became a committed researcher, pouring over erudite tomes, assiduously cribbing ideas. During the years Scorsese did his extensive reading, revisionist histories were redrawing the portrait of Christ's ministry. The Dead Sea Scrolls were being evaluated, artifacts were being uncovered, and modern research methodologies were creating new visions. Christ's ministry, passion, and crucifixion took place, commentators were beginning to agree, in a society as unsettled as today's Middle East: "Judaism in Jesus's time was wracked by sectarian rivalry. The Pharisees, a lay reform movement strong in the village synagogues but not in

Jerusalem were at odds with the Sadducees, the priests who dominated the temple. In the countryside were the Essenes, a radical
monastic sect that rejected the Temple establishment, and the insur-
rectionist Zealots, whose main objective was throwing off Roman
rule. Each had different expectations for the Messiah: a military deliverer, a priestly king who would restore Israel's religious fervor, a mystical figure who would usher in a new age."[7] Scorsese found in this
divided society the model for his conflicted Christ. Merging his research with his rereading of Kazantzakis, Scorsese envisioned a human
Christ, unsure whether he was merely an ordinary mortal or a divinity
incarnated, and equally uncertain whether his mission was to engen-
der a family, save a nation, reform a religion, or forge a new path to
salvation. Scorsese's Christ is buffeted by Romans and Zealots, attracted by Essenes and Pharisees, and reviled by both Sadducees and
reformers. His path to Golgotha is rocky and uneven, and his time on
the cross unsettled and confused. Scorsese had long since rejected a
plastic, glow-in-the-dark Jesus; he now wanted all of America to forget Sunday-school bookmarkers, saccharine pieties, and Hollywood's
glossy, airbrushed, backlighted saviors. Scorsese embraced the theological speculations of Kazantzakis and embedded them in the confusing Jerusalem uncovered by modern archaeologists. His Christ
wavered between roles, as savior and loving husband, as Messiah and
worldly patriarch, as military deliverer and Prince of Peace, as mystical visionary and disturbed carpenter, as priestly king and as humble
homesteader. Scorsese was not about to make Kazantzakis more ac-
cessible; he was to wallow in the agonies, the perplexities, and, to use
his Greek mentor's favorite word, the struggle of Christ.

Where Kazantzakis relied on interior monologues to define Christ's
struggle, Schrader and Scorsese turned to dialogue, confrontation,
and almost-allegorical characterizations. The major scenes with Judas,
for example, emphasize the narrative's political dimensions. Judas
(Harvey Keitel) initially upbraids Jesus the carpenter for his collaboration with Imperial Rome: "You're a disgrace. Romans can't find
anybody to make crosses, except for you. *You* do it. You're worse
than them! You're a Jew killing Jews. You're a coward!" Then Judas
prods Jesus the preacher to take up the sword and ax, to assemble a
large band of apostles and disciples, and to destroy the temple, only
to see Christ's nerve fail at a critical juncture and his rebellion against
Rome fizzle. Perplexed and inconsolable, this red-haired rabble-rouser
cannot understand Christ's acceptance of a divine plan and rejection

of an armed insurrection. Their heated exchanges propel Judas to his betrayal as they confirm the Messiah's rejection of radical politics and rebellion:

> Jesus: I wish there were some other way. I'm sorry, but there isn't. I have to die on the cross.
>
> Judas: I won't let you die!
>
> Jesus: You have no choice. Neither do I. Remember, we're bringing God and man together. They'll never be together, unless I die. I'm the sacrifice. Without you there can be no redemption. Forget everything else, understand that.
>
> Judas: No! I can't. Get somebody stronger.
>
> Jesus: You promised me. Remember, you once told me that if I moved one step from revolution you'd kill me. Remember?
>
> Judas: Yes.
>
> Jesus: I've strayed, haven't I? Then you must keep your promise, you have to kill me.
>
> Judas: If that's what God wants, then let God do it. I won't.
>
> Jesus: He will do it, through you. The temple guards will be looking for me where there aren't any crowds. Go to Gethsemane and I'll make sure that they find me there. I am going to die. But after three days, I'll come back in victory. You can't leave me. You have to give me strength.
>
> Judas: If you were me, could you betray your master?
>
> Jesus: No. That's why God gave me the easier job, to be crucified.[8]

Many Christians find the theme here unsettling, for it makes Judas's treachery a heroic part of a supernatural teleology. But in the context of the film and the novel, it is the apotheosis of Judas's valor. After fighting so unsparingly for Jewish freedom and the defeat of Rome, the unrelenting Judas delivers Jesus to his condemnation by Pontius Pilate.

While Schrader and Scorsese use the scenes between Judas and Jesus to explore the social and political dimensions of Christ's public life, they rely on the episodes with John the Baptist and the Essenes to explore the Savior's mystical religious dimension. Before he confronts the holy men in the desert, Jesus is convinced of his insanity and struggles to quiet the voices bombarding his consciousness. All of God's promptings, he confesses to one member of the ascetic religious community, merely reinforce his feelings of powerlessness and guilt:

Jesus: You think it's a blessing to know what God wants? I'll tell you
what he wants; He wants to push me over [a nearby cliff]. Can't you
see what's inside of me? My sins.
Ascetic: We all sin.
Jesus: Not my sins, I'm a liar, a hypocrite. I'm afraid of everything. I
don't ever tell the truth, I don't have the courage. . . . I want to rebel
against you, against everything, against God, but I'm afraid. You
want to know who my mother and father is? You want to know who
my God is? Fear! You look inside me and that's all you find. (*Temptation*, 19)

Yet, once Jesus meets John the Baptist and his inspired hordes (pictured in Scorsese's film as gyrating, seemingly possessed nude and
seminude devotees), he accepts his visions, craves John's baptism, and
looks for purification in the desert. Jesus's enlightenment at the camp
of John the Baptist reflects Scorsese's research. Echoing many revi-
sionists, Scorsese's film postulates John's importance in opening the
gates of heaven to non-Gentiles, heathens, and pagans. As Scorsese
explained to journalists, the bizarre rituals at John's camp suggest his
desire to convert all nations: "You have to understand, the Baptist
didn't just preach to the Israelites, he preached to everybody around:
the Chaldeans, the Ethiopians, etc. It must have looked and sounded
like a wild medicine show. The point is that, through the use of their
own pagan rituals, he was transforming them and leading them into
his own eschatological philosophy" (press kit).

During his temptations in the wilderness, Jesus is assailed by
tongues of fire, hypnotic snakes, and raging lions; girded in faith, Jesus vanquishes these tempters, though he is warned the Devil will test
him again. At the Essene community and with John the Baptist, Jesus
discerns the divine in the voices he wanted to ignore as delusions. He
speaks with the dead elders of the Essene community, convinces John
of his divinity, and conquers demons handily. These inspirations prepare Christ for his role as rabbi, preacher, and savior; yet they are
presented so matter-of-factly that they are disarming. Scorsese later
realized that these scenes elicit the wrong responses from audiences.
His talking snake and stalking lion, rendered through ineffective trick
shots, evoke boisterous laughter rather than reverence. Catastrophi-
cally, it proved impossible for Scorsese to convey his subtle religious
symbolism on the starkly realistic big screen.

Similar problems plagued Schrader and Scorsese's treatment of Saint Paul, for sophisticated audiences immediately saw cult hero–actor Harry Dean Stanton as doing a "guest star" bit in the role of Paul (a perception that also shaded audience reactions to singer David Bowie as Pontius Pilate, director Andre Gregory as John the Baptist, and Barbara Hershey as Mary Magdalene). Schrader was fascinated by Paul and a decade earlier had outlined his own trilogy of films, beginning with *Taxi Driver,* continuing with a biography of singer Hank Williams, and culminating in a study of Paul the Christian apologist. Discussing his proposed treatment of the author of Christianity's most controversial epistles, Schrader declared, "I'd like to do the St. Paul story, where the need to transform one's surroundings, to recreate the world, becomes so great that he changes the entire history of Western civilization. What we know of Christianity is to my mind Paulism" (Schrader 1976, 18).

Schrader felt such an affinity for his namesake that Paul's martyrdom interested him more than Christ's. Schrader believed that Paul's inspiration filled the Gospels: "Christ is like Socrates: a mysterious figure we only know about through Plato, just as we only know about Christ through Paul. Paul had his hands in all the Gospels. There's good reason to believe he wrote Luke and he supervised the rewriting of the others" (Schrader 1990, 3). Scorsese made Schrader's conception central to the "last temptation" theme, expanding broadly on Kazantzakis's treatment of Paul. In the film Paul preaches traditional Christianity to the alternate Christ of the last temptation, the imagined Christ who rejects death on the cross and instead chooses domestic bliss first with Mary Magdalene and then with Mary and Martha. In a sharp exchange Paul confronts the nonmessianic Jesus with humanity's need for a savior:

> Paul: Just a minute, what's the matter with you? Look around you. Look around you. Look at all these people, look at their faces. You see how unhappy they are? Do you see how much they're suffering? Their only hope is the resurrected Jesus. I don't care whether you're Jesus or not, the resurrected Jesus will save the world and that's what matters.
> Jesus: Those are lies. You can't save the world by lying.
> Paul: I created the truth out of what people needed and what they believed. If I have to crucify you to save the world, then I'll crucify you. And if I have to resurrect you, then I'll do that too, whether you like it or not.

Jesus: I won't let you. I'll tell everyone the truth.

Paul: Go ahead, go on, tell them now. Who's going to believe you? You started all this. Now you can't stop it. All these people who believe me will grab you and kill you.

Jesus: No, that wouldn't happen.

Paul: You see, you don't know how much people need God. You don't know how happy He can make them. He can make them happy to do anything. He can make them happy to die and they'll die—all for the sake of Christ, Jesus Christ, Jesus of Nazareth, the Son of God, the Messiah, not you. Not for your sake. You know I'm glad I met you because now I can forget all about you. My Jesus is so much more important and more powerful. Thank you. It's a good thing thing I met you. (*Temptation*, 97–98)

These lines, even in the context of an alternate reality—episodes in a world that might have been had Christ yielded to the Devil's last temptation—still challenge audience perceptions of the development of Christianity. Schrader and Scorsese clearly suggest that the promulgation of the Christian message depended less on the truth or falsity of Christ's Passion and Resurrection than on the impassioned preaching of his apologist Paul. These themes are implicit in Kazantzakis, but they are amplified by Schrader's and Scorsese's commitment to new biblical scholarship and revisionist histories. In carrying this sophisticated analysis to popular audiences, they risked a backlash from the conservative, less erudite faithful.

At the other end of the spectrum, intellectual critics like Jewish mystagogue Phillip Lopate would castigate Schrader and Scorsese for attempting to provide too many quandaries and too little synthesis. Lopate isolates the flaw in *The Last Temptation of Christ* as being its eclectic approach to Christ, charging that the film "picks up stray nail-filings of Hebrew politics, theological contradictions, and psychological conflicts without resolving them in a thoughtful, intellectually responsible manner."[9] For Scorsese and Schrader, the theological contradictions, psychological conflicts, and Hebrew politics are no idle "nail-filings"; they are the heart of the matter. Their Christ finds no easy resolution for his travails; only on the cross can this Savior proclaim, "It is accomplished." For Lopate, the film's exultation at this moment, clumsily signaled in a loud burst of joyous music and a dizzying display of psychedelic imagery, does not suffice, for he has no faith in the redemption: "The idea that this guy's death has somehow redeemed the whole world, on whatever symbolic or literal terms you care to take it, makes no sense to me. The world is unredeemed, *n'est-ce pas?*" (Lopate, 74).

An individual's reaction to *The Last Temptation of Christ* depends on more than the normal problem of literary faith—Coleridge's "willing suspension of disbelief." This film, by choosing a fictional Christ as its protagonist and an imaginary "last temptation" as its crisis, constantly challenges a viewer's belief in the biblical Christ and in mysteries like the incarnation and the redemption. For all Scorsese's rejoinders that he is only interpreting Nikos Kazantzakis's vision of the Messiah in one controversial novel, Scorsese and his film inevitably run directly into the mythology of Christ, established theologies, dogmatic moralities, and inflexible orthodoxies. Scorsese's Christ never bears his cross alone, for he walks the *via doloroso* with two millennia of companions, all the images of the Messiah conjured up by the faithful everywhere. When Scorsese's Christ climbs down from the cross to contemplate another fate, a different Gospel, he drags with him the New Testament and centuries of sermons, scholarship, and exegesis.

Critic Andrew Sarris eloquently makes the crucial distinction central to any just evaluation of *The Last Temptation of Christ* when he asserts that audiences "should be able to accept Scorsese's eminently serious and toweringly ambitious effort as a meditation on *a* Christ and not *the* Christ."[10] The image of Jesus Scorsese presents emphasizes the duality of his nature, fully realizing both his humanity and his divinity. This complex Jesus stands in marked distinction to the Monophysite Jesus Scorsese recalls as central to his Catholic school indoctrination—a Jesus so ethereally divine that he glowed in the dark and carried his celestial choir everywhere with him. Scorsese's Christ resists spirituality at the outset, only gradually yielding to his divine mission. The process of his salvation and his redemption of all sinners is the grist of Scorsese's film. In that gradual process of Christ's evolution, Scorsese told Gene Siskel, this film mirrors the rest of the works in his canon: "Most of my films have been circling around the theme of how a flawed man can become saved. Now I've tackled the same subject head on."[11]

In *The Last Temptation of Christ* Scorsese echoes traditional Christian dogma as he develops the themes of incarnation, atonement, and redemption. Scorsese, however, explores the concept of Christ's humanity more fully than most Christians, trying to fathom the essence of incarnation and to explore the psychological and theological implications of a deity made flesh, of a God in a man's body. These questions of Christ's humanity and divinity, screenwriter Schrader declares, cut to the heart of Christianity and haunted the early church: "The two major heresies which emerged in the early Christian Church were the Arian heresy, from Arius, which essentially said that Jesus was a man who pretended to be God, and the other was the Docetan heresy, which said Jesus was really a God who, like a very clever actor, pretended to be a man. . . . *The Last Temptation of Christ* may err on the side of Arianism, but it does little to counteract the 2,000 years of erring on the other side, and it was pleasant to see this debate from the early Church splashed all over the front pages" (Schrader 1990, 139).

Defending his foray into theology, Scorsese told the "NBC Evening News" audience that he was "trying to push the concept of Jesus into the 21st century" and to understand what "temptations" could have meant to Christ. For him, he told television viewers, there had always been the paradox that "If he's God, when he had temptation brought in front of him, it was easy—he was God, it was easy to reject." On the other hand, Scorsese continued, "If he has the human foibles, if he has all the parts of human nature that we have, then it was just as tough for him as it is for us."[12] The human Arian Christ fascinated Scorsese, and his struggles and foibles are the essence of Scorsese's film.

Willem Dafoe, who plays the troubled Christ in Scorsese's *Last Temptation of Christ,* acknowledged that Scorsese's conception was the wellspring of his portrayal. As he told Richard Woodward, "Once we started, we didn't have time to reflect. This was [Scorsese's] labor of love and I put myself in his hands. And the story suited that approach because all this stuff is working through this guy."[13] Defining "all this stuff" in other interviews, Dafoe constantly came back to the theme that Scorsese pictured a human Christ working his way to the acceptance of his divinity and his redemptive mission. The key, Dafoe suggested to Kenneth Chanka, is to understand that the miscues, hesitations, difficulties, temptations, and struggles enrich the eventual triumph and do not undercut the glory of Christ's achievement. *The Last Temptation of Christ* remains, its star certifies, "a deeply religious movie for Marty. It's not a debunking. It's not a riff. It's a way to

Willem Dafoe as the Messiah in *The Last Temptation of Christ* (1988). Universal Pictures. The Museum of Modern Art/Film Stills Archive.

articulate his deep feelings. Sure part of the idea was to humanize Christ. It's short on Heavenly angels. But, in the end, it's triumphant in the way people who subscribe to the Jesus story want it to be."[14]

Scorsese shot *The Last Temptation of Christ* in sequence, an unusual way of proceeding, but as a result Dafoe more fully participated in the gradual evolution of Christ's character and endured the physical struggle of Christ's passion near the end of the production. The demands of the crucifixion scenes were so great that Dafoe could not remain on the cross more than a few minutes or he would begin to asphyxiate. After being mounted on the cross dozens of times, Dafoe was so exhausted that he felt, he admitted, that "a certain kind of martyrdom was creeping into every crevice" of his body and mind,[15] yet these trying scenes finally helped him to appreciate the triumph his character felt in conquering the cross and in enduring "The Passion," which was, after all, the working title of the whole production.

The final title of Scorsese's work, *The Last Temptation of Christ,* adds one last psychological trial to Jesus's physical ordeal. Adapting Kazantzakis's grandest conceit, Scorsese and Schrader introduce a young girl who approaches the crucified Christ and tells him he doesn't have to die, that he can climb down from the cross, reenter the world, marry Mary Magdalene, and raise a family. In the sequence that follows, Christ seems to pursue that alternate reality and to spend a full life on earth until Judas comes and rebukes his aged rabbi on his deathbed. The nature of this entire sequence is rather cloudy. In Schrader's earliest script it is clear there were to be two actors playing Christ, one who remained young on the cross and the other who matured, aged, and lay on his deathbed. The whole interlude was characterized in the shooting script as a dream. But when Scorsese talked about this sequence in his autobiography, he seemed less focused on the idea of a dream and more intent on the concept of a vivid temptation: "I imagined it as a series of literal visual tableaux which the Devil shows Christ, so that thirty-six years might go by in a second" (*Scorsese* 1989, 126). Analyzing the sequence later with Richard Corliss, Scorsese hammered at the idea that this "fantasy" or "hallucination" was really "a diabolical temptation" analogous to unwanted sexual arousal: "You know, the one sexual thing the priests told Catholic boys they could not be held responsible for was nocturnal emission. It was like an involuntary fantasy. And with Jesus it's the same thing. How can you hold him responsible for this fantasy? Of course, Catholic boys were taught that, if you entertained fantasy for a while, it became an occasion of sin. That's another good title for a movie: *Occasion of Sin!*" (Corliss, 38). In this outing, however, Scorsese rested with the concept of temptation, a word he used in the strictest theological sense, "a test" of virtue.

Many criticisms of *The Last Temptation of Christ* focus on this last sequence and its candid treatment of sexual intercourse between Jesus and Mary Magdalene. Earlier scenes in the film of Jesus with Magdalene in her brothel had suggested a childhood dalliance between the pair, one that is explicitly described in Kazantzakis' novel, but only in this "temptation" sequence does the sexual nature of Christ's humanity take center stage. The interlude is so carefully lighted and filmed that most commentators agreed with conservative James J. Kirkpatrick's remarks in his tirade "*The Last Temptation of Christ* Stinks" that "the scene is about as pornographic as the embrace of Dagwood and Blondie.[16] Some more liberal and comedic essayists, however, couldn't resist a few apposite hyperboles. The irrepressible Harlan Jacobson, for example, in *Film Comment* emphasized sexual elements in his catalog of the ways Scorsese's *Last Temptation* violated fundamentalist Christians' conceptions of the Redeemer: "Where fundamentalists see Christ as experiencing temptation but not sin (meaning he knew Magdalene was a peach but there is nothing about 'peach' that says 'bite me'), Marty's Christ is Johnny Wadd (in fact, *Spy* magazine put Willem Dafoe in its Big Dick list along with Secretariat and Milton Berle). Where the fundamentalist Christ is a good son who loved his mother, Marty's is Portnoy. And where the fundamentalist Christ aims for the finish line like a mudder at Hialeah, Marty's Christ is *The Loneliness of the Long Distance Runner.*"[17] For his part Scorsese did everything possible to avoid the lurid emphasis on Jesus's carnal relations. Scorsese widely proclaimed his desire that audiences see that "the last temptation" really involved the choice between superhuman sacrifice on the cross as a divine Messiah and ordinary life as a human: "This is not the sex life of Jesus. That's shallow. It's a temptation to live your life as an ordinary man, to come down from the Cross and marry, to make love so that you have children and to live out a normal life and to die a sweet death in bed."[18] Scorsese's Jesus and his cross join a long line of Scorsese heroes—Alice Hyatt and her songs, Jake La Motta and his boxing gloves, Jimmy Doyle and his horn, Fast Eddie and his pool cue—all torn between a larger mission and a yearning for a normal life, torn between their inspiration and their common sense, just as Scorsese himself felt torn between his camera and his domestic life. *The Last Temptation of Christ* forms yet another chapter in the autobiography Scorsese has limned in his cinema. As Charles Krauthammer perceptively concludes, "*Temptation* is a working out of Scorsese's demons, not Christ's."[19]

Many commentators denounced *The Last Temptation of Christ* for picturing so obviously confused, conflicted, and uncertain a savior. But in what must be the most peculiar *New York Times* editorial of the decade, the editors-turned-film-reviewers carefully eschewed the "he's too confused" attack in favor of a blunter personal attack on Scorsese for succumbing to other "devils." On the editorial page, in their lead editorial, under the sensational caption "Satanism in Hollywood," the august leaders of America's newspaper of record engaged in some rather purple prose to condemn both Scorsese's motives and his sensibility: "What many may find truly disturbing about the film is not its depiction of a confused, human Jesus but its director's reliance on torn and bloody flesh, human and animal, to illustrate a biblical tale. The film sins against taste. Gratuitous violence for box office gain is the temptation contrived by the devil who hides in cameras. Regrettably, Mr. Scorsese appears to have succumbed."[20] Lamentably, the *Times* succumbed to the journalistic temptation of a "holier than thou" pomposity and careless argumentation. Casual readers, who might not notice that art criticism doesn't belong on the editorial page—especially if it's shoddy vitriol full of metaphoric devils, overheated rhetoric about satanism, and ad hominem attacks—would, on the other hand, surely perceive the begging of the question in the unsupported assertion that the film contains "gratuitous violence for box office gain." Throughout his career Scorsese had frequently been identified with intense, bloody violence, but rarely if ever had thoughtful commentators charged that this violence was both "gratuitous" and solely for "box office gain." The charges ring especially hollow when leveled against *The Last Temptation of Christ*.

Both Scorsese and Schrader spent much time researching the passion of Christ and crucifixions under Roman rule. In early versions of his script, Schrader included formal notes indicating that in 4 BC 2,000 Jews were crucified in Jerusalem in one day alone. Scorsese concentrated his research on artistic renderings of the crucifixion, portrayals that convinced him that his Christ must be completely nude on the cross and that his cinematic images of the Lord's sufferings must echo the intensity Scorsese found in Renaissance renderings of Calvary. One Renaissance portrait in particular, *The Crucifixion* by Antonello da Messina, served as almost the key shot in the storyboard for Scorsese's sequence. In Schrader's later reworkings of "The Passion," the writer even creates backgrounds with the casual reference "See da Messina." The success of the filmmakers in creating a Renaissance look and intensity for their vision of Christ's bloody suffering is evidenced in David Denby's review of *The Last Temptation of Christ* and most particularly in his discussion of the intensely painful imagery: "The violence of the Crucifixion scene stirred my memory of the early Renaissance religious paintings (Mastagna? Messina?) whose mixed eroticism and blood had made me weak in the knees as an adolescent. Finally, it may be that art—the power of an *interpretation*—frightens the protestors more than anything else."[21]

Scorsese's interpretation of Christ coalesces images that haunt all his earlier films—disorienting, disturbing, and evocative archetypes of fear, guilt, and desperation; overpowering, unsettling, and visceral visions of blood, sexuality, pain, suffering, and ecstasy. Critic John Powers of the *Los Angeles Weekly* succinctly defined the film's essence when he observed that "*The Last Temptation of Christ* boldly depicts how profound religious experience overlaps with pain, madness, and sexuality" and thus "goes against the clean, orderly notion of revelation that Hollywood and organized religion like to give us."[22] Scorsese and Schrader were, by their own admission, linked by "a certain affinity about religion and life, death and guilt and sex" (DeCurtis, 108). In their filmic treatment of Christ, they could finally explore these themes definitively. Whereas earlier films allowed them glimpses of the blood that flows from Christ's side to redeem the world, in *The Last Temptation* they could confront that blood directly.

In interviews, Scorsese defended his emphasis on Christ's suffering and the ritualistic basis of religion by identifying blood as a central religious symbol: "Blood is very important in the church. Blood is the life force, the essence, the sacrifice. And in a movie you have to see it. In practically every culture, human sacrifice is very important, very widespread" (Corliss, 41). In his *Last Temptation of Christ* Scorsese defiantly asks all believers if they are bathed in the blood of the Lord.

Blood imagery becomes especially potent in the scenes Schrader and Scorsese add to Kazantzakis and in those they radically alter. Schrader, for example, was euphoric about the "Sacred Heart" scene, an episode where Jesus literally removes his heart from his chest and holds it aloft as a sign of authority and fidelity. As Schrader told Kevin Jackson,

"The one scene I did add that wasn't in the book was the one where Christ takes out his own heart. It just hit me and I loved the scene and Marty loved it, and then someone pointed out to me—I hadn't thought of it at the time—that that is the emblem of Calvin College, the heart in the hand" (Schrader 1990, 136). This sacred heart icon was also the favorite sacramental in the Scorsese household; his devout grandparents had a plaster statue of Jesus and his bleeding heart that inspired many of their grandson's religious fantasies. In fact, Scorsese confided to Amy Taubin, he especially enjoyed making "The Bleeding Heart" sequence because it was like "Digging in those wounds" (Taubin, 68). As far back as *Mean Streets,* Scorsese had wanted to include his dreams of the sacred heart in his movies. In April 1976, for example, he revealed that he had shot a dream sequence for *Mean Streets* that never made it to the screen: "I had scenes in *Mean Streets* that are [my] dreams that I actually shot. You see the way it opens now, he jumps out of bed? Well, there was a dream before that. Took a shot of him lying on the ground—with a flame going out of his heart, some sort of flame in his chest, like it was supposed to be an X-ray of him dying—you could see his soul burning up" (Goldstein and Jacobson, 29–30). The blood to quench this fire and save Charlie's soul flowed, Scorsese believed, from the inflamed and bleeding sacred heart of Jesus. Scorsese and Schrader fused their deepest religious impulses, their most mystical religious visions, their darkest sexual fantasies, their most secret guilt, their childhood fears, and their college memories; merged them with Kazantzakis's struggle and Christ's agony; and bathed these themes in blood and flesh, fire and suffering, in *The Last Temptation of Christ.*

Equally striking is the approach Scorsese and Schrader take to the Eucharist and the issue of transubstantiation and communion. Here they push the question of incarnation and the word made flesh to its most literal extremes. Their Last Supper verges on the cannibalistic. The earliest drafts of the script suggested that Christ turned the wine of the Last Supper into actual blood and the bits of bread into chunks of flesh. As the project developed, the scene was softened, but what remains still chillingly recalls the bond of blood at the center of the Christ myth. If God the Father demands the Son's blood in retribution for Adam and Eve's sin, the Son in turn leaves his blood as the fulfillment of his covenant with humanity. Filming this communion scene, Scorsese takes the most literal visions of transubstantiation as his text. In *The Last Temptation* as eventually released, when Peter drinks, he lowers his cup and touches his fingers to his lips. Rubbing the wine between his fingers, he discovers its strange consistency, the consistency of blood. This bizarre literalism can be traced to Scorsese's encounters with the Sisters of Mercy, who emphasized the sanctity of host and wine as God's real body and blood to impressionable Catholic youths. When Scorsese recalls his indoctrination, he isolates one particular anecdote that haunted him decades later: "According to the nuns, there was a woman who wanted to take home the Eucharist. And she did. She got it in her mouth, she took it back to the pew . . . went home, and put it in a trunk. And that night while she was sleeping, the trunk started to glow. Then blood started coming out of the trunk, you know? And then she was terrified, and she had a priest come in, and the priest took the host and put it back where it should be" ("Streets," 94). Scorsese carried that bloody trunk everywhere in his psyche and spent much energy trying to track down a film John Cassavetes recommended to him because it treated the same theme, Timothy Carey's unreleased *The World's Greatest Sinner.* As Cassavetes described the film to Scorsese, the protagonist takes the Eucharist from the tabernacle, only to be pursued by rivers of blood. Scorsese thought this idea of bloody retribution "wonderful" and rhapsodized about the potential power of images of blood as it "starts to follow him all through the streets as he's running" ("Streets," 94). In *The Last Temptation of Christ* Scorsese bathes his vision of Kazantzakis in that Eucharistic river of blood.

The original plans for *The Last Temptation of Christ* envisioned a European premiere at the 1988 Venice Film Festival and then an American premiere on 23 September 1988 at the New York Film Festival. Then fate intervened. In June 1988 Universal's consultant Tim Penland resigned, returning to his evangelical roots to mastermind a fierce fundamentalist attack on the film, the studio, and Scorsese. The tone for the ensuing controversy was set by director Franco Zeffirelli, who was widely quoted as assailing "the Jewish cultural scum of Los Angeles which is always spoiling for a chance to attack the Christian world" for commissioning *The Last Temptation of Christ.*[23] Zeffirelli later denied he had made these remarks, yet he redoubled his attacks on the film and the filmmakers, causing a brouhaha at the Venice festival.

The film community hadn't, in the words of the old cliché, "seen nothing yet." The summer of 1988 witnessed the most intense religious controversy in the history of Hollywood. American fundamentalists, stung by the scandals involving televangelists, turned their ire on Universal, Scorsese, and *The Last Temptation of Christ*. Emotions ran so high that all rationality and restraint soon evaporated. By 27 July 1988 *Variety* could accurately report that the "Scorsese Pic" was the "Center of a Holy War."[24] For months thereafter *Variety* was forced to feature special sections on the controversy, as legal tests, riots, and other sordid reactions greeted the openings of the film around the world.

The most influential attack in America came from former White House aide Patrick Buchanan, whose nationally syndicated column appeared on op-ed pages everywhere decrying "Hollywood's Sleazy Image of Christ" and labeling the film "an act of cinematic vandalism against the beliefs that Christians hold sacred . . . a deliberate profanation of the faith."[25] Driven to a frenzy by a propaganda blitz, the Moral Majority jammed the phones at Universal. By August 1988 almost 8,000 pickets had formed around the studio offices, security measures were instituted, and bodyguards were accompanying even minor Universal executives. The level of heat was rising as the level of light and reason declined precipitously. A measure of the controversy's effect on Scorsese may be found in the fact that his autobiography, *Scorsese on Scorsese,* contains the best summaries of the madness engulfing his film. Scorsese was at the center of a firestorm and was badly burned.

A few examples may indicate the sad direction the fray took. Reverend Donald Wildmon of the American Family Association, which garnered 60,000 new members during its campaign against *The Last Temptation of Christ,* picketed Lew Wasserman's home, preaching loudly on the doorstep of the Jewish chairman of MCA, Universal's parent corporation. Wildmon then wrote Sid Sheinberg, the Jewish president of MCA, demanding to know "How many Christians are there in the top positions of MCA/Universal? How many Christians sit on the board of directors of MCA?" (Gabler, 108) Reverend R.L. Hymes joined in this anti-Semitic onslaught, staging Passion plays outside Wasserman's home as pickets carried signs charging that "Wasserman fans Jew-hatred with *Temptation*."

Bill Bright of the Campus Crusade for Christ eschewed the stick in favor of the carrot in his crusade against *The Last Temptation*. He calmly offered Universal $10 million for the master print of the unreleased film so he could destroy it. Meanwhile Catholic Jack Valenti, chairman of the MPAA, appeared on CNN declaring that he supported Scorsese's right to free speech because "I stand first as an American citizen"; the beaming Mother Angelica, founder of the Christian Eternal Word network and Valenti's adversary in the debate, jovially reminded him, "You're a child of God first, sweetheart," as she further opined that this "movie will destroy Christianity."[26]

Shaken by such apocalyptic rhetoric and by an escalation in protests and threats, Universal blinked. On 9 August 1988 Universal sent Scorsese to debate Reverend Donald Wildmon on ABC's "Nightline," but the director's reasoned disclaimers and continued assertions that this was "a religious picture" celebrating Christ's victory could not redeem his project. On 9 August 1988 the U.S. Catholic Conference called for a nationwide boycott of the film, the first such boycott the conference had ever recommended. Urging the 53 million Catholics in America not to see the film, spokesperson Richard Hirsch called *Last Temptation* "a b-grade, muddle-headed movie."[27]

Universal could not endure the intense controversy and decided to release the film six weeks prematurely. Thomas Pollock, chairman of Universal, offered a practical justification, arguing that "we have no way of defending the movie by what we say. This isn't rhetoric about the First Amendment. It doesn't mean anything for me to say that Martin Scorsese believes in this movie or feels it's a religious movie. The movie has to talk for itself."[28] Universal released *The Last Temptation of Christ* on 12 August 1988, just as *Time* magazine's 15 August 1988 issue, the top seller on the newsstand that year, hit the racks with its cover story, inquiring "Who Was Jesus?"

Scorsese had brought Christ, his agony and his temptations, to the attention of the American public in the summer of 1988. Paradoxically, he had been so successful in creating a controversy that he made it impossible for Universal to market his film effectively. Initially Scorsese bitterly described the early release as a film being "thrown into the streets,"[29] and then he became uncharacteristically silent, allowing his autobiography to do his arguing. Ed Hulse, astute analyst for *Video Review,* argued that *Last Temptation* became a "hot potato" for everyone: "Few people risk talking about it—in print or in public—for fear they'll get burned."[30] Even Scorsese, Hulse asserted, "[has] scrupulously avoided trading verbal jabs with his detractors in hopes that, once the furor dies down, his movie will reach a hopefully more tolerant video audience" (Hulse, 36). It had taken Scorsese almost 30 years to bring his Jesus to the screen. Now it threatened to be another 30 years before his efforts would be adequately recognized.

10

"Life Lessons" (1989), *GoodFellas* (1990), *Cape Fear* (1991), and *The Age Of Innocence* (1993)

To put *The Last Temptation* behind him, Scorsese sought a shorter project and, much to his delight, ended up working on an anthology film, *New York Stories,* with his friend Francis Ford Coppola and fellow Manhattanite Woody Allen. The genesis of the three-part film came from comedian Allen's suggestion to his producer-confidant Robert Greenhut that it would be fun to do a feature film based on short sketches like those he regularly published in the *New Yorker.* Greenhut recommended using different artists instead of doing only his own material, and Allen agreed. For a while they toyed with the idea of an international anthology using foreign directors, and they talked of an avant-garde feature using unconventional talent; finally, however, Allen and Greenhut settled on the idea of a New York–themed collection and approached Scorsese and his friend Steven Spielberg about participating. When Spielberg couldn't find the time, they recruited Coppola and the package was in place.

Woody Allen had a contract with Orion Pictures, so that company had the first look at the package. Fearing that *New York Stories* would demonstrate the same lackluster box office performance other anthology films experienced, Orion turned the deal down. Meanwhile, however, Scorsese had gone out with his friend Jeffrey Katzenberg from Touchstone Pictures to see the Broadway show *Me and My Girl* and casually mentioned his preparation for the Woody Allen collaboration. Within days Katzenberg committed Touchstone to *New York*

Stories, gambling millions to embellish the artistic credentials of this Walt Disney subsidiary.

To allay investor fears, Katzenberg had a press release planted in the *Wall Street Journal* under the headline "Disney to Use Three Directors to Create a Single Movie"; the release quoted him as confidently declaring that *"New York Stories* wasn't intended for art houses."[1] To sweeten the deal for the filmmakers, Katzenberg winked at the nepotism involved in *New York Stories.* Coppola was allowed, for example, to share writing duties with his daughter Sofia, and Scorsese was assured that his daughter Domenica could play Zoe in Coppola's "Life without Zoe" episode. Eventually Coppola dismissed Domenica because of "artistic differences," and Heather McComb stepped into the ill-fated role.

Domenica Scorsese's aspirations to a film career were nourished by Scorsese's ex-wife and film-journalist-turned-screenwriter, Julia Cameron, who featured Domenica Cameron-Scorsese as Victoria Potter in her well-received first feature, *God's Will,* which premiered as the opening-night selection in San Francisco's "On Screen" women's film festival. The comedy, based on the Cameron-Scorsese marriage and divorce, lampoons a divorced, self-centered show business couple who die unexpectedly and end up fighting in heaven over what will happen to their daughter. Their appeals go to a female God, who consistently spouts feminist rhetoric and renders feminist judgments. No doubt *God's Will* embodied wish fulfillment for many lingering injuries Cameron felt. Her acrimonious divorce from Scorsese had divided their many friends into warring camps, as Cameron publicly assailed Scorsese for his blatantly adulterous liaison with Liza Minnelli, for his self-indulgent and ludicrously expensive drug habit, and for his using "every opportunity to make me beg and plead for money to support our child."[2]

In "Life Lessons," his segment of *New York Stories,* Scorsese grappled with the pain from his three divorces as well as with the heartache he felt from his many romances. Scorsese was brooding again on the central problem of artistic dedication versus romantic obsession, as eager journalists were prematurely reporting that "Marty is said to have split from his fourth wife"[3] and chronicling his romantic escapades with other Hollywood notables, including dates with Dawn Steel to play Trivial Pursuit with Steven Spielberg and others.[4] For this go-round, however, Scorsese's treatment of love was to be comic and whimsical, even if his inspiration was somber and intellectual.

The immediate source for "Life Lessons," Scorsese declared, was Dostoyevski's *The Gambler,* a work he had first read in 1968 and had planned for two decades to film.

Scorsese's resolve to film Dostoyevski's work was reinforced in 1973 when Jay Cocks, a frequent uncredited collaborator, gave him a Christmas present of a single volume containing a new translation of *The Gambler,* along with the *Diaries of Paulina*—the journal of Dostoyevski's mistress Apollinaria Suslova—and a short story Suslova wrote about their love affair. Scorsese had Paul Schrader prepare a treatment of *The Gambler* and of the Paulina material, but nothing came of it. Scorsese later turned to Richard Price, his collaborator on *The Color of Money* and "Bad," for a new approach. Price and Scorsese quickly decided to switch their protagonist from a writer to a painter, a fiftyish, wealthy, established Soho talent, Lionel Dobie, to be played by a physically imposing actor noted for his fiery temperament, heavy drinking, and egregious womanizing, Nick Nolte. They also agreed that their Paulina would be a tyro painter named Paulette, to be played with voluptuous sensuality by Rosanna Arquette, the love interest in *After Hours,* whom both Scorsese and Price remembered most vividly for her inflammatory nude scenes in the European version of the television miniseries "The Executioner's Song." Arquette, they felt, could bring to the role youth, innocence, mystery, and allure, yet also manage to cruelly rebuff Nolte.

The switch to painting from writing, Price argued, enabled the collaborators to deal with obsession and inspiration in purely visual terms. Scorsese had no objection whatsoever, for his earliest avocation had been painting. His asthma, unfortunately, had curtailed his "first great love,"[5] since he couldn't tolerate the fumes from oils and solvents. Even shooting "Life Lessons" in a well-ventilated, 10,000-foot loft near Astor Place in Greenwich Village proved an ordeal for Scorsese's sensitive respiratory system. He lived on his infamous atomizer and used a array of allergy medications as he filmed the dynamic process of modern painting. The more paint Nolte flung at his canvas *The Bridge to Nowhere* (actually an important art piece by New York artist Chuck Connelly), the more his frail director cowered, ducked, and wheezed.

Scorsese was intent on making his finished product a fun movie, full of life, humor, irony, romance, and zest. He told interviewers that he wanted to make "an enjoyable movie" that simultaneously dealt "with a serious issue—what's the equation of pain in our lives to the

Top. Nick Nolte and Rosanna Arquette in "Life Lessons," the Martin Scorsese section of *New York Stories* (1989). Touchstone Pictures. The Museum of Modern Art/ Film Stills Archive. *Bottom:* Martin Scorsese on location for his "Life Lessons," a segment of *New York Stories* (1989). Touchstone Pictures. The Museum of Modern Art/Film Stills Archive.

work that we do?"[6] The balance in "Life Lessons" depends on a ful-
crum of self-awareness and personal satisfaction. The trauma of romantic rejection is played off against the bliss of creative process, the
pain of loneliness is balanced with the rush that accompanies fame,
despair is countered with elation, and personal silences are overwhelmed by driving rock-and-roll. "Life Lessons" constitutes Scorsese's and Price's postmodernist version of the agony and the ecstasy,
their deconstruction of love in a narcissistic, secular, and entropic
world.

In many episodes Price and Scorsese use scenes culled from Paulina's diary that take on new dimensions in a modern context. Dostoyevski's pledges to avoid physical contact with Paulina and his romantic
idealization of her foot, chronicled in detail in Suslova's most famous
diary entry, have totally different resonances from those of Lionel's
almost-silly attempts to live in the same loft as Paulette, to ignore her
dalliances with a parade of young studs, and to keep his roving hands
off her sumptuous body. Nineteenth-century romanticism seems
quite out of place in the jumbled world of *Desperately Seeking Susan,*
where performance artists do extended monologues about paranoid
misfits as they position themselves in the middle of subway tracks,
and where Bob Dylan and the Band celebrate life's inconstancy and
confusion in "Like a Rolling Stone." A measure of the dislocation in
moving Dostoyevski's agonies to Soho comes when Lionel's obsessions and insomnia are counterpointed with Puccini's "Nessun
Dorma" from *Turandot*; audiences chuckle at the incongruity of operatic grand passion linked to modern sexual dysfunction much as
they tittered at similar juxtapositions in the immensely popular
Moonstruck.

The humorous allusions in "Life Lessons," its tongue-in-cheek
knowingness, its mild abasement of its lovers, and its willingness to
mock its own slim narrative give the film a charm that cannot be
ignored. Scorsese confronts all his main themes—sex and guilt, art
and commitment, love and personal redemption—but this time he's
smiling, elbowing audiences in the side, dancing his camera around
the set, eschewing any grand moral in favor of small lessons in the
actualities of life. If Julia Cameron finds her solace in *God's Will,*
Scorsese seeks more earthy answers in "Life Lessons." As Pauline Kael
observes, "Life Lessons" wins us with its geniality: "Scorsese has
lightened up, and in a satisfying way. He's developed a sense of horse-
play. . . . He sees the comedy of his own compulsiveness on love and
art and he's able to sustain this vision."[7]

Scorsese's comic success depends on the richness and density of characterization in his lightning-fast, 45-minute film. Each lover in "Life Lessons" is a complex, fully rounded, deeply flawed individual with remarkably human foibles. Lionel Dobie, for example, glories in his fame, assuring his "chippies" that "If you enter the party with me, you walk in with firepower, with authority," yet for all his boasting, he calls his women "chippies" because he feels that they "chip away at your art and they want to own your talent." Like all lionized artists, he's torn between the call of his pride and the danger of being consumed by admirers. He's also enough of a realist to appreciate that the insecure Paulette's paintings (created by Susan Hambleton, a graduate of the School of Visual Arts in New York) are, as John Simon notes in his review, "considerably better than Dobie's daubs."[8] Paulette threatens both Dobie's self-esteem and his reputation; this student might soon outshine her lovesick mentor.

Working closely with Nick Nolte, Scorsese makes the portrayal of the rueful and lustful Dobie a performance that Kay Larson, an art critic for the *New York Times,* lauded as "the most sophisticated cinematic under-the-skin account of an artist I've seen."[9] Nolte makes Lionel a larger-than-life, ursine, marauding enfant terrible who wallows in his paints, spilling them on Cartier watches and Armani tuxedos. Lionel ignores convention as he suffers the extremes of melancholia normally associated with puppy love. A displaced courtly lover, he creates large, tumultuous canvases inspired by Paulette's petty betrayals and by overamplified, maudlin popular ballads. Nolte explained that he "thought it was the story about beauty and the beast, and [Lionel is] the beast. Creative people are bestial; they're consumed. It's a comedy about people who don't know where their relationships are" (James 1988, 35). To increase the sense of Lionel as a dissolute character, a beast out of control, Scorsese encouraged Nolte to swill beer all day on set. As a result, Nolte recalls, the movie "was a very happy experience."[10]

For all the party-animal excesses and soulful suffering, Lionel Dobie never loses his vitality. His complaints can be so loud only because his appetites are so great. Lionel is the libido unleashed, a phallic fount of anarchy, destruction, and creativity. Like his expressionist canvases, he challenges the frame, stretching the borders of reality. He attracts students because it is clear that his lessons in life will be as exhilarating as they are gargantuan. As Jonathan Rosenbaum astutely observed, Lionel's excessive energy fuels the narrative drive of "Life Lessons":

"As in nearly all of Scorsese's best work, it is the expression and presentation of the central character's mania that gives the story life—a kind of expressionism that in this case is directly tied to the flow and texture of Dobie's painting—rather than the shape of the anecdote, which typically takes the form of a vicious circle."[11]

Even the most cockeyed optimist quickly recognizes that Lionel and Paulette make a terrible couple; there is no chance love will or should conquer all in their relationship. The closure of their narrative is preordained. As Scorsese envisioned it, the film begins "at the end and goes to the very end"[12] of their relationship. Lionel's chippies parallel the groupies who haunted Scorsese and Robbie Robertson during their post–*Last Waltz* binges. The story of a successful artist and his acolytes, Scorsese reminisced with Chris Holdenfield, is as predictable as it is tragicomic: "[Lionel] has constant relationships with these women, these assistants, and obviously these relationships are dead from the beginning. Because at a certain age—53, 54—and you're famous, doing a lot of stuff, and you keep getting involved with girls who are 23—they're kids, they're like daughters. You've got to let them go out, to let them grow. They'll hurt you. And you'll hurt them, too." (Holdenfield 1989, 51). Wisdom, Scorsese indicates in "Life Lessons," resides in recognizing the comedy behind all anguish, in relishing one of life's mysteries—the painful laugh.

Paulette crystallizes this insight for Lionel Dobie. She stimulates his erotic energy with what David Denby aptly describes as "that teenagey come-hither look—the upturned nose, downy upper lip, and golden skin."[13] She may be, as Vincent Canby complains, "a tiresome, arrogant, demanding bore," but as Canby also allows, "she has going for her . . . a slim foot and ankle that, when girded with a bracelet, make her the most erotic woman in the world, for a few minutes anyway."[14] Dobie is mesmerized by her firm breasts, white shoulders, graceful buttocks, and smooth thighs, yet he cannot paint when she is his. Her hatred, betrayals, and denunciations drive him to palette and canvas. Without her, he is tormented and inspired; with her, he's satisfied and passive. This dilemma parallels Christ's plight in *Last Temptation,* where marrying Magdalene means a failure in his divine mission; Jimmy Doyle's agonies in *New York, New York,* where embracing Francine means giving up his sound; and Jake La Motta's trials in *Raging Bull,* where making love to Vickie means losing his edge in the ring. Like all of Scorsese's special saints, Dobie must choose art to live. His proclamation about painting could stand as Scorsese's artis-

Top. Lionel Dobie (Nick Nolte) gives Paulette (Rosanna Arquette) "Life Lessons" in *New York Stories* (1989). Touchstone Pictures. The Museum of Modern Art/Film Stills Archive. *Bottom Left.* Nick Nolte as Lionel Dobie in "Life Lessons," a part of *New York Stories* (1989). Touchstone Pictures. The Museum of Modern Art/Film Stills Archive. *Bottom Right.* Rosanna Arquette as would-be artist Paulette in "Life Lessons," a story in *New York Stories* (1989). Touchstone Pictures. The Museum of Modern Art/Film Stills Archive.

tic credo: "If you give it up, you weren't a real artist to begin with."

Reviewers of "Life Lessons" proved less enamored of the film's philosophy than they were of its visual audacity. Scorsese was working once again with Nestor Almendros, his cinematographer on a black-and-white Armani commercial made immediately after *The Color of Money*. Almendros, Francois Truffaut's regular cinematographer, prodded Scorsese to make his cinematic form in "Life Lessons" as daring and vital on screen as Chuck Connelly's and Susan Hambleton's experiments were on canvas. The challenge was staggering, given the time restraints on "Life Lessons": Scorsese had only two weeks for preproduction and four weeks for actual shooting, and even the postproduction had to be rushed so his footage could be coordinated with the work of Woody Allen and Francis Ford Coppola.

An aroused Scorsese made Almendros work harder than ever before; their virtuosity approached the demonic intensity of Lionel's most violent outbursts. Even the disapproving John Simon had to acknowledge the "obsessive manner" in which Scorsese and Almendros structured visuals: "Together with his splendid cinematographer, Nestor Almendros, he puts to use every trick known to the cinema: slow motion, extreme closeups, weird changes of camera angle, monochromatic shots in various colors, zoom shots galore, iris shots, jagged editing—you name it. An entire introductory course in film-making is deployed in speeded up fore-shortening" (Simon 1989, 47).

Few professionals worldwide could deny that Scorsese ruled as America's most competent and accomplished director, a man true to his personal vision and vigorously dedicated to the craft of filmmaking. *New York Stories* was invited to open the 1989 Cannes Film Festival on 1 March 1989; that same evening the Museum of Modern Art hosted its American premiere along with a gala salute to the many accomplishments of Martin Scorsese. *New York Stories* was also chosen as the first American work to be registered for copyright after the United States became a member of the Berne Convention. Scorsese, who sported his own Armani tuxedo, Cartier watch, and Gucci loafers, now also could enter any party with the firepower and the authority his fictional counterpart Lionel Dobie exuded. Scorsese, like Lionel, would survive and thrive. He had learned how to put his pain up on the screen, how to laugh at his grief and guilt, and how to work a crowd—all without betraying his art.

Before he edited "Life Lessons," Scorsese flew to Milan to do another commercial for Armani. As so often happens in Scorsese projects, especially his short works, the motivation was loyalty to an intimate friend, Gabriella Forte, the head of Armani International, though in the course of his labors Scorsese also discovered a unique affinity for Giorgio Armani himself. This 20-second advertisement would have a large impact on Scorsese's next major film, *GoodFellas*, because, as he told Bob Strauss, "If I hadn't done [his earlier 1985 Armani commercial with Nestor Almendros and this 1988 Armani commercial with Michael Ballhaus], I wouldn't have found the style for *GoodFellas*. I learned how short a shot can be on the screen for an audience to register the image and understand its meaning. . . . The commercials crystallized my concept of moving the action much quicker."[15] The concept for this second commercial came from a French agency and emphasized a visual homage to classic Italian films by Visconti, Bellochio, and Bertolucci. Scorsese and Ballhaus admitted they "had some fun" shooting this mysterious interlude between an unseen male lover and his distraught paramour because "there are lots of shots of him peering through a door" with "the camera slowly moving in on his eyes," and the result is a film that is "all style" (*Scorsese* 1989, 150). Style began to preoccupy Scorsese as his bankability became certain. If the 1980s evidenced his labors to join the ranks of Hollywood directors, the 1990s would see his efforts to lead the pack over new horizons, beginning with the virtuoso display of new cinematic techniques in *GoodFellas*. Critics in New York, Los Angeles, Boston, and Chicago would laud *GoodFellas* as the best picture of the year and Scorsese as best director, but his peers with the Directors Guild would also find in *GoodFellas* his clarion call for a new daring and complexity in narrative technique.

Scorsese's earlier successful crusade for improved color film stocks from Kodak had brought him to the attention of Japanese director Akira Kurosawa, when in 1980 Scorsese met him in a hotel room and was allotted 10 minutes to convince Kurosawa to sign the petition to Kodak from the world's greatest filmmakers. As Scorsese recalls their conference, "I talked fast. I was very intense, and he said he would think about it."[16] Within months Scorsese learned that Kurosawa would sign. Kurosawa kept the memory of that small, bearded, seemingly possessed New Yorker in his mind's eye for years, however, and when he wrote his kaleidoscopic epic *Dreams,* he contacted Francis Ford Coppola and told him, "That's the level of intensity I want for the part of Vincent van Gogh" (Darnton, 47). Coppola made the arrangements with Scorsese, and the director once again found himself in what for him was the awkward position of acting in a major role in an important film.

Characteristically, faced with creating an image of van Gogh in a segment entitled "Crows," in which the narrator leaps into the landscapes of van Gogh to confront the artist, Scorsese drew on his vast store of film memories and imitated Kirk Douglas's performance as van Gogh in Vincente Minelli's awardwinning *Lust for Life*. Scorsese's lines proved uninspiring, as he explained the bandages covering his missing ear by declaring, "Yesterday I was trying to do a self-portrait but the ear kept getting in the way." For most critics, the hurried, clipped, nervous New York speech patterns so characteristic of the hyperactive Italian American director got in the way of his performance. *Variety* sniped at Scorsese's "rapid-fire New York patois blithely unaltered for the role,"[17] while *Entertainment Weekly* accused him of "babbling on in an unadulterated New York accent."[18] Clearly, the trip to Arles via Japan was a bumpy one for a director from Little Italy.

But Scorsese was on his way back to home base. His next feature, *GoodFellas,* would return him to the gangster-ridden "mean streets" of his childhood. Scorsese had always wanted to continue his tales of Murray, J.R., Charlie, and Johnny Boy and their milieu, but he had never found an appropriate script or adequate studio backing. With *GoodFellas* he found both.

Scorsese first learned of Nicholas Pileggi's 1985 book *Wise Guy: Life in a Mafia Family,* the source of *GoodFellas,* when he was filming *The Color of Money.* His associates procured galleys of the text for the director, and he was immediately hooked. As he told Gavin Smith of *Film Comment,* he knew Pileggi's reworking of the reminiscences of Henry Hill, a gangster cooperating with federal authorities, could make a "fascinating film" if the director respected Hill's account for "what it is," treated it in the "spirit of a documentary," and achieved a result that looked "as if you had a 16 mm camera with these guys for 20, 25 years" and screened "what you'd pick up."[19] Scorsese wanted to be that eavesdropping director and impulsively called Pileggi at *New York* magazine to see if they could make a deal. Pileggi happened to be out of the office when Scorsese called, and when he returned to find a slip of paper instructing him to "call Martin Scorsese," he behaved like the typical cynical New Yorker—he threw it in the wastebasket, sure it was a practical joke by David Denby, the film reviewer at *New York,* or one of his other colleagues. Scorsese persisted in his calls nonetheless and finally reached Pileggi at home, excitedly telling him, "My name is Martin Scorsese. I'm a film director. I've been looking for this book for years."[20] Pileggi quickly assured the director that he had "been waiting for this phone call all my life" (Denby 1990, 32), and that "I can't think of anyone I'd rather have direct *Wise Guy.*"[21] Pileggi and Scorsese couldn't make the deal immediately or directly, however, for as fate would have it, the rights to Pileggi's New York Mob material had been optioned nearly a decade before by Irwin Winkler, the producer of *New York, New York* and *Raging Bull.* Winkler sold the project to Warner Brothers, with Barbara De Fina as executive producer, Thelma Schoonmaker as editor, and Michael Ballhaus as cinematographer. With a generous budget of $25 million, Scorsese was headed back to the old neighborhood with his regular crew and with an old friend too: after almost eight years of separation, Scorsese and Robert De Niro were to be reunited, with De Niro playing the role of James Conway, Henry Hill's hero and mentor.

Pileggi's *Wise Guy* began on 22 May 1980, when Henry Hill, an ex-convict with a long rap sheet, decided he could not withstand the clear-cut evidence federal agents had amassed against him in a narcotics case. He faced a long prison term and possible assassination by Mob capos fearful that he might reveal all he knew about the inner workings of the Mafia, the fabled Lufthansa heist, point-shaving schemes in college basketball, and corpses buried all over the eastern seaboard. Hill wanted a deal—freedom and protection in exchange for his information; the federal authorities agreed, and his testimony for the United States began. As the charges and prosecutions grew, court personnel recognized that they had uncovered a unique resource and Hill discovered that in his stories there could even be loot for him. So the shrewd gunsel instructed his lawyer to find a talented ghostwriter. Pileggi, a regular on the crime beat, well regarded for his objectivity and professionalism, was Hill's attorney's first contact.

Pileggi was well aware what a treasure had been dropped in his lap. Hill had been associated with job chief Paul Vario, a kingpin in the Lucchese crime family, for more than 25 years and had been a trusted confederate of James ("Jimmy the Gent") Burke, a fabled Brooklyn criminal celebrated for his flamboyant life-style, overly generous tips, ready laughter, and brutal streak of violence. Yet Hill, because he was half-Irish, remained a bit of an outsider in this Italian organization, and that peculiarity attracted Pileggi. As he explained to Susan Linfield of the *New York Times,* "Henry was a thug, but he was a visiting thug. It's like talking to an aide-de-camp in Napoleon's headquarters. He knows how Napoleon likes his coffee. I wanted to know how these people lived."[22] In his final draft of *Wise Guy,* Pileggi emphasized Hill's special viewpoint, clearly within and yet peculiarly outside the gang: "He was a full-time working racketeer, an articulate hoodlum from organized crime, the kind of rara avis that should please social anthropologists as much as cops."[23] Pileggi's involvement with this rare bird, a gangster with self-awareness, eventually became so intense that during this same period Pileggi's wife, author-screenwriter Nora Ephron, prepared her comic film treatment of a mobster suffering from boredom in the federal Witness Protection Program, *My Blue Heaven.*

Scorsese's *GoodFellas* premiered at a time when American film screens were crowded with wiseguys; in 1990 gangsters had again emerged as cinema's tragic heroes. America, mired in an economic recession as banks collapsed and real estate values plummeted, was reliving the Great Depression and its fascination with bad guys. Machine guns rat-a-tat-tatted, tires squealed, and sirens wailed in the night as the criminals in *The Godfather, Part Three, The Krays, Miller's Crossing, The Prince of New York, State of Grace,* and *GoodFellas* splattered blood on celluloid, brandished thick wads of illicit loot, splashed champagne, and gleefully escorted awestruck molls to the Copacabana. Power was the aphrodisiac of choice in an enervated republic, and to be a "made man" in the organization of hoods, as Henry Hill rhapsodized, was to be "treated like movie stars with muscle."[24]

Several sociologists theorized that the post-Watergate, post-Irangate, post-savings-and-loan-gate United States provided a perfect atmosphere for celebrations of criminal mayhem. The consensus argued that "Like folks in the 30s, we live in the aftermath of a ruthless economic boom that enriched a few but left many feeling stunned and fiscally pinched. Some feel there's something crooked about the easy money made by the big shots and a sort of rough justice in sly underdogs slicing a bit off for themselves. While films featuring good guys collaring crooks are perennial, the true gangster movie—one that takes the gangster's point of view—tends to proliferate in times of economic stagnation and popular resentment."[25] Scorsese's analysis of *GoodFellas* reinforced these notions. He fervently declared in interviews that "The film is about money. Throughout, you constantly hear them talking about who owes who how much. It's very important, because that's what they're really in business for. The violence is not the main thing—it's just a way to consolidate power to get the money" (Linfield, 30).

GoodFellas presented Henry Hill and his colleagues as so many unwashed yuppies from hell in a black comedy parable. Instead of stock options, wiseguys had revolvers; in place of acquisition departments, goodfellas had knives, ice picks, and Molotov cocktails. Their litigators were goons and assassins, yet their values were the same: they wanted the fanciest cars, the best seats in the house, and the most succulent meals, and they despised manual labor, traditional nine-to-five jobs, mortgages, and long-term commitments. To understand the "life," the values of Henry Hill and all the hangers-on at the Pritikin Avenue cabstand, Scorsese warned the press, audiences must overcome some basic misconceptions: "What people don't understand is that a gangster's job is not to go around killing people. A gangster's job is to make money. That's the main thing—everyone makes a lot of money. Someone gets out of line, and it ruins that money making for everybody. So he's got to go. It just happens to be their line of work."[26] Denizens of the Brownsville–East New York section of Brooklyn, Henry's turf, could not accept the precept that crime doesn't pay, for they knew the central axiom of streetcorner life: crime must pay. Money, the corner boys know, is the Mob's lifeblood. When there isn't enough vigorish, some individual must pay in blood.

When Scorsese began filming *GoodFellas* on 1 May 1989, he used locations around his birthplace in Astoria, Queens, to re-create Henry Hill's Brooklyn home and early family life. Location shooting at Kennedy airport, the Hawaiian Kai restaurant, and the old Copacabana reinforced Scorsese's resolve to create an "almost anthropological study of a small criminal culture" ("Martin Scorsese Directs"). To prepare their shooting script, Scorsese and Pileggi had worked separately at first, drawing up individual lists of the items and scenes in Hill's autobiography that must appear in their film. Each working session they would compare their lists of priorities, which proved remarkably similar, and then try to cut more material. They wanted, Scorsese indicated, to pare the narrative to the bone, so they could flesh it out with the particulars of Mob life. As Scorsese saw the film, "The trick was to see how far we could get away with cutting right to the heart of the matter and compressing it all. To show [Mob life] not just through facts—'So and so was killed because he killed so and so'—but

to show it through the everyday, seemingly unimportant details . . .
how they dressed, what they ate; the food, and the ritual of eating
were very important" (Strauss, 12).

Scorsese and Pileggi edited out of *GoodFellas* all the sequences in
Wise Guy where Henry is on his own, operating away from the Mob
and away from Paulie Cicero (the Paul Vario character) and Jimmy
Conway (the Jimmy Burke character). Thus, moviegoers never see
Henry's escapades in the army, his involvement with fixed harness
racing, his misadventures procuring a Haitian housekeeper, his disastrous foray to Boston College to fix basketball games, his years "on
the farm" at Lewisburg Prison, or his sojourn at Allenwood, the federal white-collar prison. Scorsese and Pileggi use Henry Hill only as
the federal prosecutors did: he is their eyes and ears in Mob circles. As
a person he counts for little, and this aspect explains Ray Liotta's
somewhat flat performance. His director Scorsese never concerned
himself with Hill's humanity; this seemingly central character was
merely the point of access to what really interested the filmmaker, the
world of the wiseguys. Pileggi had titled his book *Wise Guy*; Scorsese's working title was *Wise Guys,* and his eventual choice was
GoodFellas. Scorsese always had his eyes and cameras on the collective, not the individual.

To ensure verisimilitude, Scorsese cast virtually all Italian American
performers in *GoodFellas,* justifying his ethnic typecasting by arguing
that "You don't have to tell an Italian American how to hold a glass
or sit down with the boys. Casting Italian Americans saves you time,
and, on one level, gives you authenticity."[27] Scorsese wanted to avoid
the mythical dimensions of Coppola's *Godfather* saga and instead capture everyday actualities. He told Gavin Smith that for him *The Godfather* was "epic poetry, like *Morte D'Arthur*"; his "stuff," Scorsese
maintained, "is like some guy on the streetcar talking" (Smith, 28).
Scorsese avoided Coppola's parallels to a medieval court in treating
his don; his Cicero clan might take limos to the Copacabana, but most
of the time the family was at the cabstand or local pseudo-Polynesian
restaurants like the Bamboo Lounge, playing poker games at smoky
social clubs, or guzzling beer-and-a-chaser at Henry Hill's bar, The
Suite. Scorsese's self-professed aim in *GoodFellas* involved convincing
the audience that "it was hanging out with these guys in a bar"
(Denby 1990, 32).

Several of the finest yet eeriest sequences in *GoodFellas* occur when
the boys congregate and their banter suddenly erupts into something
more profound and disturbing, as though all along they were a tribe

waiting for a blood sacrifice. The power of the metamorphosis depends on the visceral dynamic Scorsese carefully cultivates in seemingly frivolous scenes. All the overheated chaos of the endless conversations in bars and restaurants serves as an ongoing totem feast, and while maidens may be waiting for their young warriors, there is a constant fear of castration and exile for feebler, less macho men. Every verbal exchange involves some taunting, some testing, some trial-by-ordeal. The curses and deprecation serve, as David Denby reports, to link the Italians as bloodbrothers in a criminal tribe and to capture the fiercely primitive masculine ambience: "No one in this movie . . . seems rootless or out of place; the men talk in rhythmic profanities—a weblike pattern of words—always turning back on itself—that rise straight out of their unconsious. Pesci [playing Tommy De Vito] and De Niro [Jimmy Conway], who worked together earlier in *Raging Bull,* connect at some level below thought. De Niro's Jimmy, a cold, calculating killer, loves crazy Tommy, and De Niro selflessly keeps himself way under Pesci's gaudy excess, goading, remonstrating, observing, enjoying."[28]

For *GoodFellas* Scorsese gave Pesci but one mandate: "I don't want to see you act. I want to see you behave."[29] Pesci's most memorable scene, a tirade in which he enjoys bearbaiting a disoriented Henry, was improvised, based on his memory of a similar incident when a dangerous character made him sweat the same way. The encounter, which occurs after Tommy has spun a hilarious tall tale, depends more on the dramatic shift in mood than it does on any specific threat. Tommy just turns and suddenly becomes an implacable inquisitor:

> Henry: (chuckling) You're a pisser, you know? Really funny. Really funny.
> Tommy: What do you mean I'm funny.
> Henry: (laughs) It's funny, you know. Y-Y-You're—It's a good story. It's funny. You're a funny guy.
> Tommy: (chuckles) What do you mean, you mean the way I talk? What?
> Henry: It's just, you know, you're—It's—You're just funny. It's—It's the fun, you know, the way you tell the story and everything.
> Tommy: Funny how? I mean, what's funny about it?
> *(the atmosphere is becoming intense)*

Henry's only escape from seemingly lethal peril is to wager everything on a comic bluff, so when Tommy doggedly pursues his bizarre interrogation, Henry finally explodes in mock-rage: "Get the fuck outta here, Tommy." Tommy then retreats, relenting on his physical threat but still teasing and crowing for the benefit of his wider audience, the gang: "You mother-fucker! I almost had him. I almost had him. Ya, stuttering prick ya. Frankie, was he shaking? Huh? I wonder about you sometimes, Henry. You may fold under questioning" (*Good-Fellas*, 23–24). Henry passes this trial by fire, but ironically his idiot savant Grand Inquisitor has found the heretic, the eventual apostate, whose recantation would bring his best friends to the stake in Foley Square.

Henry's fortuitous escape from Tommy is juxtaposed with two other characters' confrontations with the diminutive hoodlum, encounters that have bloodier outcomes—the defiance by the young would-be hoodlum Spider and the savage insults from a "made man," Billy Batts. Tommy's run-in with Batts was originally conceived as the opening sequence of *GoodFellas*, as the mayhem progressed from *passatella*, the ritual insults, to a vindictively brutal murder and then an almost-slapstick burial that included the diversion of a satisfying dinner at Tommy's mother's house after she was awakened by the noise of the corner boys stumbling around her kitchen looking for a shovel and rooting in her collection of kitchen equipment for appropriate weapons and dissection tools. In the final release, however, the Batts sequence was recut, and only a snippet of his death throes in Henry's car trunk and of Tommy's vicious stabbing of his squirming torso introduces the film, as the narrative quickly flashes back to Henry's childhood adulation of wiseguys. The reediting makes Batts's murder more central to the film, since it is reenacted later in *Good-Fellas*, and it also makes the conversations at the dinner table at Tommy's mother's house more revealing. Scorsese's mother, Catherine Scorsese, plays Tommy's mother, and though she has come a long way since *Italianamerican*—including roles in Brian De Palma's *Wise Guys* and Norman Jewison's *Moonstruck*—she still looks at the camera and her son for directions and cannot effectively improvise with such masters of the impromptu as Niro and Pesci. Her awkwardness does suggest, however, how her character's domestic, ordered, regular universe, replete with hobbies like painting, endures despite its proximity to the alien world of vendettas, hits, contracts, and scams.

The key theme in the Batts murder concerns Mob conventions and taboos. As an established member of the Gambino family, Batts has unique status. As a "made man" he is sacrosanct. No wiseguy or goodfellas can kill Batts without permission of the organization. His murder, Henry Hill explains in a voiceover, "was really a touchy thing. . . . [B]efore you could touch a made guy, you had to have good reason. You had to have a sitdown, and you better get an okay or you'd be the one that got whacked" (*GoodFellas,* 60). In line with the ironic tone of the film, Tommy is destroyed by his own dream. He aspires to be a "made man", yet does the one thing that denies him the opportunity—he whacks Billy Batts. His comeuppance occurs soon thereafter. The bosses call him for his own initiation—his rite of passage into Mob protection. But when the beaming, overdressed hood gets to the ritual, he discovers he has been set up. Instead of being initiated, he is executed for his violation of the code. Tommy pays in blood for Batts's death so the order of the crew can be preserved. As the chastened Henry explains, "There was nothing we could do about it. Batts was a made man and Tommy wasn't. And we had to sit still and take it. It was among the Italians. It was the real greaseball shit. They even shot Tommy in the face so his mother couldn't give him an open coffin at the funeral" (*GoodFellas,* 108).

Tommy's earlier encounter with Spider holds equal thematic importance in *GoodFellas,* yet it may be the least understood sequence in the film. Audiences were bewildered by Tommy's seemingly random violence and almost-gratuitous murder of Spider. The setting is simple: Tommy and the boys are playing cards; Spider, their young gofer, slights Tommy; then Tommy pulls a gun, demanding that Spider dance "like they do in cowboy movies." When Tommy shoots at the floor, he hits Spider in the foot, and the boy must be carried to the doctor. Sometime later the film returns to the card game, Spider and Tommy tangle again, and this time Spider echoes Henry's earlier riposte, "Why don't you go fuck yourself, Tommy?" As Jimmy and others taunt him, Tommy rises, pulls his revolver, and shoots Spider six times in the chest.

This offhanded shooting comes in the context of allusions to movie violence and Westerns. In Scorsese's earliest drafts Tommy alludes to "the only cowboy movie Cagney ever made,"[30] Lloyd Bacon's *The Oklahoma Kid,* but in the finished film the allusion is centered on the presence of Humphrey Bogart, the bad guy, also appearing in his only Western. Tommy wants the boys to know just how bad he is when he calls Spider "You fucking varmint!" and demands that he "Dance! Dance, you fuck, ya! Dance, you little prick" (*GoodFellas,* 67). Tommy views Spider's machinations as a threat to his manhood and frames the shootout in purely phallic terms. Thus, in their second encounter, when Spider drags his wounded foot around in almost-oedipal mockery and when Jimmy tauntingly inquires, "Are you gonna let this fuckin' punk get away with that? What's the matter with you? What's the world comin' to?" (*GoodFellas,* 70), Tommy erupts and empties his oversize gun. To prepare Pesci for this scene, Scorsese had taken the actor aside and reminded him, "John Ford made Westerns. We make street movies. Let's do that" ("Pesci on Scorsese," 21).

On the other hand, Scorsese didn't want anyone too comfortable with this shooting, so he loaded Pesci's revolver with full-charge blanks. When the shots boomed across the soundstage, the cast was stunned, and the horror of the violence literally rang in their ears. Pesci later admitted that this brutal murder was the most difficult acting assignment he'd ever encountered: "It was hard for me to do, because it was hard for me to justify. I had to feel the way Tommy does. So I told myself that the kid would have grown up to be a rat anyway" (Linfield, 30). Audiences had a hard time making this identification, so the scene remained puzzling for many.

Scorsese hoped everyone would find the answer to the puzzle in the dialogue that followed the slaying, deadpan lines that reestablish the ironic tone and black humor as the gang members quarrel over who has to dig the grave for Spider. This scene, like Shakespeare's famous drunken porter and the knocking at the door in *MacBeth,* was, Scorsese told syndicated columnist Kathy Huffhines, the "turning point" for *GoodFellas*: "The story is comic. It's about guys who do an Abbott and Costello routine, then something goes wrong. Like when they kill a poor kid . . . and De Niro says 'You did this when I didn't have any lime in the place? And we hafta dig a hole?' . . . And it is funny. And it's terrible. But it's also funny. And that's the real turning point of the film. There's an order, you see, and it got out of control. And then trying to get back to order: 'OK, you killed him; you hafta dig the hole.'"[31] This sense of an order that gives meaning also applies, Scorsese further explained to Huffhines, to the narrative structure and intricate cross-cutting in *GoodFellas.* Tommy's misadventures with Spider are systematically intercut with Henry's wife Karen's discovery of Janice, Henry's svelte mistress. As Tommy struggles to defend his masculinity, Karen frantically defends her femininity and her family. Harry, Tommy, and Karen thus embody in their obsession with control, possessions, dignity, and power the frantic, violent dance of death that Scorsese wants audiences to recognize lies at the heart of

Ray Liotta as Henry Hill, Robert De Niro as Jimmy Conway, Paul Sorvino as Paul Cicero, and Joe Pesci as Tommy De Vito in *GoodFellas* (1990). Warner Brothers. The Museum of Modern Art/Film Stills Archive.

gangland life. The sequence of events, as Karen's marriage collapses and Spider dies, reveals Scorsese's major themes. He explained his intentions in detail to Huffhines:

> Liotta's wife says, 'I need some money.' They have some fun in the kitchen. Then it cuts. The boy in the bar gets shot in the foot. Cut. Liotta's wife is throwing keys out the window and Liotta is throwing a lamp at his wife. Cut. The boy in the bar gets killed. Cut. The wife is buzzing the buzzers on an apartment looking for the mistress. None of

this nonsense of confrontation. None of this stuff of 'I think my husband is being unfaithful.' Those scenes pushed together and compressed tell you more about the energy level of living a life like that. At that point they're all trapped. They can't get out. (Huffhines, 2)

The juxtaposition also reveals the uneasy mixture of *Mean Streets* and Armani commercial that *GoodFellas* relies on. *GoodFellas* celebrates the materialistic, celebrity track, brand-name life-style of the Cicero clan as it dispassionately records their compulsive violence, relentless paranoia, and inexorable deterioration.

Duality and irony reign in *GoodFellas*. The wiseguys are wised up in the most dramatic possible reversal of fortune. Capo Paulie Cicero, for example, has but one fear: that drug involvement by his associates could implicate him and land him in jail as an old man. He cautions Henry not to get involved with narcotics, warning him, "Listen, I ain't gonna get fucked like Gribbs, you understand? Gribbs is seventy years old and the fucking guy's gonna die in prison. I don't need that" (*GoodFellas,* 85). Yet Henry's drug problem does eventually topple Paulie's domain, and as an end title informs the audience, Paulie dies in Fort Worth Federal Prison at age 73.

Similarly, wiseguy Jimmy Conway's greatest pride rests in the training he has given Henry Hill in the mob's two golden precepts: "Never rat on your friends" and "Keep your mouth shut." Nevertheless, within weeks of his arrest Hill has turned on his confederates and testified against Jimmy, condemning him to a jail term in a New York prison that will extend well into Jimmy's seventies. Interestingly, *GoodFellas* shows Henry facing no crisis of conscience and harboring no illusions about a Mafia code of silence. Coauthor Pileggi justified Henry's pragmatism by noting that it reflected the actual facts of the case: "The honor code is a myth. These guys betray each other constantly. Once Henry's life is threatened, he has no qualms about testifying. He does no soul searching because he has no soul. The F.B.I., the marshalls, were all astounded at the quickness with which he turned. I mentioned this once to Henry, and he didn't know what I was talking about" (Linfield, 30). On screen, however, myths die hard, and viewed against the conventions of the gangster melodrama, Henry's quick reversals seem darkly ironic. Henry is a "dirty rat" who gets to live another day and live a normal life in the suburbs. The crowning irony, then, resides in Henry's final lament at his fate. Normalcy for this operator who so loved the life of a wiseguy is the worst

Robert De Niro as Jimmy Conway confronts Ray Liotta as Henry Hill in *GoodFellas* (1990). Warner Brothers. The Museum of Modern Art/Film Stills Archive.

fate of all: "That's the hardest part. Today everything is different. There's no action. I have to wait around like everyone else. Can't even get decent food. Right after I got here I ordered some spaghetti with marinara sauce and I got egg noodles and ketchup. I'm an average nobody. I get to live the rest of my life like a schnook" (*GoodFellas*, 131). As Henry intones these lines, there is a dazzling image of Tommy blazing away with his gun—shelling the audience. The implication of the daring, energy, and power Henry has lost is clear. The mood resembles the silence at the end of Stephen Crane's "The Bride Comes to Yellow Sky" as Scratchy Wilson, the child of the Old West, resigns himself to the coming of law and order and drags his weary feet away, making deep, fossillike tracks in the dust. Scorsese's vainglorious Henry Hill, the film's final titles inform us, is still immersed in the federal Witness Protection Program; though he did dabble again with narcotics in Seattle, since 1987, the titles note, he has been "clean."

Clean is hardly what young Henry yearned to be back in 1955. For that teenager, the life of crime was everything, for it meant being somebody in a neighborhood crowded with nobodies, brandishing power among the powerless, and enjoying extras where few had necessities. Some of the sternest criticism of *GoodFellas* charges that the film is so imbued with the youthful Henry's fascination with and awe of wiseguys that it lacks a clear moral dimension. Owen Gleiberman's roast of *GoodFellas* for *Entertainment Weekly* typifies this criticism: "Here, it's almost as if [Scorsese] is concocting a schoolboy fantasy of remorseless evil. *GoodFellas* is brilliant surface moviemaking, but it's hollow at the center. . . . What's missing is Scorsese's humanity."[32] Scorsese and Warner Brothers were fearful of just such an attack on the amorality of *GoodFellas* after a disastrous sneak preview in Sherman Oaks. At the Sherman Oaks screening, as Scorsese remembers the scene, "people got so angry that they stormed out of the theatre" because they thought "it was an outrage that I had made these people so attractive" (Taubin, 38).

Scorsese's subsequent promotional forays for *GoodFellas* addressed the question of morality and amorality, good guys and bad guys, humanity and bestiality. Scorsese freely admitted that the whole film is glazed with Henry's admiration for the Mob, his longings for the life of a wiseguy, and his glee with the privileges of a goodfella. Henry sparkles at the Copacabana, relishes fine Italian cuisine, lusts after both the madonna Karen and the whore Janice, and worships Paulie and Jimmy Conway. Scorsese identifies with this vitality, freely confessing his own love–hate reaction to "the life." In *GoodFellas,* Scorsese further allows, he was trying to relive his own youth in Little Italy and to show how the Mob became a family:

> It's a nostalgia piece from the early 1960's when I grew up. Where I grew up, the people around me, a lot them were connected that way. To me, they were cousins, or they were friends; they were friends of my father. I would eat at their houses, they were like family, it was just life. There was no moral judgment, because we weren't aware of a great deal of what they actually did when they left the block—when they went around the corner, or up on the roof, or to Brooklyn. When a gangster has to kill another gangster, it's a tragedy, because these people are like family. (Ebert, 5)

Henry's wife, Karen, a Jewish suburbanite seduced by his daring and potency, establishes Scorsese's theme when she remarks that Henry really has "two families," his biological kin and his associates in the Cicero clan.

Karen, played by Lorraine Bracco, Harvey Keitel's wife in real life, becomes Scorsese's means of defining the slippery slope into crime, demonstrating how an educated, wealthy person from a good home could embrace "the life." At first the Jewish Karen shares her close friend Diane's prejudice against all Italians, but when Henry stands her up on a date, she reflexively asserts her own worth. Henry, stunned and impressed, notices in her anger that she looks good, with her great eyes like Taylor's, and he begins his seduction with a visit to the Copacabana. This sequence involves the film's most noticeable display of virtuoso filmmaking in an extended handheld shot marching down stairs, through doors, across the kitchen, and down front in the club as the whole world accedes to Henry's VIP status. As David Thompson observes, this "four minute steadicam take glides us along with Henry and Karen into the Copacabana, spelling out the sexual allure of the criminal's omnipotence" (GoodFellas, xi). Karen admits she's never known anyone like Henry, a 20-year-year-old kid with so many connections that it seems everyone wants to be nice to him. Then in a sequence reminiscent of the basic plot of Who's That Knocking at My Door?, a neighbor tries to rape Karen. Henry's response is bloody and direct; he pistol-whips the boy mercilessly. When Henry gives the phallic gun of retribution to Karen to hide, she readily admits in a voiceover that it "turned" her on, as she places it in a milk carton, a clear vaginal symbol. Their wedding follows, despite disapproval from both biological families; the one place Mr. and Mrs. Hill do get acceptance, and a proper reception, is with the gang. Associates shower them with money and insist that they socialize exclusively with Paulie and his extended family.

For a while Karen seems hypnotized by the excitement and wealth. Scorsese details the sexual excitement and enslavement of wealth in a revealing scene between Henry and Karen in their kitchen:

Karen: I wanted to go shopping. Can I get some money?
Henry: How much do you need? How much?
Karen: (Holding her thumb and forefinger a few inches apart) That much.
Henry: What? (He takes the amount she wants from his wad.) Here.
Karen: This much. (She puts her hand to his crotch.)
Henry: Here.
Karen: Give me a kiss. (They kiss.)
Henry: Here. See you later.
Karen: No. (She goes down his body and unzips his fly.)

Henry: (Chuckles.) Oh, all right.
(*GoodFellas*, 50)

Blind to her own debasement and to Henry's evil deeds, Karen ra-
tionalizes everything by noting in a voiceover that "After a while, it
got to be all normal. None of it seemed like crimes. It was more like
Henry was enterprising and that he and the guys were making a few
bucks hustling, while the other guys were sitting on their asses waiting for hand-outs" (*GoodFellas*, 47). Soon, however, Karen tires of
coffee klatches with women in too much makeup; constant tales of
violence, betrayal, and imprisonment; and a culture where wives go
to the Copa one night and mistresses go another. Henry's liaison with
Janice destroys any love that was in the relationship and drives Karen
to a harrowing though unsuccessful attempt to shoot him. His subsequent imprisonment and drug addiction further strain their relationship. During the last drug bust, Karen must once again hide a gun for
Henry. This time, however, there's no thrill of excitement. Karen
winces conspicuously when she slides the small pistol into her panties.

In the film's final titles, Scorsese reveals that by the time the film
was made Karen and Henry had separated after 25 years of marriage.
This fact ironically underlines Paulie's injunction to Henry during his
spats with Karen: "When you come back, you go back to Karen,
huh? . . . Please, there's no other way. You're not gonna get a divorce.
We're not '*animali*'" (*GoodFellas*, 73). Karen did learn just what species
of *animali* the Cicero clan was. Lorraine Bracco told interviewers that
the key to interpreting Karen rested in her sense that Karen needed a
family to survive: "She married him and stayed with him for all the
wrong reasons. She was a mentally abused woman who felt she had
no place to go. She would have considered divorce more of a failure
than a salvation."[33] Scorsese reinforced this idea on set. When Lorraine
Bracco kept screaming in rehearsals that if she were Karen, she'd leave
Henry, Scorsese and Ray Liotta would stop and do improvisations. It
always worked out the same, she recalls: "'I'm leaving you, Henry,'
I'd say, and he'd say, 'You can't, honey. You have nowhere to go'"
(Linfield, 30). Scorsese built on this concept to define the center of
GoodFellas. The Mob is a family that embraces and contains all its
members; like a feudal fiefdom, it endures by absolute allegiance. Its
rewards are wealth and a sense of belonging; its penalties are exile and
death. Only the Mob blessed Karen and Henry's marriage; their romance cannot endure outside that limited circle. In fact, it's doubtful

that Henry or Karen can ever really be "clean" again. "The life," Scorsese forcefully indicates, is a relentless trap with little possibility of escape; the bait of wealth and power may glitter and allure, but the bars of prison soon clang down, and the boom of a pistol gives the final coup de grace.

The many gunshots, knifings, and beatings in *GoodFellas* gave Scorsese problems with the MPAA ratings board, and trade papers rumored that an X rating was imminent. Scorsese trimmed the film until "it looked better," and when asked by the press if the film was still "sensual," he replied, "Yes, it's sensual—everybody eats, there's lots of food and violence, it's all about life."[34] The rating board gave *GoodFellas* the R rating Warner Brothers and Scorsese sought, and the film premiered at the Venice Film Festival, where Scorsese won the Silver Lion for his directing. The American premiere garnered Scorsese his best box office results ever, and major urban critics unanimously praised *GoodFellas* as the finest film of the year and Scorsese as the outstanding director. The reception for *GoodFellas* by audiences and critics alike provided, as Mike Clark observed, "more proof of a long evident given—that Martin Scorsese is the greatest active U.S. filmmaker."[35]

In the early 1990s, Scorsese's status as America's premier director and his burgeoning economic fortunes encouraged him to expand his operations on the East Coast. He soon found himself engaged in every facet of the movie business: developing talent, packaging deals, producing features, acting major roles, re-releasing overlooked classics, underwriting museums and festivals, promoting American cinema abroad, and spearheading a film restoration and preservation foundation. Simultaneously, his soulmate in film, Robert De Niro, established the Tribeca Film Center, a mammoth production facility, whose seven spacious floors housed foreign film companies like Miramax and domestic operations like Steven Spielberg's Amblin' Productions as well as Manhattan's trendiest watering hole and meeting spot, the Tribeca Grill.

Once lonely outsiders, Scorsese and De Niro emerged as powerful insiders. Their amalgam of friends, associates, and colleagues was redefining the American film and revitalizing the New York art scene. De Niro could hardly ignore the symmetry here; his artist father had once nurtured a thriving salon in Greenwich Village. His son had moved the scene downtown, south of Houston Street and way east of Hollywood.

Once a shooting star in New York's galaxy, a fleeting character in Andy Warhol's diaries, Scorsese was now New York's plenipotentiary. His circle, including producers Irwin Winkler, Barbara De Fina, Steven Spielberg, Harry Ufland, and Arnon Milchan; writers Richard Price, Paul Schrader, Mardik Martin, and Wesley Strick; editor Thelma Schoonmaker; cinematographers Michael Chapman and Michael Ballhaus; actors Robert De Niro, Nick Nolte, Joe Pesci, Lorraine Bracco, and Jodie Foster; and directors Brian De Palma, Francis Ford Coppola, Stephen Frears, and Jonathan Demme, dominated the contemporary film scene.

Scorsese, once the putative saint of cinema, found it difficult to be King of New York and King of Hollywood. The crowns weighed heavily on his head in the 1990s, and the decade contains both major missteps and gigantic triumphs. His "network" (the buzz word of an earlier decade) gave him access to the screen unprecedented in American history. The boy who fought to make short films at NYU was now powerful enough to film anything he wanted. Yet the same potent network enmeshed him in many vain endeavors.

Vanity, for example, motivated his 26-minute-long tribute to his friend Giorgio Armani, *Made in Milan,* which premiered in the United States as part of a larger "Images of Man" exhibition and promotion for the designer. A special screening of the documentary at the Museum of Modern Art in November 1990 attracted luminaries like John F. Kennedy, Jr., Cindy Crawford, Michael J. Fox, Richard Gere, Susan Sarandon, Robert De Niro, and Toukie Smith to watch, as journalist Woody Hochswender described the action, Armani "draping fabric on a model, or sleeves rolled up, his burly hands ripping the insides of a jacket"; the whole film, Hochswender opined, was "on an excitement level somewhere between sewing and watching people sewing" so that employing Scorsese to direct such flimsy material was as absurd and wasteful as "hiring George Cukor to film your wedding."[36] *Newsweek* echoes this assessment, noting that Scorsese's unabashed panegyric was almost pure folly: "The 26 minute film, made by buddy Martin Scorsese (who received a reported $2 million fee), depicts the designer's work in embarrassingly egotistical detail, leading some wags to dub it 'Paid in Milan.' Though there were scattered titters in the MOMA audience, most kept their sniping under wraps."[37] Mercifully, *Made in Milan* itself was kept under wraps after the screening and remains the one almost impossible to see Scorsese film.

Scorsese's loyalty to friends also prompted his appearance in *Guilty by Suspicion,* Irwin Winkler's first attempt at directing, a chronicle of the blacklist years in Hollywood, staring Robert De Niro. The project has been intended for director Bertrand Tavernier with a politically charged script by activist Abraham Polonsky. Creative differences arose, however, over the image of communism and conformity in the film, so Irwin Winkler rewrote the story and decided to direct it himself, with Arnon Milchan as producer. Rallying to assist Winkler on screen and off, Scorsese volunteered to play Joe Lesser, a character loosely based on director Joseph Losey. For his role, Scorsese dutifully shaved his trademark beard, and he limned one successful major scene opposite De Niro in which Joe Lesser proclaims his communism and urges his colleague to flee the country. For Scorsese, however, his second scene at a Hollywood party was pure mortification; he later told interviewers about his agony: "There's another [scene] at a party that I didn't like myself in because I talk very quickly and you also wonder what that short person's doing up there on the screen. It's true, I had to look up to all the actors to talk to them" (Moline, 2). Scorsese willingly, nevertheless, sacrificed his beard and exposed his short stature for old friends like Winkler.

Sometimes the confluence of friends brought Scorsese real successes. *The Grifters,* for example, one of the decade's best film noir adventures, based on Jim Thompson's cult novel, was a Martin Scorsese production, for which Barbara De Fina served as executive producer. The project cemented Scorsese's friendship with Stephen Frears, put him in contact with Elmer Bernstein who did the music, and established relationships with actors John Cusack, Angelica Huston, and Annette Bening. *The Grifters* also reminded Scorsese how much he wanted to direct and to lead the process of innovation in American cinema.

The project Scorsese chose for his next feature was Thomas Keneally's true story of Oscar Schindler, a German Catholic industrialist who saved over a thousand people from the gas chambers, *Schindler's List,* an acclaimed best seller based on the testimony of *Schindlerjuden,* "Schindler's Jews." This holocaust epic, replete with large moral questions and monumental guilt and retribution, was to be produced by Scorsese's friend, the West Coast's wealthiest director, Steven Spielberg. Spielberg, meanwhile, was planning to direct a remake of J. Lee Thompson's 1962 thriller *Cape Fear,* a classic Robert Mitchum, Gregory Peck confrontation based on John D. MacDonald's novel, *The Executioners*.

Fate intervened, however, when Spielberg decided he'd rather direct *Schindler's List* and when Robert De Niro committed himself to the role of the villain Max Cady in *Cape Fear*. Scorsese, who had no desire to do a re-make, especially of a simplistic though effective film like the 1962 *Cape Fear*, in which the consummate virtue of the American family is assailed by the absolute evil of a lone, crazed rapist, found himself beset on all sides by friends. Spielberg was implacable, demonstrating a tenacity legendary even in Hollywood, and De Niro ardently argued that the two old friends could put a new twist on Max Cady and *Cape Fear*.

Scorsese eventually blinked, seeing in *Cape Fear* a sure-fire commercial property that would make lots of money for Universal and repay the studio in part for its support of *The Last Temptation of Christ*, an opportunity to pay back some of the religious fundamentalists from the South who had lambasted his religious epic, and a chance to improvise again with Robert De Niro, whose work on *GoodFellas* had helped to secure Scorsese his economic base. Bargaining with Spielberg, Scorsese obtained his largest production budget ever, a commitment to his first wide-screen Panavision project, and a free hand to reshape the script as he saw fit. Scorsese told Spielberg that he would do *Cape Fear* only if "we can make the crux of the film internal."[38] Assured that Scorsese would allow the Bowden family to survive their ordeal, Spielberg conceded that "Well, then you can do anything you want up to that point."[39] Spielberg knew the happy ending was Hollywood's ace in the hole; Scorsese was content to stack the rest of the deck. *Cape Fear* would fulfill all the requirements of the thriller genre, and Scorsese was free to add whatever layers of personal vision and concern he wished.

Scorsese's basic approach to re-working *Cape Fear* eliminated the white hats and the black hats, the good guys versus bad guys dualism. Scorsese's Sam Bowden (Nick Nolte) was an attorney prone to cutting corners for powerful clients, cheating on his wife, and alternately ignoring then abusing his adolescent daughter. Scorsese's Max Cady was a demon who had been cheated by Sam, when Sam buried exculpatory evidence in a rape case, brutalized and sodomized in a Georgia prison, and warped by a childhood in an evangelical fundamentalist "Pentecostal cracker" family. These stunted characters seem fated for one last confrontation, one final baptism of fire, blood, and purification.

If the tenor of Scorsese's new metaphor in *Cape Fear* was judgment and truth by ordeal, the vehicle was sexuality; Sam's libidinal excesses, Max's animalistic perversions, Sam's wife Leigh's (Jessica Lange) raging sexual jealousy, and Sam's daughter Danielle's (Juliette Lewis) awakening sensuality propel Scorsese's camera toward the raging waters at Cape Fear and the fragile houseboat adrift in a tumultuous storm. Explaining his central concept to Peter Biskind, Scorsese intimated that in his vision of the film "Cady was sort of the malignant spirit of guilt, in a way, of the family—the avenging angel. Punishment for everything you ever felt sexually. It is the basic moral battleground of Christian ethics."[40] In Scorsese's *Cape Fear,* the best parts were "the dirty parts," the moments when each character's id impulses broke through and faced the x-ray of moral evaluations. Each character took Job's place as pawn of God and demon, as creature shaped for divinity but locked in a mortal frame. For Scorsese, the thunder of the Apocalypse roared when Max Cady entered New Essex, the blue skies of rationality were beset by furious clouds of doubt, and the waters of the unconscious were set roiling. Max, in the words of Richard Corliss, became the "evil twin to Jesus in Scorsese's *The Last Temptation of Christ.*"[41]

Max Cady's sexual allure involves no subtlety whatsoever. His garish pocket lighter ignites an enormous cigar as little electric lights on its side illuminate the red nipples of its nude figurine. Max's raucous laughter knows no bounds; his tropical shirt is equally loud and offensive. His greasy hair, stubbly beard, white Greek sailor's cap, convertible car, and polyester pants are all part of his smarmy come-on; he's a good old boy, an alcohol soaked Mr. Goodbar, with a hard muscled body and primitive tattoos, celebrating Loretta and his broken heart, promising lightning bolts down his abdomen and crotch, and threatening Biblical vengeance, truth, and justice. Max is all Freudian tension, suggesting countervailing impulses of life and death, pleasure and pain, bliss and desolation. Max comes ready for love with sweet talk and handcuffs, a sardonic chuckle and boundless brutality. In one widely discussed scene, Max raises brutality to a level of intensity unprecedented on the American screen when he assaults Sam's latest love interest Lori Davis (Illeana Douglas). Audiences were unnerved by Max's savagery, and theater owners, journalist Meredith Berkman reported, found themselves providing "therapy" and "emo-

Robert De Niro as Max Cady and Nick Nolte as Sam Bowden in *Cape Fear*. The Museum of Modern Art/Film Stills Archive.

tional first aid" along with cold water and paper towels; Berkman discovered this phenomenon when she too was overcome and sought assistance.[42]

Scorsese explores the limits of film narrative technique to suggest the cathexis of unbridled sexuality in *Cape Fear*. For example, when Sam and Leigh make love, Scorsese switches to x-ray footage to suggest the hidden dimensions of their passion. When Leigh then wanders around, listless and unfulfilled, Scorsese has the screen go red, an idea he borrowed from Michael Powell's *Black Narcissus,* in which a nun faints from sexual desire and the screen goes orange.[43] When Leigh puts on lipstick, the x-ray footage recurs.

Some insight into how calculated this sexual imagery was comes in a discussion of these scenes which Jessica Lange and Martin Scorsese had with Janet Maslin. Their elaborations on the action echo the interactions with performers that Scorsese encourages on the set before and after each take. As Lange analyzed the scene with the lipstick and mirror, she felt her character was being introspective: "at that moment, I think she feels a dissatisfaction with everything she's surrounded herself with. She really looks at herself, takes a moment to sit down and try to figure out why she's there" (Maslin 1991, 14). For Scorsese, the scene was more visceral, loaded with unconscious and irrational urges: "It's as if the husband doesn't exist and she's going out on a date—but unfortunately the date is with Max" (Maslin 1991, 15). Throughout the film, Scorsese's framing and editing subliminally establish his psychosexual theme. Cady is competing with Sam for his wife and his daughter. The two flawed men are acting out Freud's primal dream.

Max's attempted seduction of Danny (the family's diminutive and androgynous nickname for Danielle) begins with a phone call in which he pretends to be her drama teacher. In a torrent of psychobabble, Max suggests that she use the pain of menstruation and of misunderstandings with parents who won't let her be a woman in her artistic work. Danny, whose off the shoulder blouses constantly threaten to expose her pert breasts and whose sleepwear provokes her father to demand she cover her thighs and legs because she's not a little girl anymore, incessantly gestures to her mouth, covering and uncovering it as she attempts to conceal and expose her own appetites. During this phone conversation, Scorsese had his camera mounted on a panatate, which did a full 360 degree turn, following Max, who was working out physically as he worked Danny over psychically. J. Hoberman of the *Village Voice* called this scene "the movie's most daring set piece" though he was disturbed by its almost "hot dog" appeal to contemporary critical concerns: "De Niro makes a call to Lewis in the guise of her new drama coach (subtext overwhelming narrative). The stunt nature of this self reflexive turn is literalized by having the actor chat on the phone and even cue records while dangling upside down on his chinning bar. . . ."[44] Continuing the many metaphors concerning sexuality, maturity, and communication, Scorsese has Danny pop her orthodontic retainer into her mouth quite dramatically at the end of the phone call.

In his next encounter with Danny, Max, still disguised as a drama teacher, is revealed as a Big Bad Wolf tempting a modern, pot-smoking Little Red Riding Hood, and the barrier to Danny's mouth is dramatically penetrated. Aroused, she then engages in the first sustained passionate kiss of her life. This scene in the school basement (the underworld) with its stage scenery (dreams and illusions) garnered an Academy Award nomination for Scorsese's latest discovery, Juliette Lewis, a worldly 17-year-old beauty who could play an innocent 15 year old.

Owen Glieberman pinpointed the physical characteristics that made Juliette Lewis perfect for the role of Danielle: "Lewis, with her full lips, flashing eyes, and unexpectedly throaty voice, shows us Danny's child-woman precocity—the fact that, for all her MTV generation smarts, she still has the eerie guilelessness of a young girl."[45] Everyone on the set was so taken by Juliette Lewis's physical youthfulness that they felt the dangerous erotic tension Scorsese was exploiting. As Wesley Strick the screenwriter recalled the production, the atmosphere was charged with apprehension: "Juliette Lewis looks like a kid, but she has these really sensual lips. After a take, she would literally skip back to her trailer; you'd feel like a pervert just looking at her."[46]

Much of the nine-minute theater seduction sequence between Max and Danny was improvised, yet Scorsese managed to capture everything he needed in one inspired take. Before the scene, he warned Juliette Lewis that De Niro was going to do something unusual and erotic, but that's all the information she had before De Niro as Max coaxed her as Danny to take his thumb in her mouth in a symbolic act of fellatio. Discussing the episode with Chris Smith, Lewis revealed that "they didn't tell me they were going to do that. Marty and Bob—they're sick, they're sick together."[47] Lewis managed the scene admirably, however, and the result was aptly described by critic Eleanor Sullivan: "When he sticks his thumb in her mouthful of braces, twice, it's a moment to stop time."[48]

Scorsese recognized the power of the performances and later lauded his actors in an interview with Janet Maslin, observing that "Something happened between the two of them, and it was just great" (Maslin 1991, 15). De Niro went out of his way to promote Lewis's career during the press conferences for the film. And Lewis herself admitted that the episode left her tingling with excitement: "When we finished shooting, I realized, God, this is what acting is supposed to feel like."[49] Scorsese's one problem was how to edit the sequence. During the improvisation, he had two cameras running, and immediately afterward he told screenwriter Strick that "there was such an embarrassment of good footage that he was almost considering dividing the screen in half and just running both of them the whole time."[50] Editor Thelma Schoonmaker, however, showed Scorsese how seamlessly the footage from both cameras could be melded, and the result is a classic sequence that dazzled audiences and critics alike and will long be grist for scholars and film students.

Unfortunately, horror film conventions demanded that Scorsese's subtle sexual threats and implied triangles be fleshed out in physical confrontations. So the last encounters in *Cape Fear* go way over the top, mimicking the worst of slasher films and the dementia of Freddy Kruger's nightmares. Max no longer cajoles and manipulates; instead he tears at clothing, manacles his victims, fondles wife and daughter, and orders the women to "Get down on your knees and take off your clothes" as he threatens that "Tonight you're gonna learn to be an animal—to live like one and to die like one."

Animalism does reign in this scene, as pots of boiling water, lighter fluid, chains, rocks, and handcuffs become primitive weapons. Max, the id gone wild, seemingly cannot be killed; he is resurrected and reborn again and again. Only when the raging river of the unconscious surrounds him can the moral order be restored, as he slowly drowns, singing the hymns of his tortured religious youth. Scorsese obviously relished dispatching a Bible-belter to the strains of hymns; it was poetic justice for the treatment of his *The Last Temptation of Christ*.

Audiences loved Scorsese's "in your face" conclusion, the legacy of his deal with Spielberg, but his normally supportive critics were disturbed. Mark Goodman, for example, argued that "You have two options here: hire a baby-sitter and pay good money to go see this movie or stay home and puncture a spurting vein with the family screwdriver. The effect will be much the same either way, and with the screwdriver you'll have saved yourself a trip."[51] Terrence Rafferty, Pauline Kael's successor at the *New Yorker* entitled his article on *Cape Fear* "Mud" and spent most of his time slinging the same at the film, charging that "the movie is a disgrace: an ugly, incoherent, dishonest piece of work."[52] For all his vitriol, however, Rafferty did hit on the paradox central to *Cape Fear* and much of Scorsese's canon when he called Scorsese's presentation of Max's violence as the wrath of God chastising a feckless Job, a "consecration of something debased and profane" (Rafferty 1991, 158). As he had done so often in the past, Scorsese was bathing his audience in the blood from Christ's side, reminding them that the deep river of blood coursing through the Gospels presents evil and temptation as part of God's plan for salvation.

If, on a sexual level, carnality and violence, the pleasure principle and the death urge, are linked yet constantly in tension in *Cape Fear,* so also on a moral plane evil and good are commingled and intertwined in their opposition. Scorsese developed these themes in a revealing interview with David Rensin in which the filmmaker declared

Cape Fear his most "Catholic" work: "Max is the avenging angel in a way. Nick Nolte and Jessica Lange's characters, Sam and Leigh, are representative, for me, of humanity. They're basically good people who have had some hard times and are trying to go through them and piece their lives together. Now they're being tested, like Job, by Max. . . . I have to ground everything in a bedrock of spiritual motivation."[53] Terrence Rafferty suggests that this moral "consecration" of evil is the boulder on which the houseboat of *Cape Fear* smashes and becomes mired in the mud; for Scorsese, the rock of morality is Peter's rock, the bastion of civilization holding back the swelling tide and raging storm of human passion. Max Cady and his evangelical friends may pervert Christianity into a violent, hateful, and destructive force, Scorsese suggests, but eventually God's plan will be manifest in swamps and on mean streets.

As he approached fifty, Scorsese meditated somberly on sexuality, passion, restraint, repression, and redemption. His marriage with Barbara De Fina was rumored to be terminating, even though they agreed to continue working together as director and producer. The now gray haired iconoclast, who admitted wanly that he didn't have enough time to read anything, startled his co-workers by announcing a new twist to his career: his next film was to be an adaptation of Edith Wharton's 1920 Pulitzer Prize winning novel, *The Age of Innocence*, featuring Daniel Day Lewis, Michelle Pfeiffer, and Winona Ryder in a moving tale of a late-nineteenth-century New York romance.

Somewhat disingenuously, producer De Fina, recently separated from Scorsese, told Rachel Abramowitz that *The Age of Innocence* was perfect for the middle-aged director: "It's about three people—a young woman, her marriage to someone a little older, and this third mysterious beautiful woman who arrives. It's about missed opportunity, which is a perfect subject for Marty. It's about repression. People think it's weird, but it's really just perfect for Marty."[54] Scorsese himself was less prone to suggest a roman à clef and emphasized his desire to make a costume drama, in the manner of Visconti's *Senso* or *The Leopard*. He had to admit, however, that since *Cape Fear,* sexual frustration, repression, and expression had been on his mind. Working with co-author Jay Cocks, Scorsese indicated he would emphasize the "yearning for sex" in Wharton's measured prose: "the subject matter that I seem to be attracted to—for example, Edith Wharton's *Age of Innocence* . . . has the *yearning* for sex, which I believe at times can be more satisfying than the actual consummation. I'm exploring those areas—

material that has to do more with the repression of sexuality than the actual sex itself" (Rensin, 72). Scorsese's "yearning for sex" surely leads back to *What's a Nice Girl Like You Doing in a Place Like This?*, *Who's That Knocking?*, and *Mean Streets*. J.R. always seems to inhabit part of the Scorsese consciousness, as do Charlie, Johnny Boy, Jake La Motta, and Jesus Christ. Curiously, however, it was his taxi driver, Travis Bickle, that Scorsese consciously linked to his Wharton project, suggesting to interviewers that "For me, it's the sense of poignancy—the sense of loss—in *The Age of Innocence* that I like. This man is in love with his wife's cousin, and he has to stay in his own world. I really identify with the way he covers up the obsessive love he has for this woman. Maybe I've gotten old or something. For me, it's not that far a cry from Travis Bickle's obsession with Betsy. It's very funny to think of these two stories together. They're several worlds apart. But they're both New York" (Fuller, 18).

And Scorsese himself will always be all New York—the Big Apple—the Damon Runyonesque metropolis with millions of untold stories. After *Cape Fear*, he signed with Universal Pictures and their Park Avenue office to do six pictures, one a year, as well as to produce several more each year. Already announced are two Martin Scorsese Productions, *Mad Dog and Glory*, a gangster film written by Richard Price, starring Robert De Niro, and directed by John McNaughton, and *Pure Heart*, a tale of two brothers, played by John Cusack and Nicholas Cage, in love with the same girl, directed by Wesley Strick. Scorsese is then slated to direct *Clockers*, a tale of drugs and guilt in the urban ghetto, scripted by Richard Price.

Asked why he continues to create at such a furious pace, Scorsese gave an answer that cuts to the heart of his career: "The only thing you *can* do is make more pictures. In other words, it's the same old story: you keep proving yourself time after time after time" (Rensin, 58). For one of America's greatest film directors, cinema is salvation and retribution. This saint of cinema pays for his sins, image by image, in the streets and on the silver screen.

NOTES AND REFERENCES

Preface

1. David McClintick, *Indecent Exposure: A True Story of Hollywood and Wall Street* (New York: Dell, 1982); hereafter cited in text.

2. Bob Woodward, *Wired: The Short Life and Fast Times of John Belushi* (New York: Simon & Shuster, 1984); hereafter cited in text.

3. Julia Phillips, *You'll Never Eat Lunch in This Town Again* (New York: Random House, 1991); hereafter cited in text.

4. Steven Bach, *Final Cut: Dreams and Disaster in the Making of Heaven's Gate* (New York: William Morrow, 1985); hereafter cited in text.

Chapter One

1. Richard Gambino, *Blood of My Blood: the Dilemma of the Italian Americans* (New York: Doubleday, 1974); hereafter cited in text.

2. David Ansen, "Martin Scorsese," *Interview,* January 1987, 50; hereafter cited in text as Ansen 1987.

3. J. Hoberman, "King of Outsiders," *Village Voice,* 15 February 1983, 40; hereafter cited in text as Hoberman 1983.

4. Guy Flatley, "Martin Scorsese's Gamble," *New York Times,* 8 February 1976, 34; hereafter cited in text as Flatley 1976.

5. Paul Attanasio, "Film, Faith, and Fire," *Washington Post,* 27 October 1985, 2; hereafter cited in text.

6. Paul Schrader, "Martin Scorsese," *Cahiers du Cinema,* April 1982, 6–13; hereafter cited in text.

7. Richard Corliss, "Body and Blood: An Interview with Martin Scorsese," *Film Comment,* October 1988, 36; hereafter cited in text.

8. Diane Jacobs, *Hollywood Renaissance* (South Brunswick, N.J.: A. S. Barnes, 1977), 129; hereafter cited in text as Jacobs 1977.

9. Martin Scorsese, "In the Streets," in *Once a Catholic: Prominent Catholics and Ex-Catholics Discuss the Influence of the Church on their Lives and Work,* edited by Peter Occhiogrosso (Boston: Houghton Mifflin, 1987), 91; hereafter cited in text as "Streets."

10. James Truman, "Martin Scorsese," (London) *Face,* February 1987, 79; hereafter cited in text.

11. "Martin Scorsese," *Newsday,* 15 September 1987, pt. 2, 5; hereafter cited in text as *Newsday.*

12. Nathan Glazer and Daniel Moynihan, *Beyond the Melting Pot: The Negroes, Puerto Ricans, Jews, Italians, and Irish of New York City* (Cambridge, Mass.: MIT Press, 1970), 205; hereafter cited in text.

13. Gene Siskel, "Scorsese's Testament," *Chicago Tribune,* 14 August 1988, sec. 13, 4; hereafter cited in text.

14. Diane Jacobs, "Martin Scorsese Doesn't Live Here Anymore: Hollywood's Successful Young Director Has Walked Some Pretty Mean Streets," *Viva,* March 1976, 89; hereafter cited in text.

15. *People Weekly,* 8 August 1988, 42.

16. Maureen Orth, "The Temptation of Martin Scorsese," *Vogue,* September 1985, 17; hereafter cited in text.

17. *Scorsese on Scorsese,* edited by David Thompson and Ian Christie (London: Faber & Faber, 1989), 13; hereafter cited in text as *Scorsese* 1989.

18. Haig P. Manoogian, *The Filmmaker's Art* (New York: Basic Books, 1966), 29; hereafter cited in text.

19. Pauline Kael, *Taking It All In* (New York: Holt, Rinehart & Winston, 1983), 110; hereafter cited in text as Kael 1983.

Chapter Two

1. Stanley Kaufman, *A World on Film* (New York: Dell, 1966), 428.

2. Esther B. Fein, "Martin Scorsese: The Film Director as a Local Alien," *New York Times,* 29 September 1985, sec. 2, 19; hereafter cited in text.

3. William S. Bayer, *Breaking through, Selling out, Dropping Dead* (New York: Macmillan, 1971), 97; hereafter cited in text.

4. Andrew C. Brobrow, "The Filming of *Mean Streets*: An Interview with Director Martin Scorsese," *Filmmakers Newsletter,* January 1974, 30; hereafter cited in text.

5. Mary Pat Kelly, *Martin Scorsese: the First Decade* (Pleasantville, N.Y.: Redgrave, 1980), 11–12; hereafter cited in text as Kelly, 1980.

6. Kathleen Carroll, "A Director in the Family," *New York Daily News,* 17 August 1975, 71; hereafter cited in text.

7. Archer Winston, "Rages and Outrages," *New York Post,* 4 March 1974, 17.

8. All the direct quotations from Joey Morale are cited in John Lombardi, "Scorsese's Complaint," *New York,* 8 September 1975, 48–53.

9. Martin Scorsese, "Confessions of a Movie Brat," in *Anatomy of the Movies,* ed. David Pirie (New York: Macmillan, 1981), 134; hereafter cited in text as "Confessions."

10. Michael Bliss, *Martin Scorsese and Michael Cimino* (Metuchen, N.J.: Scarecrow Press, 1985), 110; hereafter cited in text.

11. Mark Jacobson, "Pictures of Marty," *Rolling Stone,* 14 April 1983, 44; hereafter cited in text.

12. Lesley Robinson, "*Who's That Knocking at My Door?*" (London) *Film,* December 1976, 6.

13. Press release for *Who's That Knocking at My Door?* (New York: Joseph Brenner Associates, 1969); hereafter cited in text as Brenner. Scorsese made uncredited contributions to the text of this press release.

14. "Almost Making It," *Time,* 19 September 1969, 95–96.

15. Holly McLennan, "*Who's That Knocking at My Door?*" *Sexology,* January 1970, 71.

16. A. H. Weiler, "That's Who," *New York Times,* 3 August 1969, 32.

17. Martin Scorsese, *Dialogue on Film,* Vol. 4, no. 7, April 1975, edited by Rochelle Reed (Los Angeles: American Film Institute, 1975), 84; hereafter cited in text as *Dialogue.*

18. Terence Rafferty, "His Girl Friday," *Village Voice,* 30 November 1982, 83; hereafter cited in text.

19. Kathleen Carroll, "Youth Served in New York Film Festival," *New York Sunday News,* sec. 4, 3.

20. Bella Taylor, "Martin Scorsese," *Closeup: The Contemporary Director,* ed. Jon Tuska (Metuchen, N.J.: Scarecrow Press, 1981), 315; hereafter cited in text as B. Taylor.

21. Mark Carducci, "Martin Scorsese," *Millimeter,* May 1975, 12; hereafter cited in text.

22. Joe Bob Briggs, *Joe Bob Goes to the Drive-In* (New York: Delacorte, 1987), 10.

23. Quoted in Stephen Schiff, "Married to the Movies," *Vanity Fair,* September 1988, 88.

24. "Review of *Box Car Bertha,*" *Variety,* 30 June 1972, 11.

25. Jeffrey Lyons, "*Boxcar Bertha,*" *Rock,* 25 September 1972, 8.

26. Archer Winston, "*Boxcar Bertha,*" *New York Post,* 17 August 1972, 32.

27. Chris Holdenfield, "*New York, New York*: Martin Scorsese's Back Lot Sonata," *Rolling Stone,* 16 June 1977, 38; hereafter cited in text as Holdenfield 1977.

28. Amy Taubin, "Scorsese: A Bicoastal Story," *Village Voice,* 25 October 1988, 67–68; hereafter cited in text.

29. Marion Weiss, *Martin Scorsese: A Guide to References and Resources* (Boston: G. K. Hall, 1987), 10; hereafter cited in text.

30. Scorsese isolated the actual shooting locations for *Mean Streets* in a wide-ranging interview with Paul Gardner published under the title "Martin Scorsese," *Action,* May–June 1975, 30–36; hereafter cited in text.

31. Vincent Canby, "*Mean Streets* at Film Festival," *New York Times,* 3 October 1973, 22.

32. "Calendar," *Los Angeles Times,* 14 March 1976, 4.

33. F. Anthony Macklin, "It's a Personal Thing for Me: An Interview with Marty Scorsese," *Film Heritage* (Spring 1975): 27; hereafter cited in text.

34. Harry Haun, "You Can Take Him out of Little Italy but . . . ," *Los Angeles Times,* 16 December 1973, sec. 2, 1–2; hereafter cited in text.

35. Pauline Kael, *Reeling* (Boston: Little, Brown, 1976), 172.

36. Jon Landau, "*Mean Streets*," *Rolling Stone*, 8 November 1973, 80.

37. Leo Braudy, "The Sacraments of Genre: Coppola, De Palma, and Scorsese," *Film Quarterly* (Spring 1986): 28; hereafter cited in text as L. Braudy.

38. Rex Reed, "*Mean Streets*," *New York Daily News*, 12 October 1973, 11.

39. Robert Phillip Kolker, *A Cinema of Loneliness* (New York: Oxford University Press, 1988), 164; hereafter cited in text.

40. Janet Maslin, "More on *Mean Streets*," *Boston Phoenix*, 13 November 1973, sec. 3, 2.

Chapter Three

1. "Director Finds Local Crazies," *New York Times*, 2 September 1975, 37.

2. Mel Gussow, "Ellen Burstyn," *New York Times*, 31 March 1975, 38; hereafter cited in text.

3. Michel Cieutat, *Martin Scorsese* (Paris: Rivages, 1986), 240; hereafter cited in text.

4. Richard Thompson, "In the American Grain: An Interview with Robert Getchell," *Sight and Sound* 45, no. 2 (Summer 1976): 141; hereafter cited in text.

5. James Monaco, *American Film Now* (New York: Oxford University Press, 1979), 153; hereafter cited in text.

6. Molly Haskell, "Character in Search of an Author," *Viva*, May 1975, 38; hereafter cited in text.

7. Arnold Abrams, "Harvey Keitel Is Still Acting Up," *Newsday*, 15 July 1984, 4–5.

8. Scorsese discusses these improvisations in Steve Howard's article "The Making of *Alice Doesn't Live Here Anymore*: An Interview with Martin Scorsese," *Filmmakers Newsletter*, March 1975, 24; hereafter cited in text.

9. Joan Barthel, "Ellen Burstyn Plays *Alice* from the Inside Out," *New York Times*, 2 March 1975, sec. C, 3; hereafter cited in text.

10. John Simon, "*Alice Doesn't Live Here Anymore*," *Esquire*, May 1975, 45; hereafter cited in text as Simon 1975.

11. Pauline Kael, "Woman on the Road," *New York*, 13 January 1975, 80.

12. Arthur Bell, "Shooting with Scorsese: Ready When You Are, Paisan," *Village Voice*, 18 August 1975, 69; hereafter cited in text.

13. William S. Pechter, "*Alice Doesn't Live Here Anymore*," *Commentary*, May 1975, 68.

14. Judith Crist, "A Star Outshining Its Galaxy," *New York*, 27 January 1975, 64.

Chapter Four

1. John Gregory Dunne and Paul Schrader, "The Conversation: On Fame, Guilt, and the Wars of Hollywood," *Esquire,* July 1982, 85; hereafter cited in text.

2. Richard Thompson, "Screen Writer: *Taxi Driver's* Paul Schrader," *Film Comment,* March–April 1976, 13; hereafter cited in text.

3. Rex Reed, "Making a Movie Here Is a Movie in Itself," *Sunday News,* 3 August 1975, "Leisure" sec. 5; hereafter cited in text.

4. Martin Scorsese, "Tapping the Intensity of the City: Creativity as a Natural Resource" *New York Times Magazine,* pt. 2, 9 November 1986, 85; hereafter cited in text as "Tapping."

5. Carmie Amata, "Scorsese on *Taxi Driver* and Herrmann," *Focus on Film,* Summer–Autumn 1976, 7; hereafter cited in text.

6. Norman McLain Stoop, "Martin Scorsese and *Taxi Driver*: In the Middle of the Street in the Middle of the Night," *After Dark,* March 1976, 36.

7. Ann Powell, "Transcendental Travis: Conversations with and about Paul Schrader," *Cinemabook* 1, no. 1 (Spring 1976): 21–22.

8. Pauline Kael, *When the Lights Go Down* (New York: Holt, Rinehart & Winston, 1979), 132; hereafter cited in text as Kael, 1979.

9. Gregg Kilday, "Scorsese: Virtuoso of Urban Angst," *Los Angeles Times,* 14 March 1976, 38; hereafter cited in text.

10. Laurence Grobel, "*Playboy* Interview: Robert De Niro," *Playboy,* January 1989, 78; hereafter cited in text.

11. Ann Guarino, "To Hell and Back with *Taxi Driver's* Author," *New York Sunday News,* 22 February 1976, 17.

12. Photocopies of Paul Schrader's draft script dated 29 April 1975 are available for purchase from Script City, 1765 North Highland Avenue, Suite 760, Hollywood CA 90028; hereafter cited in text.

13. Colin L. Westerbeck, "Beauties and the Beast: *Seven Beauties* and *Taxi Driver,*" *Sight and Sound* 45, No. 3 (Summer 1976): 137.

14. Marianne Sinclair, *Hollywood Lolitas: The Nymphet Syndrome in the Movies* (New York: Henry Holt, 1988), 150.

15. Kathy Huffhines, "Jodie Foster's Life Is Really Far from Simple," *Asbury Park Press,* 17 April 1989, sec. A, 7.

16. Paul Schrader, *Schrader on Schrader,* ed. Kevin Jackson (London: Faber & Faber, 1990), 120; hereafter cited in text as Schrader 1990.

17. Susan Braudy, "Robert DeNiro—The Return of the Silent Screen Star," *New York Times,* 6 March 1977, D13, D31.

18. Flannery O'Connor, *Three by Flannery O'Connor* (New York: Signet Classics, 1983), xxi.

19. Richard Goldstein and Mark Jacobson, "Martin Scorsese Tells All: 'Blood and Guts Turn Me On!'" *Village Voice,* 9 April 1976, 29; hereafter cited in text.

20. Paul Schrader, "Dialogue on Film," *American Film*, July–August 1989, 20; hereafter cited in text.

21. Robert F. Moss, "The Brutalists: Making Movies Mean and Ugly," *Saturday Review*, October 1980, 17–18.

22. Lawrence Wright, *In the New World* (New York: Alfred A. Knopf, 1988), 296.

23. Michael Blowen, "A Chronicler of Urban Misfits," *Boston Globe*, 13 March 1983, B1, B9; hereafter cited in text.

Chapter Five

1. Mark Goodman, "Tripping with Martin Scorsese," *Penthouse*, May 1977, 69; hereafter cited in text.

2. Seth Cagin, "Tracking," *Soho Weekly News*, 22 July 1981, 40; hereafter cited in text.

3. Jack Kroll, "Martin Scorsese: The Movie Brat," 16 May 1977, 84; hereafter cited in text.

4. Robert Lindsey, "The Director of *Taxi Driver* Shifts Gears," *New York Times*, 8 August 1976, sec. 2, 11.

5. Beverly Walker, "Is Martin Scorsese Making a Musical?" *Real Paper*, 11 September 1976, 22; hereafter cited in text.

6. Earl MacRauch, *New York, New York* (New York: Simon & Schuster, 1977), 5; hereafter cited in text.

7. Guy Flatley, "At the Movies," *New York Times*, 24 June 1977, C8; hereafter cited in text as Flatley 1977.

8. Karin Winner, "New York, New York—At a Wonderful Time," *Women's Wear Daily*, 5 August 1976, 32.

9. Hilary Ostlere, "*New York, New York*, a Terrible Down," *Westsider*, 30 June 1977, 13.

10. Arthur Bell, "Bell Tells," *Village Voice*, 19 August 1981, 33.

11. Earl MacRauth, "New York, New York," an unpublished screenplay dated 12 May 1976, 105C; photocopies of the script are available for purchase from Script City, 1765 North Highland Avenue, Suite 760, Hollywood, CA 90028.

12. Terence Rafferty, "Martin Scorsese's Still Life," *Sight and Sound* 52, no. 3 (Summer 1983): 188; hereafter cited in text.

13. Tom Allen, "Manhattan Downbeat," *Soho Weekly News*, 23 June 1977, 42.

14. Chris Holdenfield, "Martin Scorsese: the Art of Noncompromise," *American Film*, March 1989, 49; hereafter cited in text.

15. Jonathan Kaplan, "*Taxi Driver*: Martin Scorsese Interviewed," *Film Comment*, July–August 1977, 43; hereafter cited in text.

16. "*Shine It On,*" *Variety,* 6 July 1977, 72.

17. "The Liza and Marty Show," *Newsweek,* 5 September 1977, 49.

18. "*The Act,*" *New York Post,* 31 October 1977, 6.

19. Interview in "Martin Scorsese Directs," produced and directed by his former students Joel Sucher and Steven Fischler and broadcast on 16 July 1990 as part of the Public Broadcasting Service's "American Masters" series; hereafter cited in text as "Martin Scorsese Directs."

20. Stephen Silverman, "Why Scorsese Made *The Last Waltz,*" *New York Post,* 25 April 1978, 17.

21. Michel Ciment and Michael Henry, "Nouvel Entretien avec Martin Scorsese," *Positif,* December 1978, 7.

22. Stuart Byron, "Back Talk," *Film Comment,* May–June 1978, 82.

23. David Sterritt, "Scorsese Makes Offbeat Films," *Christian Science Monitor,* 1 June 1978, 14.

24. "Notes on *The Last Waltz,*" *Rolling Stone,* 30 December 1976, 71.

25. Roger Greenspun, "Grand Finale," *Penthouse,* August 1978, 38.

26. Stephen Harvey, "*The Last Waltz,*" *Inquiry,* 12 June 1978, 31.

Chapter Six

1. Jack McKinney, "La Motta Lacked De Niro's Determination," *Philadelphia Daily News,* 9 January 1981, 39.

2. Jake La Motta with Joseph Carter and Peter Savage, *Raging Bull* (New York: Prentice Hall, 1970), 85; hereafter cited in text as La Motta.

3. Paul Schrader and Mardik Martin, *Raging Bull,* a revised version of the draft script dated 18 April 1979, 94–95; hereafter cited in text as Schrader and Martin. The script is available for purchase from Script City, 1765 North Highland Avenue, Suite 760, Hollywood, CA 90028.

4. Joe Baltaks, "*Raging Bull,*" *Philadelphia Daily News,* 19 December 1980, 27.

5. Barry Paris, "Maximum Expression: De Niro Talks," *American Film,* October 1989, 36; hereafter cited in text.

6. Clarke Taylor, "Scorsese and Salvation," *Calendar,* 14 December 1980, 48; hereafter cited in text as C. Taylor.

7. Thomas Wiener, "Martin Scorsese Fights Back," *American Film,* November 1982, 31; hereafter cited in text.

8. Andrew Sarris, "Mean Fighter from Mean Streets," *Village Voice,* 25 November 1980, 55; hereafter cited in text.

9. Philip French, "In the Ring with Scorsese," (London) *Observer,* 15 February 1981, 14; hereafter cited in text.

10. Stephen Schiff, "Fists of Fury," *Boston Phoenix,* 16 December 1980, sec. 3, 3; hereafter cited in text.

11. Veronica Geng, "Taurus Trap," *Soho News,* 19 November 1980, 59; hereafter cited in text.

12. "Review of *Raging Bull*," *Variety,* 12 November 1980, 26; hereafter cited in text.

13. David Rosenbaum, "The Pain's the Thing," (Boston) *Real Paper,* 25 December 1980, 22.

14. Howard Kissel, "Martin Scorsese: Back on Lean Street," *Women's Wear Daily,* 9 September 1985, 24; hereafter cited in text as Kissel 1985.

15. Martin Scorsese, "The Second Screen," *Video Review,* April 1990, 24; hereafter cited in text as "Second Screen." Scorsese's commitment to video and its place in the study of film is evidenced in his preparation of interactive videodiscs for both *Raging Bull* and *Taxi Driver.* These discs allow viewers to view the film and hear commentary and analysis at the same time. They also permit students to see setups, outtakes, and alternative editings.

16. Michael Blowen, "Scorsese and the Symbol of Christ," *Boston Globe,* 2 September 1988, 19; hereafter cited in text.

17. Rex Reed, "*Raging Bull*," *New York Daily News,* 14 November 1980, 3, 21.

18. John Simon, "Of Force and Finesse," *National Review,* 20 March 1981, 303.

19. Steven Harvey, "Against Interpretations," *Inquiry,* 12–26 January 1981, 31.

Chapter Seven

1. Anthony DeCurtis, "Martin Scorsese," *Rolling Stone,* 1 November 1990, 106; hereafter cited in text.

2. Mark Litwak, *Reel Power: The Struggle for Influence and Success in the New Hollywood* (New York: William Morrow, 1986), 113; hereafter cited in text.

3. Susan Shapiro, "The Color of Marty," *New York Daily News Magazine,* 12 October 1988, 19; hereafter cited in text.

4. Todd McCarthy, "Are Today's A's Yesterday's B's?" *Variety,* 15 October 1990, 9.

5. Karen Moline, "The Good Fella from New York's Mean Streets," (London) *Sunday Times,* 30 September 1990, sec. 7, 4; hereafter cited in text.

6. Georgia Brown, "Paul Zimmerman: Screenwriting Is like the Priesthood," *American Film,* November 1982, 72; hereafter cited in text.

7. Carrie Rickey, "Marty," *American Film,* November 1982, 68; hereafter cited in text.

8. Dave Kehr, "*The King of Comedy*," *Chicago Reader,* February 1983, 40.

9. "Scorsese and De Niro: A Partnership Sealed in Artistry," Twentieth

Century-Fox press release dated 21 February 1983; hereafter cited in text as "Scorsese and De Niro."

10. Stephen Farber, "Five Horsemen after the Apocalypse," *Film Comment*, July–August 1985, 34; hereafter cited in text.

11. Stephen Schiff, "Let Us Not Praise Famous Men," *Boston Phoenix*, 22 March 1983, sec. 3, 4.

12. Janet Maslin, "Scorsese's Past Colors *The King of Comedy*," *New York Times*, 13 February 1983, 23; hereafter cited in text.

13. Scorsese even appears in director Robert Benarzoun's documentary tribute to Lewis, *Bonjour, Monsieur Lewis*, released in 1982.

14. Allan Arkush, "I Remember Film School," *Film Comment*, November–December 1983, 58.

15. Jack Kroll, "Diary of a Mad Comedian," *Newsweek*, 21 February 1983, 60.

16. David Denby, "This Will Kill You," *New York*, 21 February 1983, 74.

17. Stephen Harvey, "The Joker's Wild," *Inquiry*, May 1983, 44; hereafter cited in text.

18. Krin Gabbard and Glen Gabbard, *Psychiatry and the Cinema* (Chicago: University of Chicago Press, 1978), 212; hereafter cited in text.

19. Howard Kissel, "*The King of Comedy*," *Women's Wear Daily*, 16 February 1983, 8; hereafter cited in text as Kissel 1983.

20. John Simon, "Grating Comedy," *National Review*, 13 May 1983, 575; hereafter cited in text as Simon 1983.

21. Dave Kehr, "*The King of Comedy*," *Chicago Reader*, February 1983, sec. 1, 14.

22. Richard Schickel, "Beyond the Fringe of Fandom," *Time*, 14 February 1983, 80.

23. Marilyn Beck, "Is Greed Killing Broadway Shows?" *New York Daily News*, 21 January 1982, 64.

24. "Scorsese Shoots an Extra Sequence for Unreleased *King of Comedy*," *New York Daily News*, 3 November 1982, 48.

25. "Review of *The King of Comedy*," *Variety*, 9 February 1983, 19; hereafter cited in text as *Variety* 1983.

26. Marilyn Beck, "*The King of Comedy*," *New York Daily News*, 2 February 1983, 37.

27. Marilyn Beck, "The Big Screen Scene," *New York Daily News*, 29 August 1983, 37.

Chapter Eight

1. James L. Franklin, "*Last Temptation* True to Author's Message," *Boston Globe*, 1 September 1988, 28.

2. Nikos Kazantzakis, *The Last Temptation of Christ* (New York: Simon & Schuster, 1960), 2; hereafter cited in text.

3. Alan Mirabella, "The Man in the Eye of the Storm," *New York Daily News*, 11 August 1988, 56.

4. Ed Naha, "Screen Scoops," *New York Post*, 14 April 1982, 119.

5. Richard Gehr, "God's Lonely Man," *Video*, March 1990, 108.

6. Paul Schrader, "*The Last Temptation of Christ*," an unpublished working script dated March 25, 1982; hereafter cited in text as Schrader 1982.

7. David Grogan, "In the Name of Jesus," *People Weekly*, 8 August 1988, 42; hereafter cited in text.

8. Joseph Minion, *After Hours*, an unpublished fourth draft dated 6 June 1984; hereafter cited in text. The draft is available for purchase from Script City, Suite 760, 1765 North Highland Avenue, Hollywood, CA 90028.

9. Andrew Sarris, "Stranded in Soho's Mean Streets," *Village Voice*, 17 September 1985, 54.

10. "Review of *After Hours*," *Variety*, 30 August 1985, 14.

11. Ed Siegel, "Martin Scorsese's Amazing Story," *Boston Globe*, 8 March 1986, 16; hereafter cited in text.

12. Peter Biskind, "Chalk Talk," *American Film*, November 1986, 71; hereafter cited in text.

13. Myra Forsberg, "*The Color of Money*: Three Men and a Sequel," *New York Times*, 19 October 1986, 21; hereafter cited in text.

14. David Denby, "Martin Scorsese Updates *The Hustler*," *New York*, 15 September 1986, 36; hereafter cited in text as Denby 1986.

15. David Ansen, "The Big Hustle," *Newsweek*, 13 October 1986, 69; hereafter cited in text as Ansen 1986.

16. Bruce Cook, "Shooting for the Right Angle in *The Color of Money*," *Philadelphia Inquirer*, 12 November 1986, 18.

17. Unpublished press release from Touchstone Pictures, n.d.

18. David Denby, "Son of *The Hustler*," *New York*, 27 October 1986, 129–30.

19. Vincent Canby, "Paul Newman in *The Color of Money*," *New York Times*, 19 October 1986, sec. C, 12.

20. Robert Goldberg, "'Bad' Prime Time," *Wall Street Journal*, 31 August 1987, 87.

Chapter Nine

1. Caryn James, "Paul Schrader Talks on *Last Temptation* and His New Films," *New York Times*, 1 September 1988, sec. C, 19; hereafter cited in text.

2. Aljean Harmetz, "How Studio Maneuvered *Temptation* into a Hit," *New York Times*, 24 August 1988, sec. C, 15.

3. Richard Lacayo, "Days of Ire and Brimstone," *Time*, 23 July 1988, 73.

4. Universal press release, n.d.

5. Universal press kit for *The Last Temptation of Christ,* n.d.; hereafter cited in text as press kit.

6. Michael Morris, "Of God and Man: a Theological and Artistic Scrutiny of Martin Scorsese's *The Last Temptation of Christ,*" *American Film,* October 1988, 49.

7. "The Last Days of Jesus," *Newsweek,* 16 April 1990, 48.

8. Paul Schrader, *The Last Temptation of Christ,* an unpublished script, dated November 23, 1983, 75–76; hereafter cited in text as *Temptation.*

9. Phillip Lopate, "Fourteen Koans by a Levite on Scorsese's *The Last Temptation of Christ,*" *Tikkum,* November–December 1988, 76; hereafter cited in text.

10. Andrew Sarris, "*The Last Temptation of Christ,*" *Video Review,* September 1989, 57.

11. Gene Siskel, "Scorsese's Testament," *Chicago Tribune,* 14 August 1988, sec. 13, 4.

12. "NBC Evening News," 25 July 1988.

13. Richard Woodward, "Going to Extremes with Willem Dafoe: The Wild One," *New York,* 27 August 1990, 40.

14. Kenneth Chanka, "For Dafoe, Playing Christ Was a Risk—but No Gamble," *Chicago Tribune,* 14 August 1988, sec. B, 5.

15. Lori J. Smith, "Willem Dafoe and Scorsese's *Temptation,*" *American Film,* October 1988, 52.

16. James J. Kilpatrick, "*The Last Temptation of Christ* Stinks," *Asbury Park Press,* 5 October 1988, sec. A, 16.

17. Harlan Jacobson, "You Talkin' to Me?," *Film Comment,* October–November 1988, 33.

18. Chuck Conconi, "Personalities," *Washington Post,* 11 August 1988, sec. D, 3.

19. Charles Krauthammer, "*The Temptation* of Martin Scorsese," *Washington Post,* 19 September 1988, sec. A, 23.

20. "Satanism in Hollywood?" *New York Times,* 12 August 1988, sec. A, 26.

21. David Denby, "Time on the Cross," *New York,* 29 August 1988, 50.

22. John Powers, "Jesus Doesn't Live Here Anymore," *Los Angeles Weekly,* 12 August 1988, 40; hereafter cited in text.

23. Neal Gabler, "*Temptation*: Protests Verge on Censorship," *Video Review,* September 1989, 108; hereafter cited in text.

24. "Scorsese Pic Center of a Holy War," *Variety,* 27 July 1988, 3.

25. Patrick J. Buchanan, "Hollywood's Sleazy Image of Christ," *Philadelphia Inquirer,* 27 July 1988, sec. A, 15.

26. This debate was broadcast on CNN on 27 July 1988.

27. "Film Is Not a Critical Success," *Asbury Park Press,* 8 October 1988, sec. C, 15.

28. Aljean Harmetz, "*The Last Temptation*," *New York Times*, 5 August 1988, sec. C, 13.

29. Caryn James, "Scorsese's Passion Now: Dostoyevsky," *New York Times*, 20 October 1988, sec. C, 25; hereafter cited in text.

30. Ed Hulse, "Best Drama Citation for *Last Temptation*," *Video Review*, May 1990, 36; hereafter cited in text.

Chapter Ten

1. "Disney to Use Three Directors to Create a Single Movie," *Wall Street Journal*, 29 March 1988, 20.

2. Amy Pagnozzi, "Wife Says Scorsese Had Affair with Liza Minelli," *New York Post*, 4 October 1983, 9.

3. Deborah Mitchell, "Family Business," *Seven Days*, 5 April 1989, 78.

4. "Nerves of Steel," *Interview*, August 1989, 113.

5. Roger Ebert, "Martin Scorsese and His 'New York' Story," *Chicago Sun-Times*, 5 March 1989, sec. 2, 1; hereafter cited in text.

6. Terri Minsky, "Martin Scorsese 'Life Lessons,'" *Premiere*, April 1989, 111.

7. Pauline Kael, "Two Base Hit," *New Yorker*, 20 March 1989, 93–94.

8. John Simon, "Three New Yorkers Are a Crowd," *National Review*, 16 June 1989, 47; hereafter cited in text as Simon 1989.

9. Kay Larson, "Moving Pictures," *New York Times*, 24 April 1989, 86.

10. Jeannie Williams, "Nolte, the Cannes Artist," *USA Today*, 12 May 1989, sec. D, 2.

11. Jonathan Rosenbaum, "Three of a Kind," *Reader*, 5 March 1989, 32.

12. Press release, Touchstone Pictures, n.d.

13. David Denby, "Slaves of New York," *New York*, 13 March 1989, 63–64.

14. Vincent Canby, "Anthologies Can Be a Bargain," *New York Times*, sec. H, 23.

15. Bob Strauss, "Martin Scorsese: A Kaleidoscope of Intelligence and Honesty," *Knoxville News Sentinel*, 28 September 1990, 12; hereafter cited in text.

16. Nina Darnton, "Best Fella," *Mirabella*, October 1990, 47; hereafter cited in text.

17. "Review of *Dreams*," *Variety*, 16 May 1990, 25.

18. "Kurosawa's *Dreams*," *Entertainment Weekly*, 1 July 1990, 23.

19. Gavin Smith, "Martin Scorsese Interview [on *GoodFellas*]," *Film Comment*, September–October 1990, 27–28; hereafter cited in text.

20. David Denby, "Fall Preview—Movies," *New York*, 10 September 1990, 32; hereafter cited in text as Denby 1990.

21. Warner Brothers press kit for *GoodFellas*, "Production Information," 3.

22. Susan Linfield, "*GoodFellas* Looks at the Banality of Mob Life," *New York Times,* 6 September 1990, sec. H, 19; hereafter cited in text.

23. Nicholas Pileggi, *Wise Guy* (New York: Pocket Books, 1987), 4; hereafter cited in text.

24. Martin Scorsese and Nicholas Pileggi, *GoodFellas,* edited by David Thompson (London: Faber and Faber, 1990), 130; hereafter cited in text as *GoodFellas.*

25. "Public Enemies: A Cinematic Gangster Guide," *Entertainment Weekly,* 12 October 1990, 32.

26. Warner Brothers press release, n.d.

27. Joyce C. Persico, "De Niro and Scorsese on the Same Wave Length," *Staten Island Advance,* 25 September 1990, sec. B, 14; hereafter cited in text.

28. David Denby, "Meaner Streets," *New York,* 24 September 1990, 82.

29. "Pesci on Scorsese," *Variety,* 17 October 1989, 21; hereafter cited in text.

30. "Revised draft of *GoodFellas,* 12 January 1989, 58. The draft is available for purchase from Script City, Suite 1500, 8033 Sunset Boulevard, Hollywood, CA 90028.

31. Kathy Huffhines, "Film Gets Martin Scorsese Talking," *Asbury Park Press,* 30 September 1990, sec. E, 20; hereafter cited in text.

32. Owen Glieberman, "GoodFellas," *Entertainment Weekly,* 22 September 1990, 19.

33. Alex Witchel, "A Mafia Wife Makes Larraine Bracco a Princess," *New York Times,* 27 September 1990, sec. C, 13.

34. Jeannie Williams, "Scorsese Minds his P's and Q's and Gets an R," *USA Today,* 28 June 1990, sec. D, 2.

35. Mike Clark, "Critics Raise a House Divided," *USA Today,* 28 December 1990, sec. D, 4.

36. Woody Hockswender, "Images of Man, Labeled Armani," *New York Times,* 21 December 1990, Sec. C, 1.

37. "Giorgio Takes Manhattan," *Newsweek,* 12 November 1990, 51.

38. Graham Fuller, "Martin Scorsese," *Interview,* November 1991, 17; hereafter cited in text.

39. Janet Maslin, "Martin Scorsese Ventures Back to Cape Fear," *New York Times,* 11 November 1991, Sec. C, 14; hereafter cited in text.

40. Peter Biskind, "Slouching Toward Hollywood," *Premiere,* November 1991, 73; hereafter cited in text.

41. Richard Corliss, "Filming at Full Throttle," *Time,* 11 November 1991, 84.

42. Meredith Berkman, "Exorcising 'Cape Fear'," *Entertainment Weekly,* 13 December 1991, 20.

43. Scorsese identifies this device of a solid color screen as a "wonderful way to express desire" in Maureen Dowd's article, "The Impact on Scorsese of a British Film Team," *New York Times,* 18 May 1991, sec. C, 16.

44. J. Hoberman, "Swamp Thing," *Village Voice,* 19 November 1991, 57; hereafter cited in text.

45. Owen Gleiberman, "With a Vengeance," *Entertainment Weekly,* 22 November 1991, 58.

46. "Ultimate Fall Preview," *Premiere,* October 1991, 79.

47. Chris Smith, "Fair Juliette," *New York,* 25 November 1991, 32.

48. Eleanor O'Sullivan, "Just a Tonier Slice-Dice Movie," *Asbury Park Press,* 15 November 1991, sec. C, 5.

49. Jeannie Park, "She's Got a Foot in the Door," *People,* 9 December 1991, 106.

50. Mary Pat Kelly, *Martin Scorsese; A Journey* (New York: Thunder's Mouth Press, 1991), 290; hereafter cited in text.

51. Mark Goodman, "Review of *Cape Fear,*" *People,* 25 November 1991, 19.

52. Terrence Rafferty, "Mud," *New Yorker,* 2 December 1991, 158; hereafter cited in text.

53. David Rensin, "The Raging Talent of Martin Scorsese, A Playboy Interview," *Playboy,* April 1991, 64; hereafter cited in text.

54. Rachel Abramowitz, "In the Works," *Premiere,* December 1991, 9.

SELECTED BIBLIOGRAPHY

Primary Sources

Books and Pamphlets

Dialogue on Film: Martin Scorsese, vol. 4, no. 7, April 1975. Edited by Rochelle Reed. Los Angeles: American Film Institute, 1975. A transcript of a 12 February 1975 seminar with the fellows of the American Film Institute's Center for Advanced Film Studies. This early monograph contains many indications of the images, themes, and concerns of Scorsese's film canon.

Scorsese, Martin, and Nicholas Pileggi. *GoodFellas.* Edited by David Thompson. Introduction by David Thompson. London: Faber & Faber, 1990. A reworking of the final draft of the screenplay, not a shooting script. *Scorsese on Scorsese.* Edited by David Thompson and Ian Christie. Introduction by Michael Powell. London: Faber & Faber, 1989. An excellent arrangement of lectures Scorsese gave in England during the controversy over *The Last Temptation of Christ.*

Parts of Books

Scorsese, Martin. "Confessions of a Movie Brat." In *Anatomy of the Movies,* edited by David Pirie, 81–100. New York: Macmillan, 1981. An illuminating essay on the craft of filmmaking.

Scorsese, Martin. "In the Streets." In *Once a Catholic: Prominent Catholics and Ex-Catholics Discuss the Influence of the Church on their Lives and Works,* edited by Peter Occhiogrosso, 88–101. Boston: Houghton Mifflin, 1987. A little-known but essential interview that treats Scorsese's youth in great detail.

Articles

Scorsese, Martin. "*A mes amis et collegues: Au sujet de nos film.*" *Positif,* nos. 232–33, (July–August 1980): 126–27. Scorsese's famous petition to Eastman Kodak to improve color stock so that films will be preserved. Kodak denied any culpability, but the company did improve its film.

Scorsese, Martin. "Guilty Pleasures." *Film Comment,* September–October 1978, 63–66. Scorsese's list of his favorite films, with some amusing observations.

Scorsese, Martin. "The Second Screen." *Video Review,* April 1990, 24–25. Perceptive comments on the impact of the videocassette market on film style.

Scorsese, Martin. "Tapping the Intensity of the City." *New York Times Magazine,* 9 November 1986, 28, 82–85. Musings on New York City's impact on Scorsese's psychology and works.

Videodiscs

Scorsese, Martin. *Raging Bull.* The Voyager Company. A state-of-the-art research tool, including a transfer of the film, an alternate soundtrack with Scorsese offering a running commentary on the techniques of filming and his thematic concern, a complete shooting script, a collection of storyboards, an interview with Jake La Motta, an anthology of scenes from other films that influenced Scorsese, and a collection of outtakes and screen tests. Indispensable.

Scorsese, Martin. *Taxi Driver.* The Voyager Company. Michael Chapman supervised this inspired transfer of the film to videodisc. In addition, there are an alternate soundtrack with a shot-by-shot analysis by Scorsese, a supplementary analysis by Paul Schrader, and an anthology of production photos, storyboards, and screenplay drafts. The videodisc also details the editing of the film and the response to rating-board suggestions. Indispensable.

Secondary Sources

Books

Bliss, Michael. *Martin Scorsese and Michael Cimino.* Metuchen, N.J.: Scarecrow Press, 1985. An early study that Scorsese has praised for its thoroughness and attention to detail.

Cieutat, Michel. *Martin Scorsese.* Paris: Rivages, 1988. A compact French overview of the director's themes, including much of the interview material Scorsese and Schrader have provided for *Positif* and *Cahiers du Cinema.*

Kelly, Mary Pat. *Martin Scorsese: The First Decade.* Pleasantville, N.Y.: Redgrave, 1980. A treasure trove of interviews, photographs, scripts, and anecdotes treating Scorsese's earliest films. Indispensable.

Kelly, Mary Pat. *Martin Scorsese: A Journey.* New York: Thunder's Mouth Press, 1991. More interviews, photographs, and anecdotes treating some of Scorsese's recent films. Indispensable.

Schrader, Paul. *Schrader on Schrader.* Edited by Kevin Jackson. London: Faber & Faber, 1990. Schrader comments on his work with Scorsese. He is especially cogent in his discussion of *The Last Temptation of Christ* and *Taxi Driver.*

Schrader, Paul. *Taxi Driver.* London: Faber & Faber, 1990. Includes the original English text of an important interview with Scorsese, originally published in French in *Cahiers du Cinema,* as well as a complete screenplay.

Weiss, Marion. *Martin Scorsese: A Guide to References and Resources.* Boston: G. K. Hall, 1987. In this definitive bibliography for Scorsese films up to *After Hours,* Weiss lists and evaluates more than 300 items. *N.B.* Any research on Scorsese must begin with Weiss. This Selected Bibliography assumes knowledge of her work and avoids duplication as much as possible.

Parts of Books

Bach, Steven. *Final Cut: Dreams and Disaster in the Making of "Heaven's Gate."* New York: William Morrow, 1985. Bach uses Scorsese as one of the foils, contrasting his seriousness and artistry to the approach of Michael Cimino.

Gabbard, Krin, and Glen Gabbard. *Psychiatry and the Cinema.* Chicago: University of Chicago Press, 1987. These two analysts explore the two possible approaches to Scorsese's films, one by an informed audience and the other by a mass audience, arguing that Scorsese's films intentionally provide satisfaction for both audiences.

Gambino, Richard. *Blood of My Blood: The Dilemma of the Italian American.* New York: Doubleday, 1974. Though autobiographical and sociological in thrust, this text provides a firm context for understanding Little Italy in New York City and, by extension, Scorsese.

Hackett, Pat, ed. *The Andy Warhol Diaries.* New York: Warner Books, 1989. A candid and offbeat look at Scorsese's work habits, marital intrigues, social life, and drug problems.

Hickenlooper, George. *Reel Conversations: Candid Interviews with Film's Foremost Directors And Critics.* New York. Citadel Press, 1991. An informative overview of his career by the filmmaker.

Jacobs, Diane. *Hollywood Renaissance.* South Brunswick, N.J.: A. S. Barnes, 1977. A lively chapter on Scorsese includes many memorable anecdotes and bon mots as well as some perceptive analysis.

Kolker, Robert Phillip. *A Cinema of Loneliness.* 2d ed. New York: Oxford University Press, 1988. A dense, thematic approach to Scorsese that explores point of view and narrative structure as well as technical matters.

Lourdeaux, Lee. *Italian and Irish Filmmakers in America: Ford, Capra, Coppola, and Scorsese.* Philadelphia: Temple University Press, 1990. A scholarly approach to Scorsese's ethnicity and religiosity, with much new interview material.

Manoogian, Haig P. *The Filmmaker's Art.* New York: Basic Books, 1966. An important textbook by the professor Scorsese credits with teaching him to see.

Monaco, James. *American Film Now.* Rev. ed. New York: Zoetrope, 1984. An unsympathetic treatment of Scorsese, charging that the director compromised his talent to gain popular acceptance and work in Hollywood.

Naremore, James. *Acting in the Cinema.* Berkeley: University of California

Press, 1988. A major survey of acting styles, with an entire chapter on De Niro's work with Scorsese on *The King of Comedy.*

Phillips, Julia. *You'll Never Eat Lunch in This Town Again.* New York: Random House, 1991. A scorching insider's autobiography by the young female producer behind *The Sting* and *Close Encounters.* Phillips details the early days of Scorsese's Hollywood career and his contacts with Spielberg and Schrader. Much of her emphasis is on drugs, sexism, and the sensational.

Pye, Michael, and Lynda Myles. *The Movie Brats: How the Film Generation Took over Hollywood.* New York: Holt, Rinehart & Winston, 1979. This popular history of Hollywood in the late 1970s contains much inside information on preproduction dealing and on complications in the production of major films, including works by Scorsese.

Ray, Robert B. *A Certain Tendency of the Hollywood Cinema, 1930–1980.* Princeton, N.J.: Princeton University Press, 1985. Argues convincingly that Scorsese's narratives remain purposefully open to conflicting interpretations, suited to both a mass audience and an educated one.

Taylor, Bella. "Martin Scorsese." In *Closeup: The Contemporary Director,* edited by Jon Tuska, Jr. Metuchen, N.J.: Scarecrow Press, 1981. An early attempt to define the themes of Scorsese's films. Includes interesting interview material.

Articles

N.B. For the bulk of the material in periodicals on Scorsese before 1986, see Marion Weiss's *Martin Scorsese: A Guide to References and Resources* (Boston: G. K. Hall, 1987).

Ansen, David. "Martin Scorsese." *Interview,* January 1987, 49–51. A short, first-rate profile.

Biskind, Peter, and Susan Linfield. "Chalk Talk." *American Film,* November 1986, 30–34; 68–72. Price and Scorsese discuss *The Color of Money.*

Biskind, Peter. "Slouching Toward Hollywood." *Premiere,* December 1991, 60–73. Includes inside information on Scorsese's temperament and personality.

Braudy, Leo. "The Sacraments of Genre: Coppola, De Palma, Scorsese." *Film Quarterly* (Spring 1986): 17–32. The best available analysis of Scorsese's religious themes.

Cameron, Julia. "Devoted to Betrayal: Irwin Winkler." *American Film,* October 1989, 50–53. Scorsese's ex-wife profiles Scorsese's favorite producer.

Corliss, Richard. "Body and Blood: An Interview with Martin Scorsese." *Film Comment,* October 1988, 36–42. Two notable ex-Catholics discuss *The Last Temptation of Christ* and its religious themes.

De Curtis, Anthony. "Martin Scorsese." *Rolling Stone,* 1 November 1990, 58–65, 106, 108. A wide-ranging interview covering Scorsese's entire canon but focusing on *GoodFellas.*

Gehr, Richard. "God's Lonely Man." *Video,* March 1990, 57–59, 104–5. Interesting overview of Scorsese's career.

Gleiberman, Owen. "Martin Scorsese: America's Greatest Director." *Entertainment Weekly,* 6 December 1991, 33–37. Contains many original quotes from Scorsese about his major films. An important overview and assessment.

Goldstein, Richard, and Mark Jacobson. "Martin Scorsese Tells All: 'Blood and Guts Turn Me On!'" *Village Voice,* 9 April 1976, 29–31. Often-overlooked interview, containing many key ideas and insights.

Grobel, Lawrence. "*Playboy* Interview with Robert De Niro." *Playboy,* January 1989, 69–90, 326. An extended interview with Scorsese's closet collaborator.

Holdenfield, Chris. "Martin Scorsese: The Art of Noncompromise." *American Film,* March 1989, 46–51. A major article by a journalist who has followed Scorsese's career closely and who knows the best questions to ask.

Lopate, Phillip. "Fourteen Koans by a Levite on Scorsese's *The Last Temptation of Christ.*" *Tikkun,* November–December 1988, 74–78. An unusual approach that yields interesting insights.

McCarthy, Todd. "Are Today's 'A's' Yesterday's 'B's'?" *Variety,* 15 October 1990, 6. A short but provocative view of the contemporary film industry.

Moline, Karen. "The Good Fellas from New York's Mean Streets." (London) *Sunday Times,* 30 September 1990, 2–4. A major interview and analysis of Scorsese's career.

Morris, Michael. "Of God and Man: A Theological and Artistic Scrutiny of Martin Scorsese's *The Last Temptation of Christ.*" *American Film,* October 1988, 44–50. A priest evaluates Scorsese's approach to Christ's life.

Paris, Barry. "Maximum Expression: De Niro Talks." *American Film,* October 1989, 30–34, 54. Some discussion of the first version of *The Last Temptation of Christ.*

Rensin, David. "*Playboy* Interview with Martin Scorsese." *Playboy,* April 1991, 57–74, 161. Includes much discussion of Scorsese's drug use and his sexual encounters.

Schrader, Paul. "Dialogue on Film." *American Film,* July–August 1989, 16–22. Many pointed observations on Schrader's uneasy collaborations with Scorsese.

Smith, Gavin. "Martin Scorsese Interview." *Film Comment,* September–October 1990, 27–30, 69. Mainly on *GoodFellas.*

Smith, Lori J. "William Dafoe and Scorsese's *Temptation.*" *American Film,* October 1988, 51–54. Dafoe explains his approach to the character of Jesus.

Taubin, Amy. "Blood and Pasta: Martin Scorsese's Cinema of Obsessions." *Village Voice,* 18 September 1990, 37–39. Scorsese talks about Little Italy and the Mob.

Taubin, Amy. "Scorsese: A Bicoastal Story." *Village Voice,* 25 October 1988, 67–68. A visit to the set of "Life Lessons."

Truman, James. "Martin Scorsese." (London) *Face,* February 1987, 76–79, 81. A major interview covering Scorsese's entire career.

Films

You Talkin' to Me? Warner Brothers, 1987. Director Charles Winkler's narrative develops the idea that *Taxi Driver* is the one honest film to come from contemporary Hollywood, a film so important to America's artistic conscience that it has its own devotees and acolytes. Scorsese, De Niro, Mardik Martin, and Julia Cameron are all thanked in the credits for their contributions to this film.

FILMOGRAPHY

Films Directed by Martin Scorsese

What's a Nice Girl like You Doing in a Place like This? (1963)
Producer: New York University Department of Television, Motion Picture, and Radio Presentations, Summer Motion Picture Workshop
Director: Martin Scorsese
Assistant Director: Louise Stefanic
Screenplay: Martin Scorsese
Photography: Frank Truglio (black-and-white)
Cinematography: James Newman
Music: Richard H. Coll
Unit Manager: Richard Klein
Editor: Robert Hunsicker
Sound: Sandor Reich
Cast: Zeph Michaelis (Harry), Mimi Stark (Harry's Wife), Sarah Braverman (Psychoanalyst), Fred Sica (Harry's Friend), Robert Uricola (Singer)
Running time: 9 minutes

It's Not Just You, Murray! (1964)
Producer: New York University Department of Television, Motion Picture, and Radio Presentations
Faculty Advisers: John Mahan, Haig P. Manoogian
Director: Martin Scorsese
Assistant Director: Mardik Martin
Screenplay: Martin Scorsese, Mardik Martin
Cinematography: Richard H. Coll (black-and-white)
Production Design: Lancelot Braithwaite, Victor Magnotta
Production Assistants: Larraine Brennan, Edwin Grant
Music: Richard H. Coll
Editor: Eli F. Bleich
Graphics: Marjorie Rosen
Costumes: Lancelot Braithwaite
Cast: Ira Rubin (Murray), Andrea Martin (Murray's Wife), San De Fazio (Joe), Robert Uricola (Singer), Catherine Scorsese (Murray's Mother),

Bernard Weisenberger, Victor Magnotta, Richard Sweeton, John Bivona
Running Time: 15 minutes

The Big Shave (1967)
Producer: Martin Scorsese
Director: Martin Scorsese
Screenplay: Martin Scorsese
Cinematography: Ares Demertzis (Agfa color)
Art Direction: Ken Gaulin
Special Effects: Eli Bleich
Bathroom: Ken Gaulia
Whiteness: Herman Melville
Cast: Peter Bernuth (Man)
Running Time: 6 minutes

Who's That Knocking at My Door? (Joseph Brenner Associates, Trimod Films, 1969)
Producer: Joseph Weil, Betzi Manoogian, Haig Manoogian
Director: Martin Scorsese
Screenplay: Martin Scorsese
Cinematography: Michael Wadleigh, Richard H. Coll (black-and-white)
Art Director: Victor Magnotta
Editor: Thelma Schoonmaker
Cast: Harvery Keitel (J.R.), Zina Bethune (Girl), Lennard Kuras (Joey), Michael Scala (Sally Gabo), Anne Colette (Woman in Dream), Harry Northup (Rapist), Robert Uricola (Man with Gun), Catherine Scorsese (J.R.'s Mother), Martin Scorsese (Gangster), Bill Minkin (Iggy), Wendy Russell (Ga Ga's Girl), Phil Carlson (Mountain Guide), Susan Wood (Susan), Marissa Joffrey (Rosie), Anne Maieka (Dream Girl), Saskia Holleman (Dream Girl), Tsuaiyu-Lan (Dream Girl), Vic Magotta (Boy in Street), Paul De Bionde (Boy in Street)
Running Time: 90 minutes
[Began as a student project *Bring on the Dancing Girls* (1965), later screened as *I Call First* (1967), and rereleased as *J.R.* (1970)]

Street Scenes 1970 (1970)
Producer: New York Cinetracts Collective, School of the Arts, New York University
Postproduction Director: Martin Scorsese
Production Supervisor: Martin Scorsese
Photography: Don Lenzer, Harry Bolles, Danny Schneider, Peter Rea, Bob

Pitts, Bill Ezra, Tiger Graham, Fred Hadley, Ed Summer, Nat Trapp (black-and-white, color, sepia)
Editors: Peter Rea, Maggie Koven, Angela Kirby, Larry Tisdall, Gerry Pallor, Thelma Schoonmaker
Postproduction Coordinator: Nick Tanis
Postproduction Management: Rani Kaplan
Postproduction Consultants: Maggie Koven, Peter Rea, Diana Krumens
Cast: William Kunstler, Dave Dellinger, Alan W. Carter, David Z. Robinson, Harvey Keitel, Verna Bloom, Jay Cocks, Martin Scorsese
Running Time: 75 minutes

Boxcar Bertha (American International Pictures, 1972)
Producer: Roger Corman
Director: Martin Scorsese
Assistant Director: Paul Rapp
Associate Producer: Julie Corman
Screenplay: Joyce H. Corrington, John W. Corrington, based on *Sister of the Road* by Bertha Thompson as told to Dr. Ben Reitman
Production Design: David Nichols
Cinematography: John Stephens and Gayne Rescher (uncredited) (Deluxe color)
Music: Gib Builbeau, Thad Maxwell
Editor: Buzz Feitshans and Martin Scorsese (uncredited)
Sound: Don F. Johnson
Visual Consultant: David Nichols
Costumes: Bob Modes
Cast: Barbara Hershey (Bertha), David Carradine (Bill Shelley), Barry Primus (Rake Brown), Bernie Casey (Von Morton), John Carradine (H. Buckram Sartoris), David R. Osterhout (a McIver), Victor Argo (a McIver), Grahame Pratt (Emeric Pressburger), "Chicken" Holleman (Michael Powell), Marianne Dole (Mrs. Mailer), Harry Northup (Harvey Hall), Ann Morell (Tillie), Doyle Hall (Dice Player), Joe Reynolds (Joe Dreft), Martin Scorsese (client in brothel), Gayne Rescher (client in brothel)
Running Time: 88 minutes

Mean Streets (Warner Brothers, 1973)
Producer: Jonathan T. Taplin
Director: Martin Scorsese
Assistant Directors: Russell Vreeland, Ron Satloff
Executive Producer: E. Lee Perry
Screenplay: Martin Scorsese, Mardik Martin (from a story by Martin Scorsese)

Cinematography: Kent Wakeford (Technicolor)
Preproduction and Postproduction Coordinator: Sandra Weintraub
Editors: Sid Levin, Martin Scorsese (uncredited)
Sound: Don Johnson
Visual Consultant: David Nichols
Cast: Harvey Keitel (Charlie Cappa, Jr.), Robert De Niro (Johnny Boy),
     David Proval (Tony), Amy Robinson (Teresa), Richard Romanus
     (Michael), Cesare Danova (Giovanni), George Memmoli (Joey
     Cartucci), Victor Argo (Mario), Lenny Scaletta (Jimmy), Murray
     Moston (Oscar), David Carradine (drunk), Robert Carradine (assassin),
     Jeannie Bell (Diane), Lois Walden (Jewish girl at bar), Peter Fain
     (George), D'Mitch Davis (black cop), Harry Northup (soldier), Dino
     Seragusa (cold man), Catherine Scorsese (woman on landing), Nicki
     "Ack" Aquilino (man on docks), Martin Scorsese (Shorty, hired killer),
     Barbara Weintraub (Heather Weintraub), Anna Uricola (woman at
     window)
Running Time: 110 minutes

Alice Doesn't Live Here Anymore (Warner Brothers, 1974)

Producers: David Susskind, Audrey Maas
Director: Martin Scorsese
Assistant Directors: Mike Moder, Mike Kusley
Associate Producer: Sandra Weintraub
Screenplay: Robert Getchell
Cinematography: Kent Wakeford (Technicolor)
Production Designer: Toby Carr Rafelson
Music: Richard La Salle
Editor: Marcia Lucas
Sound: Don Parker
Cast: Ellen Burstyn (Alice Hyatt), Kris Kristofferson (David Barrie), Alfred
     Lutter (Tommy), Diana Ladd (Flo), Billy Green Bush (Donald), Vic
     Tayback (Mel), Jodie Foster (Audrey), Harvey Keitel (Ben), Lela
     Goldoni (Bea), Lane Bradbury (Rita), Valeria Curtin (Vera), Harry
     Northup (Bartender), Murray Mosten (Jacobs), Mia Bendixsen (Alice
     at eight), Ola Moore (old woman), Dean Casper (chicken), Henry M.
     Kendrick (shop assistant), Martin Brinton (Lenny), Mardik Martin
     (customer at club), Larry Cohewn (diner patron), Martin Scorsese
     (diner patron)
Running Time: 112 minutes

Italianamerican (National Communication Association, 1974)

Producers: Saul Rubin, Elaine Attias
Director: Martin Scorsese

Treatment: Martin Scorsese, Mardik Martin, Larry Cohen
Cinematography: Alex Hirschfield (color)
Editor: Bertram Louitt
Sound: Lee Osborne
Cast: Charles Scorsese, Catherine Scorsese, Martin Scorsese
Running Time: 48 minutes
[Part of the "Storm of Strangers" television series, sponsored by the
    National Endowment for the Humanities]

Taxi Driver (Columbia Pictures, 1976)

Producers: Michael Phillips, Julia Phillips
Director: Martin Scorsese
Assistant Director: Peter Scoppa
Associate Producer: Philip M. Goldfarb
Screenplay: Paul Schrader
Cinematography: Michael Chapman (Panavision and color)
Art Director: Charles Rosen
Music: Bernard Herrmann
Editors: Marcia Lucas, Tom Rolf, Melvin Shapiro
Visual Consultant: David Nichols
Costumes: Ruth Morley
Cast: Robert De Niro (Travis Bickle), Jodie Foster (Iris), Cybill Shepherd
    (Betsy), Harvey Keitel (Sport), Steven Prince (Andy), Albert Brooks
    (Tom), Peter Boyle (Wizard), Leonard Harris (Charles Palantine),
    Diahnne Abbott (woman at concession), Frank Adu (angry black),
    Richard Higgs (Secret Service agent), Victor Magnotta (Secret Service
    photographer), Vic Argo (Melio), Harry Northup (soldier), Gino
    Ardito (policeman at rally), Peter Savage (the john), Garth Avery (Iris's
    friend), Robert Shields (Palatine Aide), Cooper Cunningham (hooker in
    cab), Robin Utt (campaign worker), Harry Cohn (cabbie in Bellmore),
    Janice Baio (attractive girl at rally), Murray Moston (Iris's timekeeper),
    Joe Spinell (personnel officer), Jo-Anne Baio (attractive girl at rally),
    Martin Scorsese (passenger watching silhouette), Harry Fischler (cab
    dispatcher), Beau Kayser (man on soap opera), Joseph Baio (man in
    street)
Running Time: 113 minutes

New York, New York (United Artists, 1977)

Producers: Irwin Winkler, Robert Chartoff
Director: Martin Scorsese
Associate Producer: Gene Kirkwood
Screenplay: Earl MacRauch, Mardik Martin
Cinematography: Laszlo Kovacs (color)

Production Designer: Boris Leven
Art Director: Harry R. Kemm
Music: John Kander, Fred Ebb
Editors: Irving Lerner, Marcia Lucas, Tom Rolf, B. Lovitt
Choreography: Ron Field
Cast: Robert De Niro (Jimmy Doyle), Liza Minnelli (Francine Evans),
    Lionel Stander (Tony Harwell), Barry Primus (Paul Wilson), Mary Kay
    Place (Bernice), Georgie Auld (Frankie Harte), George Memmoli
    (Nicky), Dick Miller (Palm Club owner), Murray Moston (Horace
    (Morris), Lenny Gaines (Artie Kirks), Clarence Clemons (Cecil
    Powell), Kathy McGinnis (Ellen Flannery), Diahnne Abbott (singer),
    Steven Prince (record producer), Bernie Ruby (justice of the peace),
    William Tole (Tommy Dorsey), David Nichols (Arnold Trench), Harry
    Northup (Alabama), Selma Archerd (wife of justice of the peace), Gene
    Castle (dancing sailor), David Nichols (Arnold Trench), Mardik Martin
    (well-wisher at Moonlit Terrace), Peter Fain (greeter in Up Club),
    Adam David Winkler (Jimmy Doyle, Jr.), Margo Winkler
    (argumentative woman)
Running Time: 136 minutes (rerelease 163 minutes)

The Last Waltz (United Artists, 1978)
Producer: Robbie Robertson
Director: Martin Scorsese
Executive Producer: Jonathan Taplin
Cinematography: Michael Chapman, Laszlo Kovacs, Vilmos Zsigmond,
    David Myers, Bobby Byrne, Michael Watkins, Kiro Narita (Deluxe
    color)
Production Designer: Boris Leven
Editors: Yew-Bun Yee, Jan Roblee
Associate Producer: Steven Prince
Assistant Directors: Jerry Grandey, James Quinn
Cast: The Band (Robbie Robertson, Rick Danko, Levon Helm, Garth
    Hudson, Richard Manuel), Paul Butterfield, Eric Clapton, Neil
    Diamond, Bob Dylan, Emmylou Harris, Ronnie Hawkins, Dr. John,
    Joni Mitchell, Van Morrison, The Staples, Ringo Starr, Muddy Waters,
    Ron Wood, Neil Young, Martin Scorsese, Michael McClure, Lawrence
    Ferlinghetti
Running Time: 117 minutes

American Boy: A Profile of Steven Prince (New Empire Films, Scorsese Films,
1978)
Producer: Bertram Lovitt
Director: Martin Scorsese

Executive Producers: Ken Wheat, Jim Wheat, Mardik Martin, Julia
    Cameron
Cinematography: Michael Chapman (color)
Editors: Amy Jones, Bertram Lovitt
Sound: Darin Knight
Cast: Steven Prince, Martin Scorsese, George Memmoli, Mardik Martin,
    Julia Cameron, Kathy McGinnis
Running Time: 55 minutes

Raging Bull (United Artists, 1980)
Producers: Irwin Winkler, Robert Chartwell, Peter Savage
Director: Martin Scorsese
Associate Producer: Hal W. Polaire
Assistant Directors: Alan Wertheim, Jerry Grandey
Screenplay: Paul Schrader, Mardik Martin, from the book by Jake La Motta,
    with Peter Savage and Joseph Carter
Cinematography: Michael Chapman (black-and-white, color)
Production Designer: Gene Rudolf
Art Directors: Alan Manser, Kirk Aktell
Editor: Thelma Schoonmaker
Cast: Robert De Niro (Jake La Motta), Cathy Moriarty (Vickie La Motta),
    Joe Pesci (Joey La Motta), Frank Vincent (Salvy), Nicholas Colasanto
    (Tommy Como), Theresa Saldana (Lenore), Mario Gallo (Mario),
    Frank Adonis (Patsy), Joseph Bono (Guido), Frank Topham (Tappy),
    Lori Anne Flax (Irma), Charles Scorsese (Charlie), Don Dunphy
    (himself), Bill Hanrahan (Eddie Eagan), Rita Bennett (Emma, Miss
    48's), Bernie Allen (comedian), Peter Petrella (Johnny), Mardik Martin
    (Copa waiter), Peter Savage (Jackie Curtis), Joe Malanga (bodyguard),
    Robert Uricola (man outside cab), Martin Scorsese (Barbizon
    stagehand), Johnny Barnes ("Sugar" Ray Robinson), Floyd Anderson
    (Jimmy Reeves), Eddie Mestafa Muhammad (Billy Fox), Louis Raftis
    (Marcel Cerdan), Johnny Turner (Laurent Dauthville)
Running Time: 129 minutes

The King of Comedy (Twentieth Century-Fox, 1982)
Producer: Arnon Milchan
Director: Martin Scorsese
Executive Producer: Robert Greenhut
Screenplay: Paul Zimmerman
Cinematography: Fred Schuler (Deluxe color)
Production Designer: Boris Leven
Art Directors: Edward Pisoni, Lawrence Miller
Editor: Thelma Schoonmaker

Music Producer: Robbie Robertson
Associate Producer: Robert F. Colesberry
Cast: Robert De Niro (Rupert Pupkin), Jerry Lewis (Jerry Langford), Diahnne Abbott (Rita), Sanda Bernhard (Masha), Ed Herlihy (himself), Lou Brown (bandleader), Loretta Tupper (stage door fan), Peter Potulski (stage door fan), Vinnie Gonzales (stage door fan), Doc Lawless (chauffeur), Catherine Scorsese (Rupert's mother), Cathy Scorsese (Delores), Liza Minnelli (herself), Chuck Low (man in Chinese restaurant), Margo Winkler (receptionist), Shelley Hack (Cathy Long), Jay Julien (lawyer), Fred de Cordova (Bert Thomas), Dr. Joyce Brothers (herself), Victor Borge (himself), Tony Randall (himself), Harry Ufland (Langford's agent), Martin Scorsese (television director), Charles Scorsese (man at bar), Mardik Martin (man at bar), Mick Jones (street scum), Joe Strummer (street scum), Kosmo Vinyn (street scum), Ellen Foley (street scum), Pearl Harbor (street scum), Gabu Salter (street scum), Don Letts (street scum)
Running Time: 108 minutes

After Hours (Double Play, the Geffen Company, 1985)
Producers: Amy Robinson, Griffin Dunne, Robert Colesberry
Director: Martin Scorsese
Screenplay: Joseph Minion
Cinematography: Michael Ballhaus (Duart color)
Production Designer: Jeffrey Townsend
Music: Howard Shore
Editor: Thelma Schoonmaker
Costumes: Rita Ryack
Production Manager: Michael Nozik
Associate Producer: Deborah Schindler
Assistant Directors: Stephen J. Lim, Christopher Griffin
Sound: Chat Gunter
Cast: Griffin Dunne (Paul Hackett), Rosanna Arquette (Marcy), Verna Bloom (June), Thomas Chong (Pepe), Linda Fiorentino (Kiki), Teri Garr (Julie), John Heard (Tom the bartender), Cheeck Marin (Neil), Catherine O'Hara (Gail), Dick Miller (waiter), Will Patton (Hearst), Robert Plunket (Mark), Bronson Pinchot (Lloyd), Rocco Sisto (coffee shop cashier), Larry Block (taxi driver), Victor Argo (diner cashier), Murray Moston (subway attendant), John P. Codiglia (transit cop), Clarke Evans (first neighbor), Victor Magnotta (dead man), Margo Winkler (woman with gun), Robin Johnson (punk girl), Stephen J. Lim (Club Berlin bartender), Frank "Ack" Aquilino (angry mob member), Rockets Redglare (angry mob member), Martin Scorsese (man with spotlight)
Running Time: 97 minutes

"Mirror Mirror" episode of *Amazing Stories* television series (Ambin Productions, 1985)

Producer: David E. Vogel
Director: Martin Scorsese
Screenplay: Joseph Minion, story by Steven Spielberg
Cinematography: Robert Stevens (color)
Production Design: Rich Carter
Music: Michael Kamen
Editor: Joe Ann Fogle
Cast: Sam Waterston (Jordan), Helen Shaver (Karen), Dick Cavett (himself), Tim Robbins (Jordan's phantom), Dana Gladstone (producer), Valerie Grear (host), Michael C. Gwynne (jail attendant), Peter Iacangelo (limo driver), Jonathan Luria (cameraman), Harry Northup (security guard), Glenn Scarpelli (Jeffrey Gelb), Jack Thibeau (toughguy)
Running Time: 24 minutes

The Color of Money (Touchstone, 1986)

Producers: Irving Axelrad, Barbara De Fina
Director: Martin Scorsese
Screenplay: Richard Price, based on the novel by Walter Tevis
Cinematography: Michael Ballhaus (Deluxe color)
Production Designer: Boris Leven
Technical Adviser: Michael Sigel
Music: Robbie Robertson
Editor: Thelma Schoonmaker
Costumes: Richard Bruno
Production Manager: Dodie Foster
Assistant Directors: Joseph Reidy, Richard Feld
Cast: Paul Newman ("Fast" Eddie Felson), Tom Cruise (Vincent Lauria), Mary Elizabeth Mastrantonio (Carmen), Helen Shaver (Janelle), John Turtorro (Julian), Bill Cobbs (Orvis), Keith McCready (Grady Seasons), Robert Agins (Earl at Chalkies), Alvin Anastasia (Kennedy), Elizabeth Bracco (Diane at bar), Joe Guastaferro (Chuck the bartender), Grady Matthews (Dud), Steve Mizerak (Duke, Eddie's first opponent), Jerry Piller (Tom), Forest Whitaker (Amos), Bruce A. Young (Moselle), Vito D'Ambrosio (Lou), Ernest Perry (eye doctor), Iggy Pop (pool player), Richard Price (pool hall regular), Charles Scorsese (first high-roller)
Running Time: 119 minutes

Armani Commercial (Emporio Armani, 1985)

Producer: Barbara De Fina
Director: Martin Scorsese

Treatment: Martin Scorsese
Cinematography: Nestor Almendros (black-and-white)
Cast: Christophe Bouquin, Christina Marsilach
Running Time: 30 seconds

"Bad" (Optimum Productions, 1987)
Producers: Quincy Jones, Barbara De Fina
Director: Martin Scorsese
Screenplay: Richard Price
Cinematography: Michael Chapman (black-and-white, color)
Editor: Thelma Schoonmaker
Choreography: Michael Jackson, Gregg Burge, Jeffrey Daniel
Cast: Michael Jackson (Daryl), Adam Nathan (Tip), Pedro Sanchez
    (Nelson), Webley Sniper (Mini Max), Greg Holtz, Jr. (cowboy), Jaime
    Perry (Ski), Paul Calderon (dealer), Alberto Alejandrino (Hispanic
    man), Horace Daily (street bum), Marvin Foster (crack customer),
    Roberta Flack (Daryl's mother)
Running Time: 16 minutes

Somewhere Down the Crazy River (Limelight, 1988)
Producers: Amanda Pirie, Tim Clawson
Director: Martin Scorsese
Treatment: Martin Scorsese
Cinematography: Mark Plummer (color)
Production Designer: Marina Levikova
Cast: Robbie Robertson, Sammy Bo Dean, Maria McKee
Running Time: 4 minutes, 30 seconds

The Last Temptation of Christ (Universal Pictures, 1988)
Producer: Barbara De Fina
Director: Martin Scorsese
Executive Producer: Harry Ufland
Screenplay: Paul Schrader, based on the novel by Nikos Kazantzakis
Cinematography: Michael Ballhous (Technicolor)
Production Designer: John Beard
Art Director: Andrew Sanders
Music: Peter Gabriel
Editor: Thelma Schoonmaker
Production Manager: Laura Fattori
Assistant Director: Joseph Reidy
Sound: Amelio Verona
Cast: Willem Dafoe (Jesus), Harvey Keitel (Judas), Barbara Hershey (Mary
    Magdalene), Andre Gregory (John the Baptist), Harry Dean Stanton

(Saul/Paul), David Bowie (Pontius Pilate), Juliette Caton (girl angel),
Paul Greco (Zealot), Steven Shill (Centurion), Verna Bloom (Mary),
Roberts Blossom (Aged Master), Barry Miller (Jeroboam), Gary
Basaraba (Andrew), Irvin Kershner (Zebedee), Victor Argo (Peter),
Michael Been (John), Paul Herman (Philip), John Lurie (James), Leo
Burmeister (Nathaniel), Peggy Gormley (Martha), Randy Danson
(Mary), Thomas Arana (Lazarus), Alan Rosenberg (Thomas), Del
Russel (money changer), Nehemiah Persoff (Rabbi), Peter Birling
(beggar), Donald Hudson (Sadducee)
Running Time: 163 minutes

Armani Commercial (Emporio Armani, 1988)
Producer: Barbara De Fina
Director: Martin Scorsese
Treatment: Martin Scorsese
Cinematography: Michael Ballhaus (color)
Cast: Jens Peter, Elizabeth Ranella
Running Time: 20 seconds

"Life Lessons" in New York Stories (Touchstone, 1989)
Producers: Barbara De Fina, Robert Greenhut
Director: Martin Scorsese
Screenplay: Richard Price
Cinematography: Nestor Almendros (color)
Production Designer: Kristi Zea
Editor: Thelma Schoonmaker
Cast: Nick Nolte (Lionel Dobie), Rosanna Arquette (Paulette), Patrick
    O'Neal (Philip Fowler), Jesse Borrego (Reuben Toro), Steve Buscemi
    (Gregory Stark), Peter Gabriel (gallery patron), Richard Price (gallery
    patron), Michael Powell (gallery patron)
Running Time: 44 minutes

GoodFellas (Warner Brothers, 1990)
Producer: Irwin Winkler
Director: Martin Scorsese
Executive Producer: Barbara De Fina
Screenplay: Nicholas Pileggi, Martin Scorsese, based on the book Wise Guy
    by Nicholas Pileggi
Cinematography: Michael Ballhaus (color)
Production Designer: Richard Bruno
Titles: Saul Bass, Elaine Bass
Cast: Ray Liotta (Henry), Larraine Bracco (Karen), Robert De Niro (James

Conway), Joe Pesci (Tommy), Paul Sorvino (Paul Cicero), Frank Dileo
(Tuddy), Gina Mastrogiacomo (Janice Rossi), Debi Mazar (Sandy)
Running Time: 146 minutes

Cape Fear (Universal, 1991)
Producer: Barbara De Fina
Director: Martin Scorsese
Executive Producers: Kathleen Kennedy, Frank Marshall
Screenplay: Wesley Strick, based on James R. Webb's screenplay and John
    D. MacDonald's novel *The Executioners*.
Cinematography: Freddie Francis (Technicolor, Panavision)
Production Designer: Henry Bumstead
Art Director: Jack G. Taylor, Jr.
Music: Bernard Herrmann, adapted, arranged and conducted by Elmer
    Bernstein
Editor: Thelma Schoonmaker
Sound: Tod Maitland
Cast: Robert De Niro (Max Cady), Nick Nolte (Sam Bowden), Jessica
    Lange (Leigh Bowden), Juliette Lewis (Danielle Bowden), Joe Don
    Baker (Claude Kersek), Robert Mitchum (Lt. Elgart), Gregory Peck
    (Lee Heller), Martin Balsam (Judge), Illeaha Douglas (Lori Davis).
Running Time: 128 minutes

Films in Which Martin Scorsese Was Part of the Crew or Cast

Inesita: The Art of Flamenco (1963)
Producer: New York University Department of Television, Motion Picture,
    and Radio Presentations
Director: Robert Siegal
Cinematographer: Martin Scorsese (black-and-white)
Cast: Inesita (dancer)
Running Time: 9 minutes

Woodstock (Warner Brothers, 1970)
Producer: Bob Maurice
Director: Michael Wadleigh
Assistant Directors: Martin Scorsese, Thelma Schoonmaker
Editors: Thelma Schoonmaker, Martin Scorsese
Running Time: 184 minutes

Medicine Ball Caravan (Warner Brothers, 1971)
Producer: Francois Reichenbach, Tom Donahue
Director: Francois Reichenbach
Associate Producer: Martin Scorsese
Supervising Editor: Martin Scorsese
Running Time: 88 minutes

Unholy Rollers (American International Pictures, 1972)
Producers: John Pizer, Jack Bohrer
Director: Vernon Zimmerman
Supervising Editor: Martin Scorsese
Running Time: 88 minutes

Elvis on Tour (MGM, 1972)
Producers: Pierre Adidge, Robert Abel
Directors: Pierre Adidge, Robert Abel
Montage Supervisor: Martin Scorsese
Running Time: 93 minutes

Cannonball (New World, 1976)
Producer: Samuel W. Gelfman
Director: Paul Bartel
Cast: Martin Scorsese (Mafioso)
Running Time: 93 minutes

Roger Corman: Hollywood's Wild Angel (Christian Blackwood Productions, 1978)
Director: Christian Blackwood
Cast: Martin Scorsese, Paul Bartel, David Carradine

Il Pap'Occhio (In the Eye of the Pope) (1981)
Director: Renzo Arbore
Cast: Martin Scorsese (television director)

Bonjour Monsieur Lewis (Les Films Number One, Antenne 2, and Jerry Lewis Films, Inc., 1982)
Director: Robert Benayoun
Cast: Martin Scorsese, Mel Brooks, Marty Feldman

Pavlova—A Woman for All Time (1982)
Director: Emil Lotianou
Cast: Martin Scorsese (Gatti-Cassaza, director of the Metropolitan Opera
    House)

Round Midnight (Warner Brothers, 1986)
Director: Bertrand Tavernier
Cast: Martin Scorsese (Goodley, the manager of Birdland)
Running Time: 131 minutes

The Grifters (Miramax Films, 1990)
Director: Stephen Frears
Producers: Martin Scorsese, Robert Harris, James Painten
Running Time: 119 minutes

Guilty By Suspicion (Warner Brothers, 1991)
Director: Irwin Winkler
Producer: Arnon Milchan
Cast: Martin Scorsese (Joe Lesser)
Running Time: 105 minutes

Music For The Movies: Bernard Herrmann (Alternate Current, 1992)
Director: Joshua Waletzky
Producers: Margaret Smilow, Roma Barah
Cast: Martin Scorsese
Running Time: 60 minutes

Films about the Career of Martin Scorsese

Movies Are My Life: A Profile of Martin Scorsese (1978)
Producers: Steven Prince, Peter Hayden
Director: Peter Hayden
Cinematography: Joe Marquette
Editor: Carl Thompson
Sound: Michael Eiye
Cast: Martin Scorsese, John Cassavetes, Jay Cocks, Robert De Niro, Brian
    De Palma, Jodie Foster, Mardik Martin, Liza Minelli, Steven Prince,
    Robbie Robertson
Running Time: 61 minutes

"Martin Scorsese Directs" (Pacific Street Film Projects, 1990)

Producers: Joel Sucher, Steven Fischler
Directors: Joel Sucher, Steven Fischler
Executive Producer: Susan Lacy
Associate Producer: Debra Cohen
Cast: Martin Scorsese, Michael Ballhaus, Jay Cocks, Barbara Hershey, Robert De Niro, Harvey Keitel, George Lucas, Mardik Martin, Joe Pesci, Nicholas Pileggi, Robbie Robertson, Amy Robinson, Thelma Schoonmaker, Paul Schrader, Charles Scorsese, Catherine Scorsese, Irwin Winkler
Running Time: 58 minutes

The Future of Movies (Buena Vista Television, 1990)

Producer: Jim Murphy
Director: Jim Murphy
Executive Producer: Larry Dieckhaus
Cinematography: Tom Pawelko
Cast: Martin Scorsese, Roger Ebert, Gene Siskel, Steven Spielberg, George Lucas
Running Time: 60 minutes

Hollywood Mavericks (American Film Institute, 1990)

Coordinating Producer: Florence Dauman
Creative Consultants: Todd McCarthy, Stacey Foiles, Michael Henry Wilson
Cast: Martin Scorsese, Paul Schrader, John Cassavetes, Francis Coppola, Robert De Niro
Running Time: 90 minutes

Index

Page numbers in **boldface** refer to photo illustrations.

THE AUTHOR

Les Keyser is a professor of English at the College of Staten Island, a branch of the City University of New York. He received his A.B. in English magna cum laude from La Salle College; he attended La Salle on the Monsignor McGinley Scholarship and at graduation received the Charles V. Kelly Prize for English. He received his M.A. and Ph.D. in English from Tulane University, which he attended on a National Defense Education Act Fellowship. He received his M.A. in cinema studies from New York University, which he attended on a university fellowship.

Les Keyser has delivered papers on film and literature at NCTE, NEMLA, and CEA meetings. His articles have been anthologized by Oxford University Press and Southern Illinois University Press. His first book, written with Andrew Ruszkowski, was *The Cinema of Sidney Poitier*. He then published *Hollywood in the Seventies*. His most recent book, written with his wife, Barbara Keyser, is *Hollywood and the Catholic Church: The Image of Roman Catholicism in American Movies*.